CURRICULUM FOR WALES

HUMANITIES

Religion, Values and Ethics

FOR 11–14 YEARS

Lesley Parry and Jan Hayes

HODDER EDUCATION
AN HACHETTE UK COMPANY

The Publishers would like to thank the following for permission to reproduce copyright material.

Acknowledgements

This book is dedicated to Neville Gwyn Parry (1939–2022) RIP.

With thanks to Lesley Pashkin (Cydraddoldeb Cangen /Equality Branch of the Welsh Government) for linking us up with the Interfaith Council for Wales, which helped with research for the book. Thanks to the following Inter-Faith members with whom we had contact: Jason Spragg (Church of Jesus Christ of Latter Day Saints), Ainsley Griffiths (Church in Wales), Simarmeet Singh and Channi Kaler (Sikhism) and Keshav Singhal (Hinduism). Thanks also to Simon Walkling (United Reformed Church) for pointing us to a book which proved very helpful in explaining the history of Wales as a multicultural, pluralistic nation. Thanks to Sir Hamid Patel for linking us to Islamic contacts in Wales.

Especial thanks must go to the following, who worked closely with us and welcomed us into their communities. Chris Abbas and Vivian Bartlett of the Bahá'í Faith, whose guidance and revision work was a great support in writing about this newest of world religions, a religion which is not covered in other UK textbooks in spite of its growing contribution to modern society. Gurmit Singh Randhawa MBE spoke at length with us about Sikhism as a religion of service. Along with the management committee of the Cardiff Sikh Gurdwara, he welcomed us into their gurdwara, giving access and their time, welcoming us to share langar with the sangat, and to chat over tea with the gurdwara management committee. Versha Sood welcomed us to The India Centre, and shared the temple with us, while Sashtri Shanti Swarup (pandit ji) allowed us to observe an act of worship, talked to us about Hinduism, and gave us some of his wife's lovely food. Pauliina Kossi and Choje Lama Rabsang gave permission to visit and photograph Palpung Buddhist Meditation centre and its shrineroom; they gave their time, hospitality and knowledge, telling us how Palpung came about, and of its importance to the community. The work on this book has given us new friends, and we will cherish our experiences.

Writing a book for the new Welsh Key Stage 3 curriculum gave us both an excuse to research and tour the country in which we studied for our university degrees. It reminded us of our love for this country, and showed us that – in spite of what the census might say – religion and spirituality, as well as religious and spiritual values, have shaped Wales and Welsh culture and society, contributing to cynefin, and will continue to do so for the benefit of all.

The Publishers would also like to thank the following for their work reviewing this book: Peter Hulme; Reverend Shirley Murphy and Reverend Richard Davies; Humanists UK; Yomna Helmy (Centre of Islamic Studies at the University of Cambridge); the Board of Deputies of British Jews.

Every effort has been made to trace all copyright holders, but if any have been inadvertently overlooked, the Publishers will be pleased to make the necessary arrangements at the first opportunity.

Although every effort has been made to ensure that website addresses are correct at time of going to press, Hodder Education cannot be held responsible for the content of any website mentioned in this book. It is sometimes possible to find a relocated web page by typing in the address of the home page for a website in the URL window of your browser.

Hachette UK's policy is to use papers that are natural, renewable and recyclable products and made from wood grown in well-managed forests and other controlled sources. The logging and manufacturing processes are expected to conform to the environmental regulations of the country of origin.

Orders: please contact Hachette UK Distribution, Hely Hutchinson Centre, Milton Road, Didcot, Oxfordshire, OX11 7HH. Telephone: +44 (0)1235 827827. Email education@hachette.co.uk Lines are open from 9 a.m. to 5 p.m., Monday to Friday. You can also order through our website: www.hoddereducation.co.uk

ISBN: 978 1 3983 4874 5

© Lesley Parry and Jan Hayes 2022

First published in 2022 by
Hodder Education,
An Hachette UK Company
Carmelite House
50 Victoria Embankment
London EC4Y 0DZ
www.hoddereducation.co.uk

Impression number   10 9 8 7 6 5 4 3 2 1

Year   2026 2025 2024 2023 2022

All rights reserved. Apart from any use permitted under UK copyright law, no part of this publication may be reproduced or transmitted in any form or by any means, electronic or mechanical, including photocopying and recording, or held within any information storage and retrieval system, without permission in writing from the publisher or under licence from the Copyright Licensing Agency Limited. Further details of such licences (for reprographic reproduction) may be obtained from the Copyright Licensing Agency Limited, www.cla.co.uk

Cover photo © alexmia – stock.adobe.com

Illustrations by DC Graphic Design Limited and Barking Dog Art

Typeset in Myriad Pro 11/13pt by DC Graphic Design Limited, Hextable, Kent

Printed in Italy

A catalogue record for this title is available from the British Library.

Contents

Introduction..v

How Wales became a pluralistic society

The Welsh religious landscape today 2

1 Christian history of Wales
- 1.1 Christianity comes to Wales 4
- 1.2 Celtic Christianity – the Celtic Saints 6
- 1.3 Monasticism – a feature of Welsh Christianity ... 8
- 1.4 Christianity and the Welsh language 10
- 1.5 Surges in faith – the Welsh revivals of 1859 and 1904–5... 12
- 1.6 Christianity in Wales today 14

2 Other world faiths coming to Wales
- 2.1 How Judaism came to Wales 16
- 2.2 How Islam came to Wales 18
- 2.3 How Hinduism came to Wales 20
- 2.4 How Sikhism came to Wales........................ 22
- 2.5 How Buddhism came to Wales..................... 24
- 2.6 How the Bahá'í Faith came to Wales............. 26

3 The wider Welsh spiritual landscape
- 3.1 What is spirituality?..................................... 28
- 3.2 The founding of the Bahá'í Faith 30
- 3.3 Key beliefs and practices of the Bahá'í Faith.....32
- 3.4 The modern druids..................................... 34
- 3.5 What is humanism?.................................... 36
- 3.6 Exploring humanism................................... 38
- 3.7 The Spiritualist Churches of Wales 40

The major world faiths

4 Christianity
- 4.1 What Christians believe – God and the Trinity...42
- 4.2 Key Christian beliefs – moral behaviour and the afterlife 44
- 4.3 The life of Jesus – the Incarnation 46
- 4.4 The importance of Christmas 48
- 4.5 The life of Jesus – teacher 50
- 4.6 The life of Jesus – miracle worker.................52
- 4.7 Jesus – his death and resurrection................ 54
- 4.8 The importance of Easter 56
- 4.9 Where Christians worship 58
- 4.10 How Christians worship 60
- 4.11 The Bible and worship.................................62
- 4.12 The Eucharist 64
- 4.13 Baptism – joining the faith as an infant.......... 66
- 4.14 Baptism – joining the faith as an adult 68
- 4.15 Pilgrimage in Christianity 70
- 4.16 Christian beliefs into action 72

5 Judaism
- 5.1 Key beliefs in Judaism 74
- 5.2 A faith that governs life – the mitzvot 76
- 5.3 The holy books of Judaism 78
- 5.4 The Jewish place of worship – the synagogue 80
- 5.5 A Jewish home and daily life........................ 82
- 5.6 Jewish life – observing Shabbat 84
- 5.7 Jewish celebrations – Pesach (Passover)......... 86
- 5.8 Judaism in the Welsh community 88

6 Islam
- 6.1 Key beliefs in Islam 90
- 6.2 The founder of Islam – Prophet Muhammad 92
- 6.3 The holy book of Islam – the Qur'an 94
- 6.4 The Muslim place of worship – the mosque.... 96
- 6.5 Belief and prayer – the Pillars of Shahadah and Salah... 98
- 6.6 Devotion and thankfulness – the Pillars of Zakah and Sawm..................................... 100
- 6.7 Dedication and resilience – the Pillar of Hajj .. 102
- 6.8 Islam in the Welsh community 104

7 Hinduism
- 7.1 Key beliefs about God in Hinduism 106
- 7.2 Key beliefs in Hinduism – karma and reincarnation 108
- 7.3 The Hindu place of worship – the mandir 110
- 7.4 Acts of worship in Hindu temples 112
- 7.5 The home as a place of worship for Hindus ...114
- 7.6 Holy places for Hindus 116
- 7.7 Hindu celebration of Diwali.........................118
- 7.8 Hinduism in the Welsh community 120

8 Sikhism
- 8.1 Key beliefs in Sikhism 122
- 8.2 Founders of the faith – the ten gurus 124
- 8.3 The Sikh place of worship – the gurdwara ... 126
- 8.4 Worship at the gurdwara and the Guru Granth Sahib 128
- 8.5 Becoming a Khalsa Sikh – the Amrit Sanskar 130
- 8.6 Amritsar – the spiritual centre of Sikhism 132
- 8.7 Living as a Sikh 134
- 8.8 Sikhism in the Welsh community 136

9 Buddhism
- 9.1 The life of the Buddha – before enlightenment 138
- 9.2 The life of the Buddha – the enlightenment and beyond 140
- 9.3 Key teachings of the Buddha 142
- 9.4 Key beliefs in Buddhism 144
- 9.5 Monasticism in Buddhism 146
- 9.6 The Buddhist place of worship – temples 148
- 9.7 Buddhist celebration of Wesak 150
- 9.8 Buddhism in the Welsh community 152

Values and ethics

10 Identity and belonging
- 10.1 Identity and belonging 154
- 10.2 Shaping or being shaped? 156
- 10.3 What is morality, and how do we get it? 158
- 10.4 Beliefs – values – behaviour 160
- 10.5 Religious influences on morality 162

11 Rights and responsibilities
- 11.1 Human Rights – the UDHR and UNCRC 164
- 11.2 Rights and responsibilities 166
- 11.3 Religion and human rights 168
- 11.4 Social justice 170
- 11.5 Attitudes to poverty 172

12 Diversity and tolerance
- 12.1 Humanity 174
- 12.2 Prejudice and discrimination 176
- 12.3 Religious attitudes to prejudice and discrimination 178
- 12.4 Religious responses to prejudice and discrimination 180
- 12.5 Discrimination as a religious issue 182

13 The natural world
- 13.1 The creation 184
- 13.2 Science and the origins of the universe 186
- 13.3 Our wondrous world 188
- 13.4 How humans are damaging the world 190
- 13.5 Environmental ethics 192
- 13.6 Animal rights 194

14 Respect for life
- 14.1 Religious beliefs about the origins of life 196
- 14.2 Scientific beliefs about the origins of human life 198
- 14.3 How important is human life? The death penalty 200
- 14.4 How important is human life? Euthanasia 202
- 14.5 How important is human life? Victims of natural disasters 204
- 14.6 How important is human life? The refugee crisis 206

15 Peace and protest
- 15.1 Attitudes to peace 208
- 15.2 When conflicts happen 210
- 15.3 Conscientious objection 212
- 15.4 Keeping the peace 214
- 15.5 Protest 216

Glossary 218

Index 221

We have worked in collaboration with University of Wales Press to produce this resource. They have reviewed it to make sure it is tailored to the new curriculum and explores Welsh culture and heritage in an authentic way. Find out more about University of Wales Press and their resources in Welsh and English languages by visiting their websites www.uwp.co.uk and www.gwasgprifysgolcymru.org

Introduction

▶ About this book

This book has been designed to be used however you and your teacher want. The content can be used by teachers to create their own lessons, or you may work through the resources and activities on each spread more intensively.

Teachers are encouraged to design their own curriculum for their school, making sure it meets the needs of them and their students, as well as reflecting your own local area. They may decide to teach Religion, Values and Ethics (RVE) as its own discipline, or they may teach it within a Humanities context alongside or integrated with Geography, History, Social Studies and Business studies.

Whether you study RVE as its own subject, or within a Humanities context, it is important to everyone to gain the knowledge, understanding and skills to help us develop as ethical, informed citizens of Wales and the wider world.

This book reflects the fact that religions in Wales are in the main Christian. It allows you to explore the other main religions, spiritual paths and non-religious worldviews met in Wales today. It helps you to see how these views have contributed to Welsh history, language and culture, and to cynefin, and that they continue to have influence today. The skills honed through this enquiry, exploration and investigation will help you to develop as ambitious and capable learners.

The book covers the development of Wales as a pluralistic and multicultural society, so that you better understand how Wales has developed and continues to develop. It explores the main beliefs and practices of those living and working in Wales today. You can see some of the contributions being made by all those who live here regardless of having faith or none, and can begin to think about how you can be enterprising, creative contributors in your own right.

The book also explores some of the biggest issues facing humanity today. It is presented through a Welsh context, making each topic directly relevant to you and your community. It will challenge you to make your own opinions on these issues, and to begin to see them as multi-faceted issues. Giving you the skills to analyse and evaluate issues, situations and dilemmas will help you on the path to becoming healthy, confident individuals able to make your voice heard as a valuable member of society.

Features of the book

Each topic covers a double page spread.

Learning objectives tell you the intended learning of the topic, so you know what to expect from it.

Key terms and beliefs provide an easy reference for the topic.

It begins with a Big Question to get you thinking straight away. These can also be reviewed at the end of the lesson, as often what we learn changes our initial ideas.

Find out for yourself boxes encourage you to explore your own community, engaging more deeply in your learning.

Activities boxes test your learning on the topic. From simple to complex questions, they usually end with a statement for you to evaluate and give your opinion on.

Talk it out boxes give you opportunities for discussion with others, or self-reflection, helping you use your own knowledge and experience, and encouraging exchange of views.

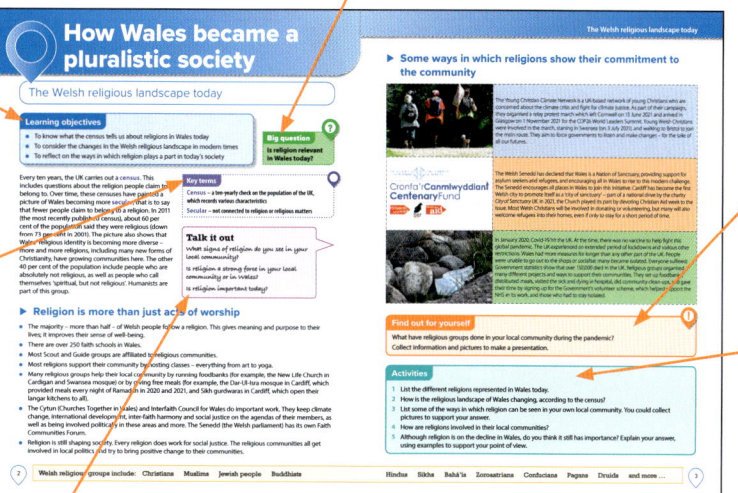

Progression in RVE

As you study different topics, your knowledge and understanding of RVE in Wales will grow. Everyone needs to be able to comprehend the world around them, to be able to analyse ideas and situations, to be able to synthesise different aspects and attitudes, and to evaluate the options they face in any dilemma. Each topic gives you the opportunity to practise these skills which are important for future life.

About this Curriculum for Wales

What Matters Statements and the Four Purposes

The content of this book will help you to gain an understanding of the five What Matters statements within the Humanities Area of Learning and Experiences.

Together, these What Matters statements contribute to the four purposes of the curriculum:

Introduction

Cross-curricular skills
The resources and activities in this book will help you to develop your cross-curricular skills.

Literacy	• Taking part in class discussions and debates. • Describing, explaining, discussing, evaluating and writing creatively. • Using critical thinking skills when analysing statements and ideas. • Evaluating interpretations and viewpoints.
Numeracy	• Analysing and representing data in various ways. • Using statistics to inform ideas and attitudes.
Spiritual, moral, ethical and cultural	• Learning about the religious and spiritual make-up of Wales. • Exploring how religious and non-religious worldviews have contributed to Welsh spirituality, morality and culture. • Exploring a range of ethical viewpoints on issues important to Welsh society today. • Being part of a tolerant, harmonious society which welcomes all, by becoming informed about its diversity.
Digital competence	• Using the internet to carry out research. • Presenting data and text.
Creativity and innovation	• Presenting information in creative ways. • Imagining possible futures. • Expressing opinions about different viewpoints and ideas.
Critical thinking and problem-solving	• Critically evaluating ideas, teachings, and evidence. • Thinking analytically to understand the past and present and to imagine possible futures.
Personal effectiveness	• Working with others to explore Big Questions and ideas. • Working as team to organise and carry out enquiries. • Evaluating, justifying and expressing your responses.
Planning and organising	• Planning and organising your own learning, including work done outside school as research, homework or presentations.

About the course planner
Our RVE course planner provides detailed information on how the content and activities of each lesson link to the elements in the Curriculum for Wales, and the Humanities Area of Learning and Experience.

It includes:
- Topic title – giving the theme of each topic
- Learning Objectives – as met in the topic pages of the book
- What Matters – the statements that relate to the content on the pages
- Progression Steps – the progression steps that you should be able to make through the activities on the pages. These will be either Progression step 3 or Progression step 4, or a mixture of step 3 and 4.
- Skills – the cross-curricular skills that will be used in the activities
- Humanities AoLE links – where the content is relevant to specific subjects of Geography, History, Business Studies or Social Studies
- Cross-curricular links – where the content is relevant to other AoLEs, including Science and Technology, Mathematics and Numeracy and Health and Wellbeing

Additional resources for approaching Humanities thematically
To support teachers who are planning a thematic approach for Humanities, teaching RVE as part of cross-subject themes, or within an integrated Humanities course, we have developed the following resources:

- A thematic course planner shows how the content of this book can be used alongside our Geography and History books so that all the subjects are taught together in themes.
- Humanities AoLE digital resources source material from our Geography, History and RVE books, alongside new content for business studies and social studies, and presents them in themes for teachers to use in their lessons if they are teaching thematically.

About the authors
Lesley Parry and Jan Hayes have both been teaching RVE for more than 30 years. As joint and solo authors of many Hodder Education books for KS3 and GCSE, their work is widely used in UK schools. Now working as Education Consultants, both Lesley and Jan support schools and teachers through training and cpd.

How Wales became a pluralistic society

The Welsh religious landscape today

Learning objectives
- To know what the census tells us about religions in Wales today
- To consider the changes in the Welsh religious landscape in modern times
- To reflect on the ways in which religion plays a part in today's society

Big question

Is religion relevant in Wales today?

Every ten years, the UK carries out a **census**. This includes questions about the religion people claim to belong to. Over time, these censuses have painted a picture of Wales becoming more **secular**, that is to say that fewer people claim to belong to a religion. In 2011 (the most recently published census), about 60 per cent of the population said they were religious (down from 73 per cent in 2001). The picture also shows that Wales' religious make-up is becoming more diverse – more and more religions, including many new forms of Christianity, have growing communities here. The other 40 per cent of the population include people who are absolutely not religious, as well as people who call themselves 'spiritual, but not religious'. Humanists are part of this group.

Key terms
Census – a ten-yearly check on the population of the UK, which records various characteristics

Secular – not connected to religion or religious matters

Pluralistic – where several different groups co-exist in a community, society or country

Talk it out
What signs of religion do you see in your local community?

Is religion a strong force in your local community or in Wales?

Is religion important today?

▶ Religion is more than just acts of worship

- The majority – more than half – of Welsh people follow a religion. This gives meaning and purpose to their lives; it improves their sense of well-being.
- There are over 250 faith schools in Wales.
- Most Scout and Guide groups are affiliated to religious communities.
- Most religions support their community by hosting classes – everything from art to yoga.
- Many religious groups help their local community by running foodbanks (for example, the New Life Church in Cardigan and Swansea mosque) or by giving free meals (for example, the Dar-Ul-Isra mosque in Cardiff, which provided meals every night of Ramadan in 2020 and 2021, and Sikh gurdwaras in Cardiff, which open their langar kitchens to all).
- The Cytun (Churches Together in Wales) and Interfaith Council for Wales do important work. They keep climate change, international development, inter-faith harmony and social justice on the agendas of their members, as well as being politically active. The Senedd (the Welsh parliament) has its own Faith Communities Forum.
- Religion is still shaping society. Every religion does work for social justice. The religious communities all get involved in local politics and try to bring positive change to their communities.

Welsh religious groups include: Christians   Muslims   Jewish people   Buddhists

The Welsh religious landscape today

▶ Some ways in which religions show their commitment to the community

The Young Christian Climate Network is a UK-based network of young Christians who are concerned about the climate crisis and fight for climate justice. As part of their campaign, they organised a relay protest march which left Cornwall on 13 June 2021 and arrived in Glasgow on 1 November 2021 for the COP26 World Leaders Summit. Young Welsh Christians were involved in the march, starting in Swansea (on 3 July 2021), and walking to Bristol to join the main route. They aim to force governments to listen and make changes – for the sake of all our futures. They are part of the voice for all our futures.

The Welsh Senedd has declared that Wales is a Nation of Sanctuary, providing support for asylum seekers and refugees, and encouraging all in Wales to rise to this modern challenge. The Senedd encourages all places in Wales to join this initiative. Cardiff has become the first Welsh city to promote itself as a 'city of sanctuary' – part of a national drive by the charity *City of Sanctuary UK*. In 2021, the Church played its part by devoting Christian Aid week to the issue. Most Welsh Christians will be involved in donating or volunteering, but many will also welcome refugees into their homes and communities, even if only to stay for a short period of time.

In January 2020, Covid-19 hit the UK. At the time, there was no vaccine to help fight this global pandemic. The UK experienced an extended period of lockdowns and various other restrictions. Wales had more measures for longer than any other part of the UK. People were unable to go out to the shops or socialise; many became isolated. Everyone suffered; Government statistics show that over 150,000 died in the UK. Religious groups organised many different projects and ways to support their communities. They set up foodbanks, distributed meals, visited the sick and dying in hospital, did community clean-ups, and gave their time by signing up for the Government's volunteer scheme, which helped support the NHS in its work, and those who had to stay isolated.

Find out for yourself
What have religious groups done in your local community during the pandemic? Collect information and pictures to make a presentation.

Activities
1. List the different religions represented in Wales today.
2. How is the religious landscape of Wales changing, according to the census?
3. List some of the ways in which religion can be seen in your own local community. You could collect pictures to support your answer.
4. How are religions involved in their local communities?
5. Although religion is on the decline in Wales, do you think it still has importance? Explain your answer, using examples to support your point of view.

Hindus   Sikhs   Bahá'ís   Zoroastrians   Confucians   Pagans   Druids   and more …

1 Christian history of Wales

1.1 Christianity comes to Wales

Learning objectives
- To learn when and how Christianity came to Wales
- To learn about the evidence of Celtic Christianity
- To explore evidence of Celtic Christianity in the local area

Big question
Does history shape our world today?

Christianity arrived in Wales just as in England, with the Romans. The Romans invaded, then occupied England and Wales from 48 until 410 CE. Their armies built forts and settlements across the two countries. Archaeologists have found evidence that the occupying Roman army brought their own culture, lifestyle and religious cults with them. One of these cults was Christianity, which some of the soldiers followed. In the third century, the Emperor Constantine ruled that everyone living in the Roman Empire had to be a Christian. This led to the building of churches and the expansion of the religion to everyone in the empire. However, it was often the wealthy who had time, or who were inspired who showed the devotion to become Christians.

When the Roman armies left Wales in the fifth century, Roman control began to fail. The local tribes retook control of their lands and re-established their own rules and culture.

Key terms
Monastery – a series of buildings that are home to a community who dedicate their lives to living under religious vows or promises to God

Consecrated ground – land that is declared sacred; usually for a religious building or graveyard

▶ Celtic Christianity

Brittany (Northern France), Cornwall, Wales and Ireland together make up the territory in which Celtic Christianity grew. During the fifth and sixth centuries, the Celtic saints travelled across the whole region spreading the Christian message. They set up many **monasteries** where people could devote themselves to the Christian faith by taking religious vows. These monasteries included colleges for learning where monks could study scriptures and theology. Some of the monks were inspired to leave their monasteries, travel and set up new communities. The Celtic saints are the reason that Christianity survived in Wales, at a time when it did not in England.

In spite of the many monasteries and Celtic saints, the fifth and sixth centuries were difficult times for Christians. The general shift in society was away from Christianity, and Christians were commonly persecuted. The old tribes had taken back their power; they remembered the religions of their ancestors and brought them back. The British Isles suffered from invasions by other peoples; for example, Saxons and Vikings. Saxon tribes also invaded Wales trying to extend their own lands. These groups did not support Christianity, and were happy to use force, often terrorising communities.

▲ A map of Celtic Christianity

Find out for yourself
What evidence is there in your local area of Celtic Christianity? Find some images to put with your notes.

| St Mellon | St Elen | St Gwynllyw | St Elian | St Dyfrig | St Non | St Sadwrn Farchog |
| St Samson | | St David | St Padarn | St Seiriol | St Cadoc | St Tyfrudog |

1 Christian history of Wales

Who were the Celtic saints?

Many of the Celtic saints were from wealthy and noble families. They gave up their wealth and status to become devoted believers. They spent their time praying, learning scripture and telling others about their beliefs. They called on people to give up wealth, turn their backs on status and devote themselves to prayer and God's work. The time they lived in was violent and unpredictable, so their choice to devote themselves to a spiritual path was brave. They often spoke out for peace, and against the things they felt to be wrong or immoral, making them targets for attack.

The Christian Church made these individuals saints in response to their work to keep the faith going in Wales and the Celtic Christian region.

▲ St Asaph's Cathedral

What evidence is there of the Celtic saints today?

▲ Llandewi is named after St David

If you live in a place whose name begins 'Llan', it is probably linked to one of the Celtic saints. 'Llan' means 'enclosure', but was originally only used for **consecrated** Christian burial grounds. This means that many of these places are either the burial site of a saint, or a place dedicated to them. For example, Llandeilo is named for St Teilo, and Llangadog for St Cadoc.

Many churches and cathedrals in Wales have their foundations in the time of the Celtic saints. The four ancient dioceses of Wales are each linked to one of the Celtic saints – for example, St David's Cathedral heads the diocese of St David, and St Asaph's Cathedral heads the diocese of St Asaph.

There are over 400 Celtic crosses in Wales. They were set up as markers for pilgrimage paths, at churches and in other holy places. Although many were created long after the last of the Celtic saints died, many of them are devoted to the saints and mark places that are linked to them.

▲ The Celtic cross at Penmon Priory Anglesey. This priory was a centre for carving these crosses for the north of Wales

Activities

1. How did Christianity come to Wales?
2. What happened when the Romans left Wales?
3. Why are the Celtic saints important in the history of Wales?
4. The Celtic saints were outsiders in their time. Explain what might have driven them on, and what would have made their lives difficult.
5. What evidence is there of the Celtic Christians in Wales today? Can you recognise any place names that are linked to the saints named on pages 4–7?

| St Teilo | St Gildas | St Erfyl | St Caffo | St Gurthiern | St Illtyd | St Cwyllog |
| St Cadfan | St Malo | St Tanwg | St Peulan | St Brioc | St Canna | St Cenydd |

1.2 Celtic Christianity – the Celtic saints

Learning objectives
- To learn about some of the people who protected Christianity in Wales
- To understand how the saints have contributed to cynefin
- To reflect on the importance of personality

Big question
Does faith in something make a person stronger?

Do some research and you will learn that there are many Celtic saints. Not all of them were born in Wales; some came to Wales from other parts of the Celtic area. St Illtyd, for example, who founded the abbey of Llanilltud Fawr (Llantwit Major) including halls of learning for over 2,000 students, was probably born in Brittany. St Elen, whose story is told in the Dream of Macsen Wledig in the *Mabinogion* (the earliest British prose stories), was born in modern-day Turkey. Some were born in Wales, but the impact they had is found in another part of the Celtic area, such as St Petroc who was born in Wales, studied in Ireland and then set up monasteries in Cornwall.

In Wales, there are many references to the saints through place names, churches and cathedrals. Their stories are still recalled in the places they lived or visited. They are part of the historical culture of Wales. The saints are part of **cynefin**.

Key term
Cynefin – habitat; a very personal sense of place, belonging and familiarity; the place of your birth and upbringing, the environment in which you live and to which you are naturally acclimatised; all the layers that make up the place in which you live and that make it unique

St Dyfrig – Dyfrig Sant (c.455–550 CE)

St Dyfrig lived at the time after the Romans had left Wales, so Christianity was on the wane and pagan religions were re-establishing themselves. He was made Archbishop of Wales, and his efforts are credited with keeping Christianity alive in south-east Wales.

Dyfrig set up a monastery at Henllan (Ross-on-Wye), and also three teaching monasteries, where over 2,000 students studied subjects such as theology, biblical studies and maths. Importantly, many of these students became missionaries, and travelled throughout the Celtic region to encourage Christians and convert others. He taught many well-known Celtic saints, including St Teilo and St Samson. Many small monastic communities and churches were set up under his guidance in Wales and Cornwall. Today you can still visit many churches dedicated to Dyfrig, for example at Llanvaches in Newport.

There are many stories about Dyfrig, which try to show how special he was – even before he was born! Legend has it that he was the illegitimate son of a princess. Her father, being ashamed, ordered her execution. At first, she was tied into a sack and thrown into the River Wye, but the sack came back to shore. Then she was burnt on a funerary pyre, but when her father returned the next day for the ashes, he found her alive and sitting on a stone among the ashes with her baby son. The baby reached out to the king and grabbed him. Immediately the king was cured of his leprosy. The king's feelings of shame turned to love and he brought his daughter and her new son back to the Royal Court. This was the first of many miracles associated with Dyfrig.

▲ Llandaff Cathedral where St Dyfrig's body lies

| St Tudwal | St Brynnach | St Baruc | St Aaron of Aleth | St Gwynno |
| St Pyr | St Elaeth | St Dyfodwg | St Branoc | St Tewdrig | St Afan | St Deiniol |

1 Christian history of Wales

St David – Dewi Sant (c.487–589 CE)

'Do the little things' ('Gwnewch y pethau bychain') – this common Welsh phrase was coined by St David, who is the patron saint of Wales and whose death date (1 March) is the national day.

St David is the Celtic saint who has most presence in today's Wales – a university, a cathedral and diocese, as well as many churches are named after him.

St David was the son of St Non, who raised him at the convent she had set up. He was very clever and a good scholar. It is said he regularly performed miracles, including curing the blindness of his teacher, St Paulinus. After becoming a priest, he began to travel as a missionary, founding twelve monasteries and more than 50 churches. He lived a very strict lifestyle and avoided all extravagance.

Alongside St Teilo and St Padarn, he made a pilgrimage to Jerusalem. On his return, he set up the monastery of Mynyw at modern-day St David's, which has become a centre for learning and has attracted many students from far and wide. Those at the monastery had to keep the same lifestyle as St David – one meal a day, drinking only water, silence at all times, days of prayer and hard labour in the fields. The monastery welcomed all pilgrims and visitors, providing them with food and shelter.

In 545, St David attended a meeting of all the bishops at Llanddewi Brefi. St Dyfrig asked him to speak to the crowds. Legend says that when he began to speak 'the ground rose up until everyone could see and hear him, and a white dove settled on his shoulder'. This legend is trying to show St David as a man of miracles; the dove represents God's blessing, showing he was chosen for the role by God. Legends are often very exaggerated stories, but with a core truth. In this case, it would be that St David had great charisma, and when he spoke everyone quietened down so that they could hear him. What he said was valued by all, and so everyone listened.

If you visit St David's cathedral, you can visit his grave – he was buried in the grounds of his own monastery on the site now occupied by the Cathedral of St David's.

▶ Stained glass window depicting St David, at St Asaph's Cathedral

Activities

1. Give the names of some Welsh Celtic saints.
2. Explain the reasons why St Dyfrig is considered one of the most important saints in Wales.
3. Explain what St David did to help strengthen Christianity in Wales.
4. Why do you think miracles are common in the legends of many saints?
5. 'The Celtic saints are part of what makes up Welsh cynefin.' Do you agree with this statement? Explain your answer.

St Melangell   St Asaph   St Dunod   St Nidan   St Cynfarwy   St Beuno
St Tysilio   St Gelert   St Gwenllwyfo   St Winefride   St Euddogwy   St Decumen

How Wales became a pluralistic society

1.3 Monasticism – a feature of Welsh Christianity

Learning objectives
- To learn about the establishment of the great monasteries of Wales
- To understand the impact of the dissolution of monasteries in Wales
- To reflect on the contribution of the monasteries to Welsh culture

Big question
Monasteries – good or bad?

Key term

Cadw – The Welsh Government historic environment service, which looks after Welsh historical monuments and sites, including more than 20 religious monuments. 'Cadw' means to keep or protect

It was because of the Celtic saints that Christianity survived in Wales when it faded away in England. Many of those saints set up monasteries and convents. Some were very large, others tiny. Men and women took religious vows to live in them, devoting their lives to their religious faith. Education was important in all the monasteries, some of which hosted hundreds of students at any one time. The monastery at Llantwit Major was the first Christian college in the UK, with over 2,000 students, including St David, and a curriculum that included theology, science and maths. Students left as missionary monks, travelling around the region spreading the Christian message.

The conditions in the monasteries were very severe. Students had little to eat, lived in small cells (rooms) without luxuries, and followed rules of silence. They supported themselves by growing their own food.

After the Norman invasion of 1066, different orders of monks including Cistercians and Benedictines set up many monasteries and convents. Different orders followed different rules of religious life. For example, the Cistercian monasteries had businesses, such as sheep farming, and grew wealthy.

One such place was Tintern Abbey (founded in 1131 by the Cistericans). The first buildings were wooden, but as the monastery became established and grew, the foundations were laid for stone buildings, including the abbey itself. The abbey was consecrated in 1301. It is set in a huge group of other buildings – including monks' quarters, a study area (cloisters), kitchens, an infirmary (hospital) and guest accommodation. The monastery was closed in 1536 in the dissolution of the monasteries. Today its ruins are cared for by **Cadw** and open to visitors.

▲ Tintern Abbey as it was, and as it is today

8

1 Christian history of Wales

▶ The dissolution of the monasteries

The Church in England and Wales was very powerful and very wealthy. Each monastery owned huge areas of land, took taxes from the locals, and controlled the craftsmen's guilds. Craftsmen's guilds were groups of men with the same skills, such as builders. The guild protected the interests of its members.

King Henry VIII (1509–47) himself was extravagant with his spending, so the Crown needed money. At this time in Western Europe, Christianity was the Catholic Church – Protestants did not even exist. All churches held allegiance to the Pope and Rome, often favouring Rome over their king prioritising Rome in any dispute, decision or debt.

Henry had wanted a divorce from his first wife, Catherine of Aragon, but this was refused by the Pope. However, in 1534 a law was passed – the Act of Supremacy – which made Henry head of the Church in England and Wales. Now he could grant his own divorce – which he did. The law also gave him absolute power over the Church. By shutting down the monasteries, Henry could confiscate their lands and wealth. At the same time, he would cut the power and influence of the Pope on his own lands.

In 1536, Henry VIII ordered the dissolution (closure) of monasteries in England and Wales. He was not the first to do this, but he certainly had most impact.

The dissolution happened in three stages:

1. Parliament was shown evidence of the corruption of the clergy, and a survey was carried out to see what lands and wealth the Church owned.
2. In 1536, any monastery designated as 'small' was closed. All buildings, property and wealth were handed over to the Crown. Many of the lands were then gifted by the Crown to Henry's supporters. Tintern Abbey was one of these small monasteries, and its lands and buildings were gifted to Henry Somerset. He rented out the properties – it is said the church at Tintern was used for playing quoits!
3. In 1539, larger monasteries and religious houses were closed.

▲ Llanthony Priory, Abergavenney (top), and Penmon Priory, Anglesey (bottom) which were closed in the dissolution, are examples of Welsh monastic ruins. Llanthony's buildings were pillaged for building stone for local farms and houses.

Henry and the Crown took huge sums of money from this process, as well as many religious relics. The monasteries of his time were quite different from those of St David's time. Rather than living in poverty, devoting their lives to study and prayer, many of the abbots lived in extreme luxury, enjoying all the trappings of great power.

After the closures, monks and nuns were given pensions. Those who refused to comply were executed, and the monastic lands were confiscated anyway. Buildings and land were gifted to Henry's supporters, and local people. The age of religious power through the monasteries was over. Many monasteries and other religious buildings, such as Tintern and Llanthony Priory, remain as ruins across Wales.

Activities

1. What was life like in the early monasteries?
2. In what ways were the early monasteries important for Christianity in Wales, the Celtic region and beyond? Are they important today?
3. What happened at the dissolution of the monasteries? Why did it happen?
4. Did Henry have to close down the monasteries? Explain your ideas.

How Wales became a pluralistic society

1.4 Christianity and the Welsh language

Learning objectives
- To explore how the laws of Wales affected the language of religion
- To learn about the first use of Welsh in religious texts
- To consider the importance of being able to worship in your own language

Big question
Does it matter what language is used in worship?

Key term
Blasphemy – insulting God; showing disrespect to God

Activities
1. Who was responsible for the first Welsh language Bible? Why did they do it?
2. How did having a Welsh version of the Bible help the Welsh language?
3. Explain how the Pope and Henry VIII in different ways suppressed the Welsh language.
4. Do you think it was important for the Bible to be translated into different languages, including Welsh? Explain your reasoning.

▲ A copy of the Welsh language Bible

The earliest written religious Welsh is on a ninth-century tombstone at St Cadfan's church in Tywyn.

It was not until 1588 that a Bible in the Welsh language existed. It was a translation by Bishop William Morgan of Tŷ Mawr Wybrnant near Llanrwst. Queen Elizabeth I had asked for a Welsh language Bible to be made and published, so that people could read it or hear it read in their own language. It took William ten years to complete. About 1,000 copies were printed, and 24 survive today.

Some people say this Bible was the most important book ever written in Welsh. When it was written, it was probably the only book ordinary people had access to. At the time, there were many versions of Welsh, but William created a standardised form – the first time that had happened. The Bible turned written Welsh into a formal language, not one which changed by region. The fact that a Bible was in Welsh also gave the language high status. As many people could access the Bible and read it, by the seventeenth century, levels of literacy in Wales had risen compared to those in other European countries. In the nineteenth century, the Sunday School movement was strong in Wales. As children were taught from the Bible, they learned to read and write – which transformed lives.

▲ Monument to the translators of the Bible and Book of Common Prayer into Welsh at St Asaph's Cathedral

1 Christian history of Wales

▶ How did religious and secular laws affect the use of Welsh?

Until the sixteenth century, the Bible was written in Latin, and church services, including the Bible readings, were carried out in Latin. A sermon then interpreted and explained it for them in Welsh. Most people could not understand the Latin language, as they had not been educated. This meant that whatever the priest said in the sermon or said was taught in the Bible, the worshippers could not check or challenge, they just had to accept. The Bible could be used to force people to be obedient and could easily be used to manipulate people. Imagine having to go to lessons where you would be taught in a language you didn't understand, with no way to opt out, and with the threat of terrible punishments if you didn't turn up. That was the position Christians were in when they went to worship. In fact, it was against the rules of the Church to translate the Bible for worship. It was seen as a kind of **blasphemy** as it meant changing God's words.

Translating the Bible

In 1539, Henry VIII had authorised the Great Bible to be used in churches. This Bible had been created by Myles Coverdale, using a Tyndale Bible (a translation into English by William Tyndale which had previously been banned in England) and translating some parts which had been left out of that. The intention was that everyone should be able to read the Bible for themselves – or at least understand what priests were saying to them in their services. However, this Bible was in English, not Welsh. Three monarchs and 49 years later, the Welsh had William Morgan's Welsh Bible.

While Henry made the first steps toward a Welsh language Bible by breaking the ban on non-Latin Bibles, he also passed laws that undermined the Welsh language. The Acts of Union (1536 and 1543) extended English laws to Wales, making one state with one legal and administrative system. In the tenth century, the Cyfraith Hywel had drawn all Welsh laws into one written collection, and these were preserved by the Cistercian monasteries in their libraries. Henry's laws now stated that English was the language to be used for all legal matters. So, while Welsh people could continue to speak Welsh in their everyday lives, any legal documents or proceedings had to be carried out in English. This undermined the status of the language, which was made worse by laws forcing teaching to be done in English. It was not until 1942 that courts allowed Welsh to be used, and 2007 before all Welsh schools by law had to teach Welsh.

Back to worshipping in Welsh

Think about it – how would it feel to be told that you had to believe in your own language but never be able to read that for yourself? You would just be blindly accepting everything. Religious faith is personal, and believers want to feel close to God. However, the need for an interpreter creates a barrier – keeping the believer at a distance from the source of their faith. Holy books are always open to interpretation. Being able to read the Bible does not stop a person's understanding of it being flawed or manipulated by others. We can say it is better to be able to read it in the first place though!

It was crucially important for the Bible to be translated – the seventeenth century saw that happen in many European languages. Today the Bible is available in almost every language of the world. Better access to education means that many more people are literate and are therefore able to read. This allows them to better understand their religion and build their faith.

How Wales became a pluralistic society

1.5 Surges in the faith – the Welsh revivals of 1859 and 1904–5

Learning objectives
- To understand why Welsh Christianity faced great change at this time
- To explore how religious beliefs can shape society and national identity
- To reflect on the importance of charismatic speakers to any movement

Big question

Does everything ebb and flow?

▶ Ebb and flow

Religious movements go through phases. Their founders are often **charismatic** so that the way they speak about things, and the way they explain, captivates people. People want to listen to them, and are moved by what they say. Very often what they say has meaning for the time they live in, showing people a clear path in difficult times. Their message inspires people because it resonates with them at that time. Over centuries, it is reasonable to expect change in how people respond to any religion – early excitement fades, understanding grows, society changes, the messages of the religion get re-interpreted, populations move and change. Religions grow and get stronger, but they can also decline and get weaker.

Wales in the eighteenth century was almost exclusively Christian. Church worship and Bibles used the Welsh language, and almost 75 per cent of Welsh people spoke only Welsh. However, many people did not have strong feelings for their religion – they attended worship, and used the church to celebrate births, marriages and deaths, but this was just what they did. Many did not think about the beliefs behind these actions – it could be said that many people were 'sleep walking' through their religion.

At times like these, a great charismatic speaker can spark the fire of new religious passion. A charismatic speaker spreads a message which gives hope to people for that time. People recommit to religion, changing their lives to be in tune with what these speakers say. In Wales, since the seventeenth century, there have been many of these leaders, and the later ones turned Welsh Christianity into a mainly **Nonconformist** faith. Welsh Nonconformist groups included Welsh Methodists, the Baptists and Congregationalists.

Key terms

Charismatic – appealing, captivating and mesmerising

Nonconformist – Christian groups that did not keep to the rules of the established Church of England, but rather created their own forms of leadership and rituals, based on their interpretation of the message of Jesus in the Bible

Meeting – here used to describe a gathering of Christians for them to listen to a speaker talk about faith and belief

Revival blessing – the belief that God blessed people when they committed themselves to him during one of the revivals, forgiving their sins and giving a new start to life

Activities

1. Why are charismatic speakers important in religion?
2. Describe the revivals of 1859 and 1904–5.
3. In what ways did these revivals have an impact on Welsh society?
4. What do you think is more important: changing how society behaves, or changing how an individual acts? Explain your answer.

1 Christian history of Wales

The 1859 revival

At this time, a Welsh identity was being built. People spoke Welsh, and worshipped in Welsh, but there were no national institutions. Due to the Acts of Union, political, social, economic and professional groups were English. Wales was a principality of England (a state ruled by the English monarch). The Industrial Revolution had brought work to Wales in mines, foundries and factories, as alternatives to farm work. Only about twenty Welsh families, some of whom were originally English, owned most of the land in the country. Society was ready for change, and change was brought about by a number of factors, including religious revivals like one in 1859.

Welshman Humphrey Jones found his faith at sixteen and began to preach locally. Having been turned down for training to be a church minister, he went to New York to preach. He was such a charismatic speaker that at many of his prayer **meetings**, people committed their lives to Jesus Christ (the **revival blessing**).

In 1858, Jones returned to Wales. Among those who heard him speak was David Morgan. David realised that in Wales the Church was in need of a boost, and that perhaps he and Jones could provide that.

In the months that followed, these two men travelled all over Wales. They led many prayer meetings as they travelled. Focusing on specific Christian messages and teachings, they urged people to be sorry for their sins, change their ways and commit to Jesus Christ. At every meeting, many people did exactly that – they were so mesmerised by the speakers and their message. More and more people went to the meetings and then later talked about them in their communities which spread that message even further. It is estimated that over 36,000 people renewed their commitment to Christ, and most went on to make long-lasting changes to their lives. They stopped drinking alcohol, worshipped more devotedly and followed the moral teachings of Jesus. They also looked to help others and make society fairer. The religious beliefs of these people impacted on society's norms, changing the way people behaved – whether they had renewed their commitment or not – and contributed to the Welsh identity. These new-found beliefs and convictions also encouraged Christians to push for social change, making life better for many.

The 1904–5 revival

The 1904–5 revival was also known as the 'Evan Roberts revival'. Evan Roberts claimed to be an instrument of the Holy Spirit – the voice for God – and he became a household name throughout Wales.

In his first meeting, Roberts explained he had been called by God to announce the spiritual revival in Wales. At every meeting, more people committed themselves to God, persuaded by this charismatic speaker with his compelling and captivating message. He told his people they needed to recommit themselves to Jesus, that – if sorry – they could be forgiven their sins, and that God welcomed them with the greatest love. His message resonated with people, moving them to have their own religious experiences.

The impact of Roberts' movement was felt across the world. People from across Europe and the USA travelled to Wales to hear him. It is estimated that over 110,000 people committed anew to Jesus Christ. The impact on society was profound: pubs emptied, Sunday sports fixtures were cancelled as teams converted and kept the Sabbath, criminality was reduced so that the magistrates' courts had very few cases, miners prayed together before their shifts began.

▶ Evan Roberts

How Wales became a pluralistic society

1.6 Christianity in Wales today

Learning objectives
- To understand the Welsh Christian landscape in the twenty-first century
- To understand the changes in denominations and numbers
- To explore how Christianity has contributed to cynefin

Key terms
Denomination – a group within Christianity that has its own interpretation of belief and its own way to practise the religion

Evangelical – those Christian groups who see scripture as the only basis for faith, and have active evangelism (taking the Christian Gospel to others) as the most important part of what they do

Pentecostal – Christian groups that stress accepting the Holy Spirit into one's life

At the time of St David, the Christian community was made up of small communities dotted all over Wales, grown from the missionary work of monks. They all believed and practised in the same way. By the time of the revivals and Evan Roberts, there were many different Christian groups, whose practices reflected their different interpretations of the Bible and its teachings. Today, the landscape is even more varied with many newer forms of Christian groups, especially **evangelicals**.

Big question
Is Christianity still relevant in Wales today?

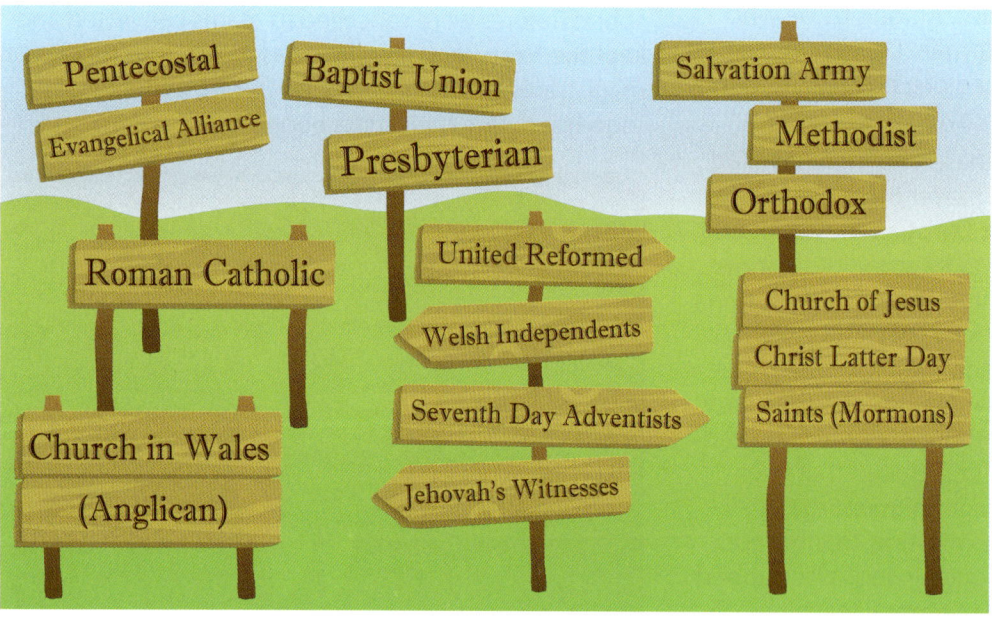

◀ Examples of the main Christian groups in Wales

Find out for yourself
Find examples of how Christianity has influenced cynefin in your local community.

Collect information and pictures to make a presentation, or to add to your notes.

Christianity in Wales appears to be on the decline. Only 48 per cent of the Welsh population claimed to be Christian in 2020 Government estimates (down from 58 per cent in the 2011 census and 72 per cent in 2001). The main Christian groups – Roman Catholic, Union of Welsh Independents, Church in Wales and Baptist Union of Wales – have smaller attendance, reduced by about 25 per cent since 2011. However, newer Christian groups, such as **Pentecostalists** and Evangelicals, are seeing massive increases in their membership. Just as with the revivals, when charismatic speakers inspired Christians to recommit, so young, active and charismatic leaders of these new church groups are doing the same today. Some churches cling to survival, some have closed altogether, others draw hundreds of followers every Sunday.

1 Christian history of Wales

▶ Christianity is part of cynefin

You could call Wales 'culturally Christian': in spite of falling numbers of practising Christians, there is much evidence of Christianity, and the influence of Christianity on society and life. Christianity plays a big part in creating cynefin for each and every person living in Wales – whether they believe in the religion or not.

Most Welsh people live in or near a place named after a saint or key person of the faith, for example, Llanbedr (St Peter), and Llandudno (St Tudno). There are churches in every town and village – often many. Many of these are no longer used for worship – it is estimated that between fifteen and twenty are converted each year – however, they still look like churches, reminding those who pass by. Other Christian monuments, such as Celtic crosses, can be spotted. Cadw encourages religious tourism and protects more than twenty religious monuments. There are at least five pilgrimage routes in Wales including the North Wales Pilgrim's Way, the Welsh Cistercian Way and the Penrhys Pilgrimage Way.

Education in Wales has a lot to thank Christianity for. The first Christian college in the UK was in Llantwit Major in the sixth century, and taught a variety of subjects. Monasteries provided education for monks and for young children throughout the Middle Ages.

Churches funded schools in the nineteenth century to give basic education to the poor at a time when the state did not. Today there are more than 250 church schools in Wales whose ethos is Christian. The motivation in these schools remains the same: firstly, that each person is unique, made in God's image; and secondly, that by providing free education, the schools are helping children to realise their potential and be successful in their future lives, thus escaping poverty and the difficulties that brings. The Welsh Government recognises the value of faith schools with their focus on human dignity, a fair society and the opportunity to explore the spiritual dimension of life.

Christmas and Easter – Christian festivals celebrating Jesus' birth and resurrection – are celebrated throughout the country. Birth, marriage and death are often still marked by Church-based services, even by many who are not Christian. The national day is named for St David.

Of course, Welsh law is based on Christian principles – as is all law in the UK. Social care comes from the same Christian heritage that gave Wales its schools. Then there is the Welsh language – formalised in writing by Bible translators, and the Bible being the only reading material most people had access to until the nineteenth century.

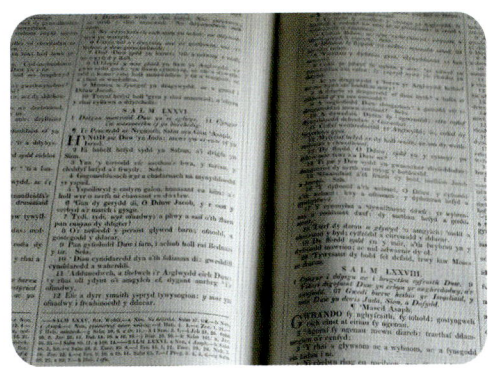

▲ Christianity is part of Welsh culture

Activities

1. How has the Christian landscape changed since St David was alive?
2. What evidence is there for Christianity declining in Wales? And for it expanding?
3. List some ways in which Christianity contributes to cynefin? Use examples from your local community to support your answer.
4. Whether a person believes in Christianity or not, the religion has shaped the Welsh landscape. Do you agree?

2 Other world faiths coming to Wales

2.1 How Judaism came to Wales

Learning objectives
- To know the historic origins of Jewish communities in Wales
- To understand why the Jewish community has declined in size
- To reflect on the importance of places of sanctuary

Big question
Is Wales a Nation of Sanctuary?

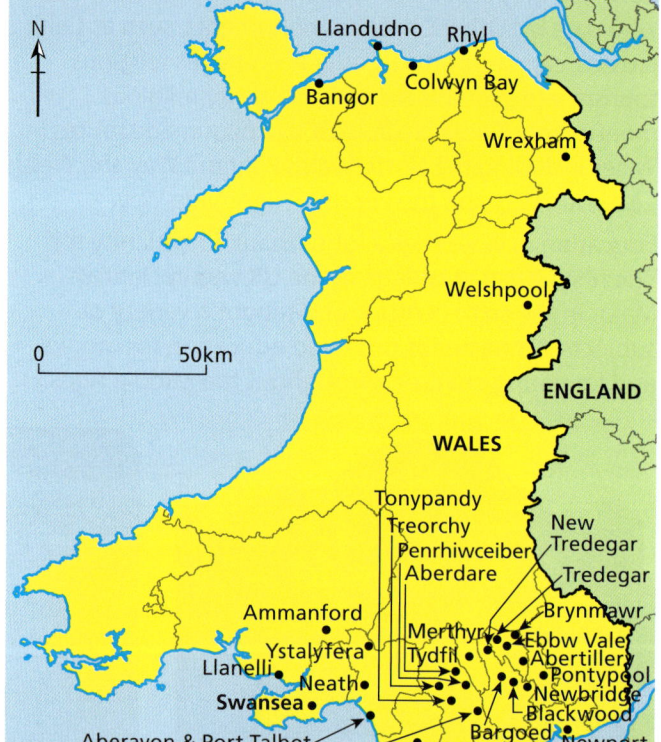

▼ Map of Wales with historic Jewish communities marked

This map on the right shows every Jewish community in Wales. You might notice your own hometown marked even though you are not aware of any Jewish people living in the area. That is because the map shows all the Jewish communities in Wales through history. Most of these communities no longer exist. A hundred years ago, there were about 6,000 Jewish people living in Wales; in the 1950s, that had risen to about 10,000; according to the 2011 Census, there were 2,064. Today, it is estimated there are around the same number, making up 0.1 per cent of the Welsh population.

▶ Why did Jewish people come to Wales?

From the eighteenth century, Jewish individuals and families moved into Wales. By 1731, there was a Jewish community in Swansea. The oldest purpose-built synagogue (still standing) in Wales was built in 1872 in Merthyr Tydfil, replacing the one established in 1848. The people in these communities had set up businesses – tailoring, pawn-broking, furniture-making, general shops, jewellery stores, music stores. The businesses served anyone, as well as including those which existed to meet the needs of the Jewish community, for example, a kosher butcher's shop to provide the meat which is acceptable under Jewish food laws.

In the second half of the nineteenth century, many more Jewish people moved to Wales. Many were escaping Eastern Europe where persecution of Jewish people (pogrom) was being driven by governments there. Not only were businesses attacked, but synagogues were destroyed, and Jewish people attacked and murdered. This led to migration west across Europe, including into Wales.

In the 1930s came another great movement of European Jews – this time away from the growing power of Nazi Germany. At first, the German leader, Hitler, passed laws which increasingly restricted life for Jewish people; ultimately the 'Final Solution' led to the rounding up and murder of millions of Jewish people. Wales was the place of refuge to which some Jewish people escaped.

After the Second World War had begun, Wales was important in supporting the war effort, though considered to be outside the focus of Nazi Germany, so a safer place. Part of the war industry (producing machinery and armaments) was relocated to Wales, and Government offices redeployed to Wales. Many people moved into Wales with their jobs or to boost the industries. Also, many people were evacuated from large English cities to Wales. Among these people were many Jewish individuals and families, plus refugees from Europe. After the war had ended, European resettlement saw more Jewish families arriving.

▶ Why have numbers of Jewish people in Wales declined?

The landscape of Wales means that much of the settlement is rural. In both the UK and the USA, Jewish communities in rural settlements are on the decline. There are a number of reasons for this:

- In small communities, people easily meet and mix with others with different beliefs. It is inevitable that some of these people will fall in love and marry. Once a person marries outside their religion, it can be a challenge to keep practising their faith, and to bring their children up in their faith.
- Many small communities do not offer everything that is needed to support a Jewish community fully. For example, there may be no kosher butcher and no synagogue. It is easier to live as a Jewish person in big communities.
- Once Israel came to exist in 1948, many Jewish people from all over the world moved there. Israel is the spiritual homeland for Jewish people. Welsh Jews – many of whom had fled from persecution in Europe, or were the children of Jewish migrants – were no exception.
- In all religions, it is the norm to marry a person from the same religion. As Welsh Jewish communities became smaller, so marriage options reduced. Hence, the Welsh communities lost members to other communities, sometimes in Wales but more often in the bigger communities of Manchester and London, for example.

The changes in the Jewish face of Wales have led to the loss of many Jewish buildings and institutes – some have been destroyed, others converted. However, in 2019 the Jewish History Association of South Wales began a project to preserve and record 250 years of Jewish history in South Wales. This included recording oral histories, digitising pictures and setting up Jewish heritage trails. The number of Jewish people in Wales might be declining, but it is now easier to find out about the Jewish history of Wales than ever before.

Activities

1. What were the reasons that brought Judaism to Wales?
2. Why has the Jewish community in Wales shrunk in size over time?
3. Explain why it is important to record the people and events of history both generally and for Jewish people.
4. Do you think the example of Jewish people in Wales shows that Wales is a 'Nation of Sanctuary'? Explain your ideas.

Find out for yourself

Check www.jewishgen.org/JCR-UK/Wales.htm to find out if there has been a Jewish community in your town or city.

Use the information there to create an info-page on the Jewish heritage of your town or city (or a part of it). Find some pictures to illustrate your page – historical or present day.

How Wales became a pluralistic society

2.2 How Islam came to Wales

Learning objectives

- To know the origins of Islam in Wales
- To understand the varied nature of the Welsh Muslim community
- To reflect on the contribution made by newcomers to any society

Big question

What do newcomers bring to a society?

In Wales today, there are at least 40 mosques. The map here shows that they are found all around Wales, reflecting the fact that there are Muslims in every part of the country. There are also communities of Muslims that are too small to have a mosque, who pray in their homes. The heaviest concentration of Muslim communities is in the south – in Cardiff, Newport and Swansea. At the time of the 2011 census, 1.5 per cent of the Welsh population (46,000) were Muslim, with an increase expected from the 2021 census.

Wales was the first British university to have a Centre for Islamic Studies – set up over 30 years ago at SDUC (St David's University College), Lampeter (now Trinity St David's). It delivers undergraduate and postgraduate courses. This has attracted Muslims from all over the UK and further afield.

There is also a growing presence within Welsh Muslim communities of those who were brought up in a different or no religious tradition. Islam calls these people 'reverts' (not 'converts') – according to Islam, they have come back to Islam, as all are born Muslim.

Find out for yourself

Find out if there is a mosque in your town, or where the nearest mosque is. Try to visit it to get pictures and information to write a short article on Islam today.

▲ Map of Wales with Muslim communities marked

Activities

1. Use the map to describe how widespread is the Welsh Muslim community in Wales today. List some of the places where you would find a Muslim community.
2. What were the main reasons for Muslims coming to Wales and settling here?
3. Why is it true to say that Muslims have contributed to Welsh society and the economy? Give examples.
4. Do you think it would be easy to go to live in another country? Explain your ideas. (Think about: different culture, language, potential contribution to society, existing community or not.)

2 Other world faiths coming to Wales

▶ Where did Muslims come to Wales from?

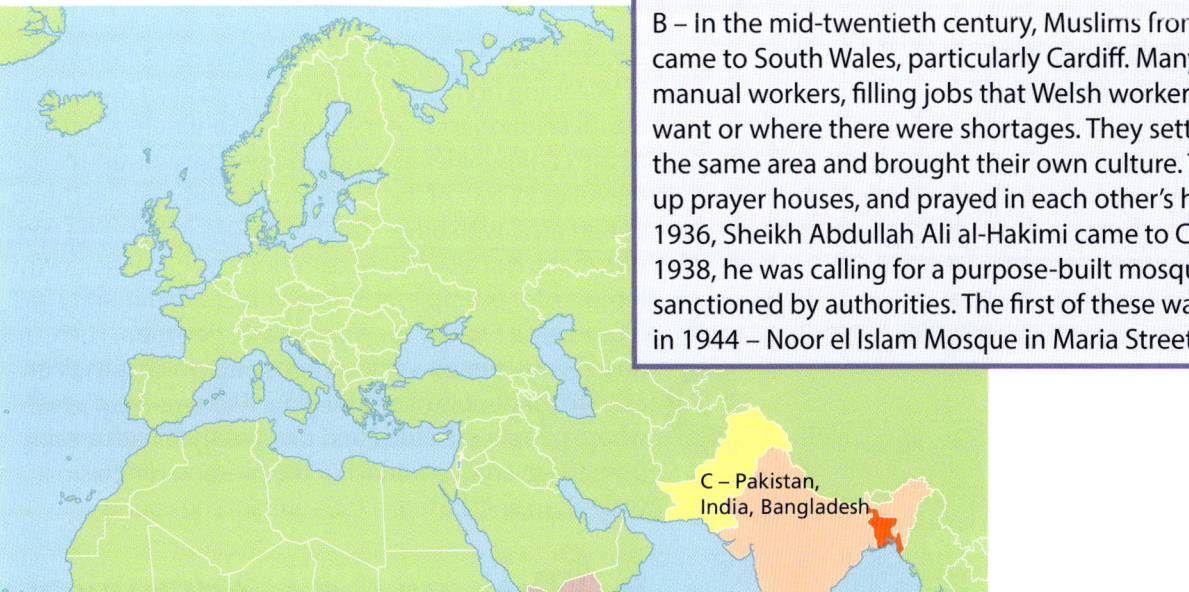

B – In the mid-twentieth century, Muslims from Somalia came to South Wales, particularly Cardiff. Many were manual workers, filling jobs that Welsh workers did not want or where there were shortages. They settled in the same area and brought their own culture. They set up prayer houses, and prayed in each other's homes. In 1936, Sheikh Abdullah Ali al-Hakimi came to Cardiff. By 1938, he was calling for a purpose-built mosque to be sanctioned by authorities. The first of these was erected in 1944 – Noor el Islam Mosque in Maria Street, Cardiff.

A – The first Muslims to arrive in Wales were sea-farers who came to Cardiff on cargo ships from all over the world. By the mid-nineteenth century, ships had changed: instead of having sails to harness wind-power, they relied on coal-powered engines. These ships needed much bigger docks than those with sails, and needed to be near big coalfields for their fuel costs to be low enough. Cardiff was a good place – a deep dock, and near the rich coalfields of South Wales. The use of engines also meant much hotter and dirtier conditions for the sailors, especially the stokers. British sailors left the sea, and found other work – leaving a shortage, which was filled by workers from colonies of the British Empire, particularly Somalia, Yemen and India, for the routes between Britain and the Far East.

These men became the first settlers, as they stayed on in port, waiting for their next ship employment after completing a journey. Boarding houses for them were built as early as 1881, and many became Muslim-owned which provided a social, cultural and religious base familiar to the sailors. Some chose to settle in Cardiff permanently in the Butetown area, having families and building communities. Some sailors married Cardiff women who converted to the religion.

In time, these communities saw themselves as British. They fought for Britain in the First and Second World Wars, even though they were, at times, subject to anti-immigrant violence.

C – Indian Independence led to the next Muslim immigration to Wales. India had been part of the British Empire, but 1947 saw partition. India was split into two states – with India in between West and East Pakistan (which in 1971 became Bangladesh). Many Indian and Pakistani men had fought for Britain during the Second World War, especially against Japanese forces, so were invited to live in the UK with their families. Britain was rebuilding after the war, and the workforce was insufficient after the loss of life sustained during the war. The new wave brought many professionals – doctors, teachers, businessmen and engineers. There were early issues for these people – it was not easy to get halal food, for example – but as the communities grew, so they came to include everything needed to live life fully and easily as a Muslim. These groups also contributed to changes in Welsh society and culture, bringing a whole new food culture, for example.

2.3 How Hinduism came to Wales

Learning objectives
- To know the origins of the Hindu communities in Wales
- To understand how Welsh Hindu communities have reached out to non-Hindus
- To reflect on how difference can be a strength

Big question
When is being different a strength?

According to the 2011 census, there were 10,434 Hindus in Wales (up from 5,439 in the 2001 census). Government estimates suggest that the number continues to increase as the communities expand, and people convert to the religion. Half of the Hindu community lives in the Cardiff area, with other sizeable groups in Swansea and Wrexham. Not all of these communities have their own temples; for example, at Tongwynlais, a community hall is used each Sunday for worship and devotion. There are three Hindu temples at Llanpumsaint, which is itself an ashram for people of any religion. Ashrams are places where people can study and practise their faith away from the everyday world. For the present, Hinduism in Wales is mainly based in the south of the country.

▶ What are the geographical origins of the Welsh Hindu community?

Throughout the twentieth century, Hindus have been coming to the UK. They have come for different reasons: some fled troubles, others came to help Britain in different ways; some came with their families, others alone. It is a very varied story and has led to a community with ties to India, Sri Lanka, Nepal, Pakistan, Bangladesh and Indonesia.

In 1947, India gained its independence from British rule and was split into two countries: India and Pakistan. This act led to a very violent transition in which many people were displaced from their homes – Hindus were pushed to India, Muslims to Pakistan. Many Hindus left their homeland and migrated to other countries including Wales.

The 1950s and early 1960s were economically difficult for these newly independent countries. A recession in India coincided with economic expansion in the UK. This expansion in the UK led to big labour shortages – there were not enough workers available for the country's needs. People from former Commonwealth countries, including Sri Lanka, Pakistan and India, moved to the UK in response to that shortage. Their arrival in the UK boosted may important sectors, such as healthcare and manufacturing.

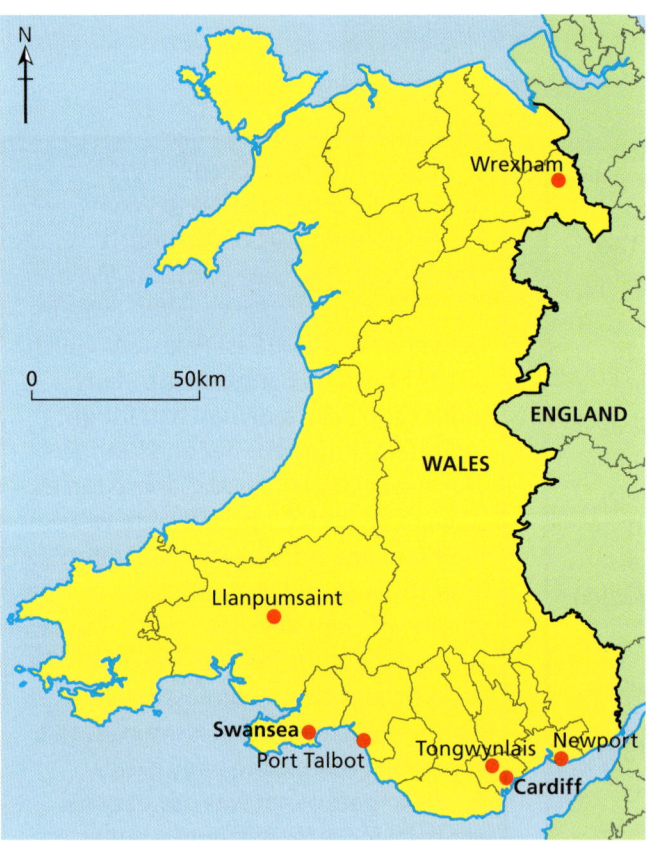

▲ Map of Wales with Hindu communities marked. There are also Hindu families and individuals scattered across all of Wales

2 Other world faiths coming to Wales

British rule in East Africa ended in the early 1960s, giving nations their independence. Kenya, Uganda and Tanzania each pushed non-Africans, who had arrived as part of British rule, out of their countries. In 1972, Uganda even passed laws of expulsion, ordering non-Africans to leave. This included Indian-Africans who had been born there. Some of these were Hindus, originally from India, who then came to Wales.

The community is completed by small numbers of Hindus from other areas of the world, including Welsh converts to the religion.

▶ A many-sided religion

There are only a small number of Hindu temples in Wales; not every Hindu community has its own temple. However, several do much to educate their non-Hindu communities about Hinduism and Hindu culture. There are two sides to this: one is that if people better understand what others do, they are more accepting of difference and less likely to be prejudiced or discriminate against Hindus. The second side is that Hindu culture is both ancient and interesting – it enriches societies so should be shared. For these reasons, Hindu communities try to be very open and welcome non-Hindus.

The first Hindus to live in Wales had to worship in each other's homes, and hire venues for bigger acts of worship, such as festivals and family celebrations. As communities grew, the need for bigger places only became greater.

The first Hindu temple in Wales started life as a Cardiff synagogue. After the synagogue closed, it became a printing press, and was then purchased in 1979 by the Hindu Swaminarayan group. This group has a strong focus on service to others. A temple is only allowed when the number of members is deemed sufficient by the leaders of the group. The temple was opened in 1982, and in 1993 a new building was consecrated across the road from it to replace it.

There are several temples in Wales that host many opportunities for Hindus and non-Hindus to learn more about Hindu and Indian culture. Bhaktidham Wales and the Hindu Cultural Association share similar aims: to educate people about Hinduism; educate the public about Indian art, culture and tradition; and improve the quality of life for those in difficulty. This also reflects the twin focuses of the Skanda Vale ashram at Llanpumsaint: devotion to God, and service to others.

In areas where there are Hindus, it is easy for non-Hindus to attend classes on meditation, yoga, dancing and music, cooking and art, as well as learning about the religion. You could check out any local temple, or Hindu temple websites to see the opportunities open to all. Hindu temples co-ordinate many projects to help those in need in their communities, for example by distributing food to the homeless and poor. Skanda Vale supports an animal sanctuary and the local hospice, showing its strong belief in the sanctity of life. All Hindu temples are open to people of any faith or none.

Those Hindus who were among the first to settle in Wales must have felt the difference of the land they had come to live in. They came from hot countries, with a different food culture, different life experiences and different beliefs. As with any newcomers, they faced all kinds of difficulties and prejudices. Their solution has been to retain their religion, even growing stronger in it, and to be very open communities, sharing insights and experiences, religion and culture with all.

▲ Sri Swarminarayan Mandir, Cardiff – the first Hindu temple in Wales

Activities

1. On a world map, label the countries with which the Welsh Hindu community has links, and add explanations of why they came to Wales from each place.
2. Hinduism is a religion that is expanding in Wales. Explain why this may be the case.
3. Explain how the Hindu community has tried to help non-Hindus to understand their faith and culture.
4. Do you think that religions should be more open to people of other or no faith? Explain your reasons.

How Wales became a pluralistic society

2.4 How Sikhism came to Wales

Learning objectives
- To know the origins of the Welsh Sikh community
- To understand what difficulties have been faced by the Sikh community in Wales
- To reflect on whether the British Sikh community is fully integrated into Welsh society

Big question
What makes you feel 'at home' somewhere?

Key beliefs

5Ks – Sikhs who have been initiated through the Amrit Sanskar ceremony have a duty to wear the 5Ks. These are uncut hair (kesh), a steel bracelet (kara), a steel dagger (kirpan), a comb (kangha) and shorts (kachhera). Other Sikhs may also choose to wear them. You can read about these on page 131.

The map on the right shows the places where Sikhs lived, according to the census of 2011 which reported 2,962 Welsh Sikhs. The majority of these were in Cardiff, Swansea and the Rhondda Valley, with three gurdwaras in Cardiff and one in Swansea. Sikhs do live in other parts of Wales, but in these other places they pray in their homes as they have no nearby gurdwara. Some of these travel on Sundays to attend gurdwara with a community.

Most Welsh Sikhs are Bhatra Sikhs, that is they come from a conservative interpretation of Sikh beliefs and practices, remaining very pukka (true or strong) in keeping the 5Ks and to Sikh traditions.

▲ Map of Wales with Sikh communities marked

◀ Welsh Sikhs worshipping in a Welsh gurdwara

◀ Announcement of Amrit Sanskar ceremony at Welsh gurdwara

2 Other world faiths coming to Wales

▶ What are the geographical origins of the Welsh Sikh community?

As early as the 1930s, some Bhatra families migrated to Cardiff from the Punjab. However, larger groups came later.

In 1947, India became independent from the British Empire. The outgoing British authorities left a very bloody and chaotic legacy by splitting the country into India and Pakistan, a process called Partition. Muslims were forced to move to Pakistan, and Hindus to India. The area of greatest chaos was the Punjab region – where most Indian Sikhs lived. They were badly affected, and many left to avoid the violence. Some of these people came to Wales, settling in Cardiff, in areas such as Adamsdown.

In the Second World War, over 100,000 Indian Sikhs fought in the British Indian Army. They were awarded fourteen Victoria Crosses. Having lived as part of the British Empire, they had an affinity for Britain, which brought some to the UK later.

The 1950s and 1960s saw young Sikhs arriving for higher education to study for degrees. Some stayed after completing their studies.

The 1960s and beyond saw a time of economic hardship in India, leading to many Sikhs emigrating to find work and earn money for their families. The UK was experiencing a booming economy at the time, with considerable labour shortages in manual jobs, so people were welcomed into the country, especially from the Commonwealth. This included staff for the then new National Health Service, and Sikh doctors and nurses moved to South Wales and the Valleys.

In 1972, after the independence of Kenya, Tanzania and Uganda from the British Empire, there was a drive for Africanisation by the leaders of those countries. Sikhs who had moved to these East African countries from India at Partition, were forced to move again, as non-Africans were expelled. Many of them came to the UK, including to Wales. They could have gone to India, but having lived as part of the British expatriate communities in East Africa often working in the British administrative systems, many felt as British as they did Indian – so the UK was an obvious choice. Many of these Sikhs were highly skilled professionals – doctors, engineers, accountants and teachers.

A Welsh community

The Sikh community in Wales grew very slowly. Wales has challenging geography and road networks that make travel more difficult. There was also limited access to the culture Sikhs were used to, for example, foods and language. In terms of religion, the first Welsh gurdwara was built at Pearl Street in Cardiff in 1976 – before that, buildings were converted or prayers were conducted in homes. Keeping to the rules and practices of the religion was hindered by the lack of understanding or presence of the religion outside their communities. This made the communities close and ensured the gurdwara was more important as a spiritual and community centre for all.

The Sikh community in Wales is strong, and growing. Of course, it faces issues, but these issues are faced by almost every community in Wales (and the UK) today, including the weakening of the extended family system; issues faced by a growing elderly community; issues from living in run-down areas; and racial harassment. The Gurdwara at Pearl Street, Cardiff, caters for community needs, provides education to children and adults, does inter-faith work and liaises with local and national Government to build community relations and cohesion.

The British Sikh Report of 2019 said that Sikhs were fully integrated into British society. The evidence for this assertion includes high levels of educational attainment (55 per cent have a degree or higher); substantial numbers in professions such as law, medicine and accountancy; and election to public office as mayors, local councillors, MPs and peers. Many Sikhs have been awarded honours such as CBE, OBE and MBE. All of the Sikh gurdwaras in Wales do sewa (service to others), helping their local communities, for example by offering food to the homeless. Sikhs in Wales see themselves as part of the solution to issues in society, and are active in trying to make positive change happen.

Activities

1. Why have Sikhs come to live in Wales?
2. Why was it difficult for the first Sikhs who came to Wales?
3. The British Sikh Report of 2019 said that Sikhs were fully integrated into British society. Do you think this is true of Sikhs in Wales? Give reasons for your answer.

How Wales became a pluralistic society

2.5 How Buddhism came to Wales

Learning objectives
- To know how Buddhism came to Wales
- To understand the varied nature of Buddhism in Wales
- To reflect on why Buddhism has established monastic centres in Wales

Big question
Does Buddhism suit Wales?

The map here shows places in Wales that have Buddhist communities. You may notice that these are scattered all over Wales. Other than Christianity, this religion has the widest coverage across the country. There are Buddhists in other areas as well – the places marked are those that have a temple, Buddhist centre, monastery, place for retreat or meeting place. Many Buddhists practise their faith in their own homes, and through connecting via the internet to groups, meditation sessions and temples. The 2011 census recorded more than 9,000 Welsh Buddhists.

Buddhism in Wales is a very varied religion. There are several main schools of Buddhism – many of which are represented in Wales. There are places of worship for the Theravadin tradition of India and South East Asia, several Tibetan Buddhist traditions, Japanese Zen Buddhism and the Western Triratna tradition. Buddhism has come to the whole of the UK in diverse ways – hence the different traditions.

▼ A Buddhist home shrine, allowing daily veneration of the Buddha

▲ Map of Wales with Buddhist communities marked

▶ Waves of Buddhism and Buddhists

The religion of Buddhism first came to the UK in the nineteenth century, though Buddhists would have lived and travelled in the UK before that, for example as Chinese immigrants, and as businessmen and travellers. It is traditional to have a home shrine, so families could still practise their faith, and pay respects to the Buddha without access to a temple. In the nineteenth century, government ministers, army officers and others who had spent time in the Far Eastern countries of the British Empire brought back information about the religion. At first, Buddhism was the subject of academic study; Buddhism is a philosophy as much as being a religion, and this made it attractive as a focus of study. Later, when its practices became more widely known, it attracted believers.

2 Other world faiths coming to Wales

Some countries in the Commonwealth were Buddhist countries; for example, Sri Lanka. After the Second World War, the UK needed to rebuild, and its economy expanded, causing huge labour shortages. This meant the country opened up to people of Commonwealth nations to help with both issues.

Political upheaval in several Asian countries also led to the arrival of families and communities who practised Buddhism. The Chinese Communist revolution of 1949 saw Chinese people arrive. The Chinese invasion of Tibet in 1950, and the flight of the Dalai Lama (spiritual leader of Tibetan Buddhism) in 1959, meant that Tibetans fled their home country, scattering across the world, including to the UK. Several rinpoches (reincarnated spiritual masters) and lamas (respected teachers) have established monasteries and centres in Wales. Civil unrest in Sri Lanka has contributed to movement from that country of Theravada Buddhists.

The 1960s was a time of great cultural change in the Western world. New ideas were being explored by younger generations who had not been alive in the Second World War. This included new religious ideas – the writings of DT Suzuki introduced Zen Buddhism to this audience.

Economic need has also seen individuals and families move from other Far Eastern Buddhist countries, such as Vietnam and Thailand, to make better lives for themselves and their families in the UK. Some were practising Buddhists, for example of the Thai Theravada tradition.

▶ A very British religion?

Nearly 60 per cent of Welsh Buddhists were born in Wales. It is a religion that has attracted many people to its fold. Being Buddhist can mean going to temples to venerate the Buddha through acts of worship; however, for more people it is about practising meditation regularly. Some Buddhist temples are converted churches. Many of the Buddhist venues in Wales are old houses set up as monasteries or places to learn to meditate or go on **retreat**. Many are in remote areas of Wales, surrounded by countryside, which makes them the perfect place for a religious community to live and work, and for people to escape life in a materialistic world. They are quiet, peaceful, surrounded by nature, and away from the noise and hubbub of daily life. Most of these were set up by Buddhist religious leaders from other countries, though some now have British leaders; most of the monks and nuns in them are British, as are most of those who visit for retreats.

▲ Brynmawr Palpung temple, whose lead and teacher is an exiled Tibetan Buddhist monk, Choje Lama Rabsang

Key term

Retreat – Buddhist practice of taking oneself away from everyday life, often to a secluded place, to spend time focused on spiritual development

Find out for yourself

Do some research to find out about a Welsh Buddhist centre. Imagine you have visited this place. Write a review of the centre – its history, how it is used today, what the atmosphere is like – for 'spiritual tourists'.

Activities

1 Describe the Buddhist landscape of Wales.
2 Explain the reasons why different forms of Buddhism are now found in Wales.
3 Give some reasons why Buddhism is interesting to some Welsh people.
4 Wales is well-suited to having Buddhist monasteries and places for retreat. Do you agree? Explain your reasoning.

How Wales became a pluralistic society

2.6 How the Bahá'í Faith came to Wales

Learning objectives

- To know the Welsh beginnings of the youngest of the world faiths
- To understand the development of the Bahá'í community in Wales
- To explore the role of believers in their local communities

Big question

What makes change happen?

▲ Bahá'í communities in Wales. The Bahá'í Assemblies are shown as nine-pointed stars. The towns marked all have Bahá'í residents. The shaded areas on the map show regions where Bahá'í individuals and families also live.

◀ The nine-pointed star is a symbol used to represent the Bahá'í Faith. It symbolises unity and perfection.

The Bahá'í religion began in Persia in the nineteenth Century. Persia is now known as Iran, but Persia was a powerful empire not just a country. The Empire covered modern Iran, parts of Turkey, Afghanistan and Pakistan. The Faith was begun by the Báb and then Bahá'u'lláh in Persia in the nineteenth century (see pages 30–1). Bahá'u'lláh chose his son – Abdu'l-Bahá – to lead after his death, because he was the perfect role model of Bahá'í living. As he understood his father's teachings perfectly, Abdu'l-Bahá was appointed the authoritative interpreter of the teachings. This was done to keep the religion united. His mission was to spread the message around the world, to serve others and to make clear the message of the Faith, as well as to ensure understanding of the relevance of the religion in the modern age. This would be important until the coming of the next Divine Messenger of God.

Before his death in 1921, Abdu'l-Bahá named his grandson, Shoghi Effendi, as successor. He is known as the Guardian of the religion, being the only one allowed to authoritatively interpret and explain the words of the scriptures. This means that his interpretations were to be considered the most correct, and the ones to be followed. This doesn't mean that Bahá'ís cannot make their own interpretations – indeed they are encouraged to explore and discuss the teachings. However, those interpretations are their own personal opinions – only the interpretations of Shoghi Effendi are to be respected as authoritative. He was also tasked to take the religion worldwide.

The mission to take the religion worldwide triggered believers to travel and tell others about their beliefs. Two such believers were women, Martha L Root of the USA, and Florence Schopflocher, a Canadian, who independently travelled worldwide giving public presentations. Having met in England, they travelled to Wales for a weekend where they gave a joint presentation at the Park Hotel in Cardiff in 1925.

It was not until 1942 that the first Bahá'í person came to live in Wales – Rose Jones, who came to Cardiff. At the time, believers were being encouraged to leave their communities to take the religion further afield, to settle there and begin to build new local Spiritual Assemblies (which require nine members). The first Assembly in Wales was established in 1948 in Cardiff. As Welsh people began to embrace the Bahá'í Faith, other Assemblies were established; for example, in Pontypridd in 1961, then Swansea in 1966.

In 1997, the international Bahá'í governing body set up Regional Bahá'í Councils, so in 2000 the first elected, nine-member Bahá'í Council of Wales was established. Its main role is to work to grow the faith and to deal with complex issues at a regional level on behalf of the National Spiritual Assembly.

▶ Making change happen

Being a Bahá'í means believing in God and the oneness of humanity, and the capacity of every person to contribute to making society better for all. Bahá'ís give money voluntarily to the Bahá'í fund, and are also encouraged to live lives of generous giving to others in service to God. Bahá'u'lláh taught that real change comes about from the grassroots of society – it cannot be imposed from the top down. The worldwide Bahá'í community has created grassroots education programmes for this purpose. It teaches that humanity is diverse – there are different cultures, languages, nationalities and histories – but that diversity is not a problem, rather part of the rich tapestry which is humanity; it is prejudice that is the problem. When people understand this and let go of prejudices, there is a common ground from which people can work together to bring change to their communities. Central to the education programme is the belief that cultural change comes when people accept each other, and speak to, treat and help each other as equals. When ideas and projects are set out, discussed as guided in the holy writings and reflected on in a community, the results are better and more people involve themselves.

Believers spend time every day in prayer, reading scripture and reflecting on it. Every nineteen days, believers meet together for the Nineteen Day Feast of prayer, consultation and fellowship. Many of these happen in people's homes when the community is too small to have a House of Worship or Centre. These gatherings follow the Bahá'í calendar of nineteen months of nineteen days, each named after one of the names of God. Time within these gatherings is given to discuss the process of community development, and projects to make those developments happen. Special Bahá'í holy days are also discussed at these gatherings.

In Wales, some Bahá'í deliver presentations about community development in the Gwent valleys, entitled 'Meaningful conversations – Valleys Unity Chats'. This is the first step – discussing those shared principles, as a way to find a common ground and to contribute to improving life for those in the Welsh valleys.

▶ A Religion for Peace

The Bahá'í Faith has a very strong tradition of peace; it is one of the basic teachings of the Faith. Bahá'ís accept the validity of all religions, believing all come from one source. They also believe that all people are part of one family. These beliefs mean that they work for peace and through peaceful means in every aspect of living. The Valleys Unity Chats are about communities working together for the betterment of all – something that can only be done peaceably, if it is to be long-lasting and effective. Bahá'í gatherings are open to those of any or no faith, as are their Houses of Worship. This is a form of welcome and openness which comes from an attitude of peace. Bahá'ís are pacifists, refusing to take up arms, instead supporting mediation and peace-keeping efforts. The Faith is against the killing of other people, and so members can enlist in armies, but only in non-combatant roles, e.g. as medics. The founders of the Bahá'í faith suffered great persecution (you can read about them on pages 30–31) but responded without violence. Their message was clearly one of peace. Members of the Bahá'í Faith believe that universal peace is possible, and within reach with effort. They see part of their role to be helping bring about that universal peace.

Activities

1. Describe the process that brought the Bahá'í Faith to Wales.
2. Draw a map of Wales. On it label the local Bahá'í assemblies and communities.
3. Outline some of the features of life as a member of the Bahá'í Faith.
4. Do you think change is more effective when it comes from the grassroots? Explain your answer.

3 The wider Welsh spiritual landscape

3.1 What is spirituality?

Learning objectives
- To understand the term 'spirituality'
- To understand that not all people who are spiritual are also religious
- To reflect on the power of spirituality

Big question
Is everyone spiritual?

Key term
Spirituality – the quality of being concerned with the human spirit or soul. It is about internal calm, health and well-being, not external and material things. It is often expressed through being connected to other people, the world, life and so on

Wales is home to communities of all the major world faiths, and some of the smaller ones, such as Bahá'í and Zoroastrianism. So, it is true to say that organised religion is easy to find in Wales. This is a form of **spirituality** which is easy to spot – if only by its religious buildings and signs.

As with almost everywhere in the world today, some Welsh people see themselves as spiritual but not religious. Historically, 'spirituality' and 'religion' were seen as one and the same, but that is no longer true in our modern world. Spirituality has come to be about mind-body-spirit, the internal life of a person. It is personal and individual, as people look for meaning, connectedness and values in their lives and relationships with the world around them and with others. In contrast, 'religion' is now seen as being a part of an established organisation or community. Wales has a very broad reflection of spirituality.

Activities
1. Explain what 'spirituality' means.
2. Choose two of the questions which can lead to a spiritual search. In as much detail as you can, give your own answers to those questions.
3. Choose another question. What extra questions does it lead to when you think about it?
4. Explain how feeling connected to God, others or the world might influence the way a person lives, and the projects they get involved in.
5. Is it true to say that everyone is spiritual? Explain your ideas.

▶ Why might people be 'spiritual but not religious'?

Some people, for whatever reason, do not feel that organised religion is for them. They might even dislike or distrust religion. They do not see religion as useful to them personally, as they feel no connection or sense of well-being in practising a religion. These people can still be spiritual in the way they think and live; they just do it outside a religious context.

Some people are part of religious organisations, but their sense of spirituality is much broader. It comes from how their religion and religious values and relationships give them a sense of well-being.

Some people might take ideas from many different religions. Different ideas from different religions each make sense to them. Some of these people might eventually settle for one religion as being more meaningful to them – but some might never do that. Others might follow different religions at different times – a sort of 'spiritual seeker'.

Spirituality includes a sense of being connected to something much bigger than yourself. It often includes searching for meaning in life – making it personal to each of us. It makes everything make sense; the sense of 'I am in the right place, doing the right thing'. Lots of people talk about destiny and fate – believing things happen because they were 'meant to' is part of spirituality.

3 The wider Welsh spiritual landscape

▶ Can we define spirituality?

Of course! You have read a definition here, or could go online to find one. It is not that simple, though – a web search provides many different definitions. It might feel as if the more you search, the further you get from a definition!

Different people have different ideas of what spirituality means – and that makes sense. Spirituality is deeply personal, a personal search – so it must have a personal meaning as well. Spirituality is often connected to ultimate questions and personal identity. A person who wonders if they have a special role in the world might think really carefully about what job they might do; for example, becoming a doctor in order to be able to help others.

Of course, each ultimate question just leads to others – the spiritual search. For example, Am I special? What makes me special? Why am I alive? Have I got a role in the world? How am I connected to others? And so on ... These questions do not have to involve religion or a god – most people who are not religious actually do experience spirituality, or call themselves 'spiritual'.

Spirituality is as much about the search for answers, as it is a way of living. Some people spend their entire lives searching and never get an answer they are properly satisfied with (but they don't give up, they keep on searching).

Being spiritual is about explaining these kinds of questions. They are called 'ultimate questions' because there is no single or fixed answer, and often the answers are not meaningful to everyone. Religions might even have started because of trying to answer those questions. Answers to them can often be very personal. Exploring these questions can shape the way a person lives and behaves, as well as the contribution they make to the wider community and world. If their spiritual search tells them there is a God, they might be more actively religious in order to be able to connect to God. If they feel connected to the world, they might be more environmentally active, showing respect to all life and the world. Connection to others might make them help out in crises, showing compassion for others – even those they will never know or meet. Being spiritual does not mean a person believes in a god.

> Can you think of any other questions like these?

> What questions do these questions bring up?

- Am I a good person?
- How am I connected to others?
- Is there a God?
- How am I connected to the world?
- Why is there suffering?
- Is there such a thing as fate?

> Discuss this with a partner, or as a group.

I am a spiritual person. I feel connected to this amazing, beautiful, inter-connected world, which we need to appreciate and care for more than we do. We rely on the world for our survival; we can learn so much from nature; we are part of one complex system – not the rulers of it. I try to live as part of that system – hurt not harm.

I am a spiritual person. I am a Christian. I feel connected to God, loved by God – that relationship and the way I feel special is my spirituality. I show it through worship of God, and through living a life by the morals and teachings of my religion. I know life is special, so I respect life and the creation.

I am spiritual as I feel connected to the whole of humanity. I always try to help others, and I feel empathy for those in difficulty across the world. The world has enough of everything – if we all share. By listening to each other, we can solve any problem, or support those in need. As a race, we have to be more caring and less selfish – and I try to live by that mantra.

How Wales became a pluralistic society

3.2 The founding of the Bahá'í Faith

Learning objectives
- To know about the origins of the Bahá'í Faith
- To learn about the Báb and Bahá'u'lláh – Divine Messengers of God
- To reflect on the importance of religious authority

Big question
What is more important – a person or their message?

Key term
Kitab-i-Aqdas – 'most holy book'; holy book of the Bahá'í Faith, written by Bahá'u'lláh while imprisoned

The Bahá'í Faith began in the nineteenth century in Persia (modern-day Iran). It is the youngest of the world faiths. Today, there are more than 7,000,000 members of the faith across 236 countries and territories in the world – only Christianity is more widespread in the world. The Bahá'í Faith is a growing, worldwide religion. The beliefs and practices of the Bahá'í Faith come from the teachings of two people (the Báb and Bahá'u'lláh), who are believed to be Divine Messengers from God.

▶ The Báb ('gate')

The Báb was born in Persia in 1819. His father died while he was young so he was brought up by relatives to be a merchant. He was brought up as a Muslim. In 1844, he made pilgrimages to Mecca and Medina. He did this to respect his duty as a Muslim to do hajj, but more specifically to openly proclaim his role as the Promised one of Islam. He did this in front of thousands of pilgrims.

The Báb returned home to continue to proclaim his message – that he was the 'gate' preparing the way for a still greater Divine Messenger to come. This was his most important message referred to in many books, letters and articles. Thousands became followers of his ideas and message, finding it compelling and beautiful. It wasn't just his words – his actions showed that he believed what he said; he lived by his words, and was willing to die for them. He revealed laws to help the poor and give women greater freedom, and said education should be for all.

The Báb's message angered the authorities. Thousands of his followers were arrested, imprisoned, tortured and gruesomely executed. He himself was arrested and detained; several times whilst detained, he had the sole of his feet whipped. The authorities said he was claiming to be a prophet and that he was 'spreading mischief in the land', inciting disobedience – a crime that is punishable by death in Islamic law.

Eventually, he was imprisoned. He was executed by a 750-strong firing squad in 1850. His followers managed to rescue his remains and keep them safe. The Báb was laid to rest in 1909, in a shrine in Haifa (in modern-day Israel), at a monument which is a pilgrimage site for all Bahá'ís. The Báb is considered by Bahá'í to be a Divine Messenger in his own right, not just the herald for one.

▼ The Shrine of the Báb in Haifa, Israel

Bahá'u'lláh (1817–1892)

Bahá'u'lláh means 'Glory of God'. Bahá'u'lláh was the promised Divine Messenger of whom the Báb spoke. His mission was to spiritually reawaken humankind, and unite all of humanity as one.

As the son of a wealthy, high-ranking government minister, he was well-educated for the time. He never attended school, but was taught such subjects as calligraphy, swordsmanship, horse-riding and classical poetry. When he was 22, his father died, but Bahá'u'lláh turned down the chance to replace him in Government, instead focusing on his love for God in service to others and helping the oppressed, sick and poor. Aged 27, he was already called 'Father of the poor', and was a follower of the Báb.

▲ One of the symbols of Bahá'í – it reads 'Ya Bahá'u'l-Abha' meaning 'O Thou, the Glory of the most Glorious', and also known as 'The Greatest Name'

In 1852, Bahá'u'lláh was imprisoned and tortured in an underground dungeon. He had several religious experiences and began to understand his divine mission – 'the breezes of the all-glorious were wafted over me, and taught me the knowledge of all that has been.' He suddenly knew truths, not because of education or intellect, but because they had been revealed to him by God, by the grace of God. He used this experience to write many letters and books, including the **Kitab-i-Aqdas**. This most holy book was written in two nights, in Arabic – a language he had never studied. Bahá'u'lláh was a Divine Messenger, the mouthpiece for God, sharing what God wanted humans to know (not what he himself knew). He proclaimed himself the Divine Messenger for the age, and that all should unite in 'one common cause, one universal Faith'. After his release, he was banished from Persia. He continued to spread his message and gain followers, but – as with the Báb – his message was not received well by the authorities. Banished three more times, he was again imprisoned, and in 1868 sent to Akka (Acre on maps of modern Israel) with his family and some followers. This did not stop him from claiming that his mission was to educate humanity for the next stage of human civilisation, which would be an era of worldwide unity, peace and justice. He continued this work.

For the last twelve years of his life, Bahá'u'lláh lived in Bahji, near Akka. He visited Mount Carmel (Israel), pointing out the permanent resting place for the remains of the Báb. He died in 1892, and his remains are enshrined at Bahji, now a site of pilgrimage for Bahá'ís.

Activities

1. Describe the key events in the lives of the Báb and Bahá'u'lláh.
2. Give some reasons why both men were imprisoned.
3. Do you think that Bahá'u'lláh's experience in prison changed his life? Explain why.
4. Religious founders like the Báb and Bahá'u'lláh gained many followers. How important might each of these have been in making this happen – their words, their actions or their personality? Which do you think was most important? Explain your ideas.

3.3 Key beliefs and practices of the Bahá'í Faith

Learning objectives
- To learn the key beliefs of the Bahá'í Faith
- To understand how these beliefs affect believers' lives
- To reflect on the openness of Bahá'í worship

Big question
Does what people believe change the way that they behave?

▶ Key beliefs

1. The Báb and Bahá'u'lláh taught that there is only one God, creator of everything, eternal, limitless, all-knowing, all-powerful, all-loving and beyond human understanding. Humans can gain some idea of God through God's messengers, scripture and God's creation. The purpose of human life is to acquire virtues by recognising and growing closer to God.

2. Humanity is one – an equal, great and diverse family, with each person having their own unique role. Any form of prejudice is wrong. Every single person has the capacity to change for the better. Humans live in an interconnected world – where they harm the world, they harm each other; only by unity can humans solve problems.

3. The world's religions come from the one God. The Bahá'í Faith teaches that God revealed his message to each of the founders of the faiths, including Krishna, Abraham, Buddha, Moses, Jesus and Muhammad. They are Divine Messengers, or Educators with a two-fold message: one part covering the ethical development and spiritual progress of humanity (an unchanging message); the other part covering laws about how people live and behave (fit for the age in which they live).

4. Science and religion are two different but complementary knowledge systems, which in combination can bring people together and can solve humanity's problems. Science (discovered by humans) is practical; whereas religion (revealed by God) brings moral and spiritual guidance.

5. The soul is eternal and not part of the body. Made in the image of God, it is on a journey back to God. Personal qualities such as love and compassion for others reflect the soul. Bahá'ís believe that the soul lives on after death in a spiritual existence which can be closer to or further from God – depending on the level of spiritual development made in this life.

These beliefs translate into a two-fold moral purpose for all people:

1. Everyone should work to transform their own character for the better – 'developing the soul'. This is done through prayer and devotion, alone and with others.

2. Everyone should contribute to making the world a better place, which advances humanity – 'walking a path of service towards God'. This is done through generous giving (to the religion and to others) and service to the community.

> 'The peoples of the world – whatever race or religion – derive [get] their inspiration from one heavenly source, and are the subjects of one God.' (*Bahá'u'lláh*)

> "You are the fruits of one tree, and the leaves of one branch. Deal with each other with love and harmony, with friendship and fellowship." (*Bahá'u'lláh*)

> "Any religion which is not a cause of love and unity is not a religion." (*Abdu'l-Bahá*)

3 The wider Welsh spiritual landscape

> **Bahá'í daily prayer (shortest of three obligatory prayers)**
>
> I bear witness, O my God, that Thou hast created me to know Thee and to worship Thee. I testify at this moment to my powerlessness and to Thy might, to my poverty and to Thy wealth. There is none other God but Thee, the Help in Peril, the Self-Subsisting.

'The earth is but one country and mankind its citizens' (*Bahá'u'lláh*)

'The well-being of mankind, its peace and security, are unattainable unless and until its unity is firmly established.' (*Bahá'u'lláh*)

▶ Worship in the Bahá'í Faith

Believers pray together in each other's homes and in Bahá'í centres. Every nineteen days, a community will host a 'gathering' to worship. Around the world there are ten Bahá'í Houses of Worship, eight continental and two local. Plans are in place to build a number of National and Local Houses of Worship across more than 130 countries. Devotional programmes take place daily in these places.

Each House of Worship is built to fit in with the local landscape and culture, so they are all unique. There are features which are common: the symbol for 'The Greatest Name', a nine-sided design (perfection and unity), nine entrances (everyone is welcome), a single dome and gardens. The House of Worship is the central building with the intention of creating other satellite buildings near it – school, hospital and so on. Anyone – of any religion – is welcome.

The Bahá'í Faith has no clergy – each person is responsible for their own spiritual journey. There are no fixed acts of worship; instead, there are devotional programmes – the recitation of scriptures from Bahá'í and other religions. Bahá'ís attend gatherings to listen to these, share prayers and meditate, sometimes with music. Bahá'ís are encouraged to pray daily and read scriptures – as spiritual nourishment. Training institutes organise study circles, open to all various ones to discuss and understand the teachings of the founders, and how these can be applied to advance society. Wales has various ones of these. Worldwide, about a million non-Bahá'ís (known by Bahá'ís as 'friends of the Faith') are also involved.

Activities

1. Create a poster to explain the key beliefs of the Bahá'í Faith.
2. Explain how these beliefs affect the way a person might behave in their daily life.
3. Find an image of a Bahá'í House of Worship. Label it to show the key elements.
4. In the Bahá'í Faith, anyone may visit the House of Worship and be part of the devotions. Do you think all religious buildings should be open to anyone for prayer and devotion? Explain your answer.

▲ New Delhi is home to one of the eight Continental Bahá'í Houses of Worship

How Wales became a pluralistic society

3.4 The modern druids

Learning objectives
- To learn about modern druidism in Wales
- To explore the key aspects of this form of spirituality
- To consider why spirituality is a 'growth industry' in today's world

Big question
Is our world too focused on money?

Druidry is a spiritual practice with ancient roots. The first historical record is from the time of the Romans; Julius Caesar, in about 50 BCE, wrote about druids, saying they were the scholarly and religious masters of their people, that chieftains used them as advisors, that they were pacifists – even to the point of talking down armies who were about to fight – and that they gave ethical guidance to their people based on great wisdom.

The modern practice of Druidry has only really emerged in the last fifty years. It has strong Celtic roots, but is found worldwide. There are three main traditions which make up Druidry today: a cultural enterprise to foster the Welsh, Cornish and Breton languages, like the Eisteddfod; a way to generate support and monies for good causes; and a spiritual path. Each one draws inspiration from the ancient druids.

Trees are symbolic of Druidry. Many people today have rejected the main religions, but still want to feel a spiritual connection to the world around them. Druidry has been described as a natural philosophy of living, a circle of all beings and a wonderful web of people. These people share a deep respect for the Earth and all life on it. Druidry teaches that the biggest problem in the world today is that humans have separated themselves from nature – in our minds, we feel we are the single most important part of the world, which allows us to do whatever we want. Druidry contrasts this with a firm belief that humans are just one part of a world in which everything has equal rights and value. Druid spirituality and philosophy aim to get a person back in touch with nature, to make them feel grounded and at one with the world.

▶ Living as a druid today

Druids are no different from most other people. Their beliefs are, in the main, not unusual. The values they hold are in fact what society expects of decent people.

Many druids are active in local issues, especially environmental issues, because of their belief in the connectedness of all, and the need to respect the world. They try to be a force for good, living ethically sound lives, acting responsibly towards others and the world.

Druids believe in the power of Awen. Awen is awareness on a physical and mental level as well as a 'soul-deep' level of the entirety of existence, and the inter-connectedness of all. All religions believe there is a sense of peace deep within each of us – reaching this is to feel Awen.

Druids have eight celebrations each year – at each of the equinoxes and solstices, and at the start of each of the four seasons. Celebrations might be small and take place at home, or huge and shared with others. The summer solstice celebration at Stonehenge is a good example of the latter, when druids wear their robes and complete formal rituals on the eve and day of the solstice. It is almost always an outdoor celebration, linked to nature. The main point is to take a break from busy lives, and re-connect to the world which nourishes all life.

Druids hold celebrations outdoors for key life events; for example, blessing a baby, marriage or death.

Activities
1. Explain the role of the ancient druids?
2. What are the common beliefs of modern druids?
3. Using a dictionary, explain the Druid virtues. Which are the most important for the world today? Why?
4. 'The biggest problem in the world is that humans think they are more important than anything else.' Explore this statement.

3 The wider Welsh spiritual landscape

▶ What Druidry believes

There is no holy book for Druidry. Inspiration and wisdom can come from any source, including and especially from the legends and myths which include the *Mabinogion* and *Taliesin*.

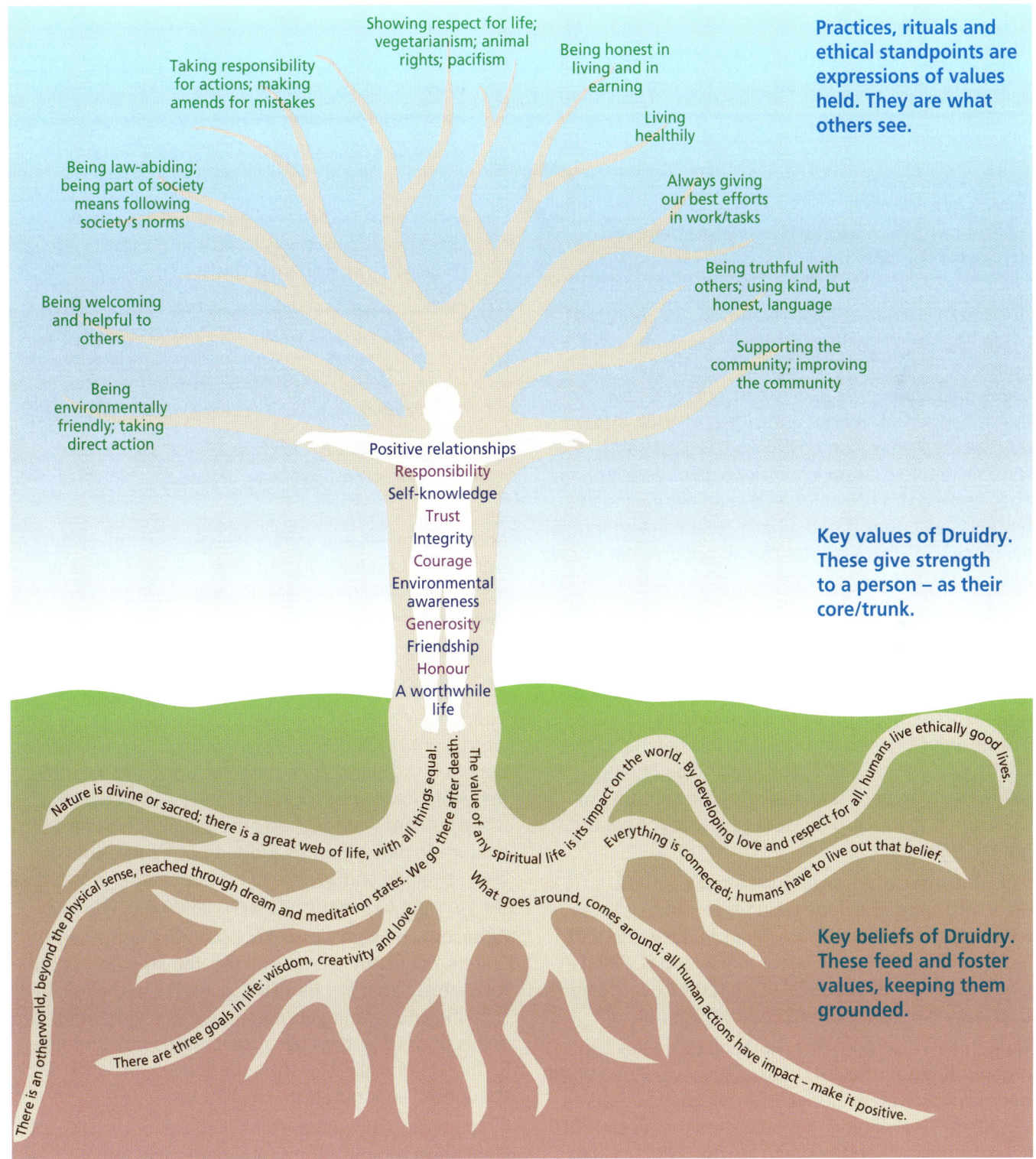

3.5 What is humanism?

Learning objectives
- To understand the origins of humanist thinking
- To learn about the Amsterdam Declaration
- To reflect on the importance of humanist thinking today

Big question
What might life be like if everyone believed this was the only life?

Talk it out
It is generally agreed that the four principles of humanism are:

- human reason (our ability to think logically, sensibly and rationally to work things out)
- ethics (a sense of right and wrong which society upholds, and bases its laws on)
- social justice (believing that justice comes through levelling out wealth and opportunity in society, so working for that)
- philosophical naturalism (a worldview stating that the universe and nature is all that exists)

With a partner, discuss these questions:

1. Think of examples to fit each of the principles.
2. Do you think any of these are more important than the others? Explain reasons for that opinion.

Humanism is a non-religious worldview, or approach to life. The earliest written records show evidence of humanist ideas. 2500 years ago, Indian, Chinese and Greek philosophers explained concepts and how things happened without using ideas of gods. Instead they focused on reasoning (thinking logically and sensibly before coming to a conclusion or decision). They applied this reasoning to human nature and the natural world. They based morality (right and wrong) on evidence and what was good for all, not on what a holy book instructed.

Fast forward to the Enlightenment period of the 17th and 18th centuries, David Hume, a philosopher, said 'A wise man proportions his belief to the evidence'. Meanwhile, another philosopher called Voltaire was defending people's rights to free opinion and speech: 'I disapprove of what you say, but I will defend to the death your right to say it'. This was the beginning of the rise of science and decline in the authority of the Church. It was also the start of discussions about human rights.

Since the Industrial Revolution began, scientific discovery has made huge changes to people's lives. It has explained many of the things in the world and reduced the power of religious explanations. Belief in God has survived, but belief in what the Church said God was responsible for in the world has not.

Today, many countries have humanist societies and organisations. At the 2011 census, just over 2,000 Welsh people registered as Humanist, while many others simply put 'No religion'. It is estimated that between a third and a half of those who are not religious hold humanist beliefs and values. People may turn away from organised religion, but they still feel a sense of responsibility to others and the world. Humanism makes sense of that shift.

▶ Definitions

'Humanism' comes from the Latin word *humanitas*. This word points to high moral standards which are used to benefit humankind. *Humanitas* includes understanding, benevolence, compassion and mercy – all of which make humans want to help others. It also includes courage in difficult times, judgement, cautiousness, clear speaking and a sense of humour – all of which give the strength to help others, even when it is difficult.

A person who has *humanitas*, according to the Latin writers, could not just be isolated, thinking only of and for themselves. They had also to live life to the full. Just thinking and arguing about something, without taking any action is pointless because it makes no difference. So *humanitas* called for thought *and* action – or thoughtful action, action which helps.

Find out more by going to the website for the UK Humanism organisation: www.humanists.uk

3 The wider Welsh spiritual landscape

▶ The Amsterdam Declaration (2002)

The Amsterdam Declaration was a set of principles to define humanism and agreed upon by humanists from around the world. It was updated in 2002, reflecting the fact that what it means to be a humanist remains an ongoing conversation.

Humanism is ethical	There is value and dignity to every human life. Everyone has the right to the greatest possible freedom, as far as it does not affect other people's rights. Humans have a duty to consider all of humanity, including those in the future. A sense of right and wrong is part of human nature.
Humanism is rational	Humanism sees that science has much to give to solve problems in the world and improve lives, as long as it is used for good. Human values applied to science allow the problems of the world to be solved. Humanism does not believe in a God or divine being who intervenes in our world.
Humanism supports democracy and human rights	Democracy is the best way for the most humans to get the most success. Humanism sees democracy as a right. Human rights help every human to be able to develop and improve their lives.
Humanism insists that personal freedom must be combined with social responsibility	Humans have a responsibility to each other and to the world. There is no room for personal selfishness in humanism; social responsibility tempers personal freedom.
Humanism is a response to a widespread demand for an alternative to religions with unchanging rules	Religions are based on God revealing truths (revelations); many religions impose their views on believers, not allowing discussion or disagreement. Humanism recognises that it is possible to know about the world and everything in it through scientific study and reasoning. This is without any reference to or need for a divine authority.
Humanism values artistic creativity and imagination	Humanism recognises that literature, music, the visual and performing arts are all important for personal development. They inspire people and enrich our lives and experiences.
Humanism is a way of life that aims for the maximum possible fulfilment	Human life is better when lived in a creative and ethical way. When they behave ethically and rationally, humans can successfully face any challenge. Anyone anywhere can live a humanist way of life.

Activities

1 Why might someone say that humanism has always existed?
2 Explain what *humanitas* means.
3 Explain, using examples, why thoughtful action can be considered as the best way to live.
4 In your own words, explain each of the seven statements in the Amsterdam Declaration.
5 In your opinion, are the seven statements enough of a guide to live by? Explain your reasons.

Activity

Look at these statements. Can you work out which strand (or strands) from the Amsterdam Declaration each one fits?

a Wherever a person lives, whatever their wealth or health or status, they can live humanist lives.
b Voting rights should be for all. No person should be denied the right to vote, and the state should remove any and all barriers to voting.
c Whatever decisions a person makes, they should think not only of themselves but also of others, and how their decisions will affect them.
d The arts develop our intellect, and it benefits anyone to create or enjoy art in its different forms.
e We should not be selfish; we should look out for others.
f Solve problems through rational thought, through science, through sharing and listening.
g Times change, so our attitudes must also change, as must our methods and solutions.

37

How Wales became a pluralistic society

3.6 Exploring humanism

Learning objectives
- To explore the key ideas that make up humanism
- To explore how humanism impacts on everyday life and on special occasions
- To reflect on whether humanist thinking is just part of human nature

Big question
How much of a humanist are you?

> For me, this life is the only one we get. I try to live it well, but not so that I hurt others.

> To me, the universe is amazing – just looking at pictures of the stars blows my mind sometimes. However, I think it is just how it happened – it is what it is, nothing designed it.

> I don't believe in God or any other kind of divine power.

> It is important for people to make their decisions based on reasoning and concern for humanity – not based on some set of supernaturally based beliefs and rules.

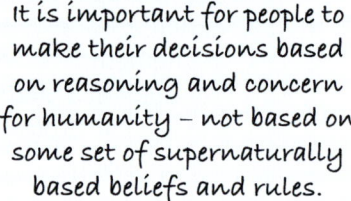

> Scientific methods help us understand the world. We shouldn't rely on religious explanations about a power outside the world who can't be proved.

> We should keep people's welfare and happiness in mind whenever we have to make a decision. I think it is human nature to be like that actually.

> I'd say being a humanist is just being a decent human being, without having any fear of God or hell to force you to be that.

Look at the statements above. They give you the key ideas behind humanist thinking. You can see that humanists do not believe in any sort of divine power. This means the only beings that can make change happen in the world are humans. By behaving responsibly and using science for good, humans can solve problems and make life better for all. By concentrating on this life – and not getting side-tracked by a potential future life – humans can make this life the best possible, for themselves and others.

3 The wider Welsh spiritual landscape

▶ Why humanism is important

- To humanists, humans – their life, dignity and development – are very important. Humanism seeks the best for all people.
- Humanism stresses the importance of science as the way to solve problems and challenges for humans and the world. Science is the best method for many people in today's world.
- Humanism connects human rights with social responsibility; it gives people an active social and political role in the world.
- Many people think now is the time for action – on climate change, to fight discrimination, to reduce poverty and so on. Humanism encourages thoughtful action, and many humanists are active in fighting these issues.
- More and more people are brought up without any religious faith or practice. Humanism is a system of thought and action that works for anyone anywhere.
- Many people today have lost trust in religious institutions, seeing them as corrupt, controlling or irrelevant.
- Many people believe that there is no God (atheist), or are unsure of God's existence (agnostic). To them, only human action can change the world and what happens in it.

▶ Celebrations in humanism

What kinds of things have you attended celebrations for?

Religiously based events	Personal and social events	Public holidays in the UK
The baptism of a baby, a church wedding, a graveside funeral	Birthday parties, New Year's Eve celebrations, anniversaries, Hallowe'en	Christmas, Easter

Humanists in Wales celebrate most or all of the important events in life, but in a secular way, that is, without religious connections. You might not be a Christian but still enjoy holidays from school at the two major Christian festivals, and join in the gift-giving and receiving for each. What about the celebrations marking stages in life, though? Non-religious people still want to celebrate the birth of a child and marriage, and to show respect at someone's death.

Humanism uses celebrants: people who lead ceremonies, but in a non-religious way. Once involved, they get to know the family or person so that they can write a unique and meaningful ceremony for them, something perfectly fitting for the event being celebrated. Celebrants in the UK have completed training to gain qualifications so that they can lead such ceremonies.

Talk it out

How far do you agree with any of the statements on page 38?

Whether you count yourself as religious or not, do you share some beliefs with humanists?

Can you explain why?

▲ Humanists caused great uproar among religious believers in the UK when they used buses and advert boards to make this statement

Activities

1. Design a poster that explains the key ideas of humanism. Use images and/or colour to make the presentation more effective.
2. Explain why humanism is important.
3. Why do people want to celebrate events – personal and social?
4. How does humanism help non-religious people to celebrate key events in life?
5. How much do you think humanist thinking is part of human nature? Explain your reasons.

3.7 The Spiritualist Churches of Wales

Learning objectives
- To learn about the Spiritualist Church in Wales
- To know the basic beliefs of the Spiritualist Church
- To reflect on how the belief that we can connect with those who have passed away helps people

Big question

Can we connect with those who have passed away?

Key terms

Awe – a sense of wonderment and amazement; linked to a sense of the divine

Medium – clairvoyant; a person who claims to be able to communicate on behalf of the dead to the living

The answer to this 'Big question', as far as Spiritualists are concerned, is definitely 'yes'. Spiritualism as a movement began in the nineteenth century, but there are references to and stories about spirit **mediums** in many texts from the ancient world. The Romans and Greeks consulted mediums for advice and guidance. The Old Testament describes a woman bringing back the spirit of the prophet Samuel to speak with the King Saul (I Samuel 28:3–25). Throughout human history there have been people claiming to be mediums; it is society's attitude to them which has kept changing.

▶ The seven principles of Spiritualism

The seven principles of spiritualism are set out by the Spiritualist's National Union, which is a UK charity bringing together all the Spiritualist Churches in the UK. The seven principles were delivered through the mediumship of Emma Hardinge Britten (1823-1899). Those people who choose spiritualism as their religion adopt these principles as a guide to belief and living.

Principle	What this means to a Spiritualist
The fatherhood of God	God exists. God is a creative force. When people look at the universe or the world around them and feel a sense of **awe**, they are experiencing evidence of God.
The brotherhood of man	Humans are one, universal family, which needs to give support and comfort to each other, and have empathy and compassion for those who suffer.
The communion of the saints and ministry of angels	This is the key principle of Spiritualism: a belief that humans can communicate with those who have passed away. There are spirit people, dedicated to the welfare and service of mankind, who teach and heal through mediums.
The continuous existence of the human soul	Matter and energy cannot be destroyed. As the spirit is energy, it is indestructible, so eternal. Mediumship is proof of this.
Personal responsibility	Humans have free will and the ability to recognise right and wrong, so are personally responsible for their words, thoughts and actions.
Compensation and retribution	'What goes around, comes around' – the natural law of cause and effect. A person must put right any wrongs they commit in this life.
Eternal progression of every soul	A person can choose to work on their spiritual development, or choose not to work on it.

In Wales, there are more than 25 Spiritualist churches, found in the north, west and south of the country. (There are nearly 350 in the UK as a whole.) Some people attend these churches regularly, others only occasionally.

Spiritualist churches offer two main practices: the divine service and spiritual healing.

3 The wider Welsh spiritual landscape

▶ A Divine Service

This group act of worship starts with a 'healing moment' when the leader asks everyone to think healing thoughts and send them out to anyone in need. There will be hymns and prayers, which are often Christian in origin. There will be at least one medium at the service, with two roles. First, they give a talk about spiritualist philosophy; this is usually unprepared and inspired by the spirit. Then they do mediumship, channelling messages from spirits to people in the congregation. Spiritualists say this is evidence of the continuous existence of the soul, as the information channelled is private to the individual (who is unknown to the medium).

Many who attend these services hope to hear messages from family or friends who have passed away, bringing comfort. The atmosphere of the service is peaceful and calm, which many in attendance enjoy for itself.

▶ Spiritual healing

Spiritualism offers the belief that it is possible to heal people through the energy from spirits. This healing can be mental, emotional, physical or spiritual, and takes place through the 'laying on of hands' or from a distance. One specific ritual for healing is called a 'healing circle', in which a group meet with trained 'spirit healers'. They sit in a circle – hence the name – and set off with a general prayer, commonly followed by the Lord's Prayer. After calling for the light of healing to touch each person in the circle, there is a short meditation before healers channel healing energy through their touch. It ends with a prayer of thanks. People attend because they believe that the circle will be able to help them, if not heal them.

'Always warm and welcoming, making me feel at peace.'

'The church is a place to go and pray, and find comfort in difficult times.'

'I have heard for myself evidence that there is life after this one; that proof makes me more concerned to do the right things in this life.'

◀ The Spiritualist church in Holywell

Activities

1. What evidence is there that humans have always believed that death is not the end for a person?
2. In your own words, explain the seven principles of the Spiritualist movement.
3. Describe the two key events for Spiritualist practice.
4. Do you think that it is helpful for people to believe that humans have a soul that lives on after the death of the body? Explain your reasons.

4 The major world faiths
Christianity

4.1 What Christians believe – God and the Trinity

Learning objectives
- To know about the Christian concept of God as the Trinity
- To understand the roles of the three 'persons' of the Trinity
- To evaluate how Christians express their belief in the Trinity

Big question
Can one thing also be three?

Most Christians believe in God as the Trinity. They believe there is one god, but that God appears in three forms or 'persons': the Father, the Son and the Holy Spirit. For Christians, this does not mean they believe in three separate gods, rather that there are three aspects of the one God. Each part of the Trinity is completely God.

In the New Testament, there are many times when the Trinity is mentioned – for example, in Matthew 28:19, the disciples are told by Jesus to go and baptise people in the name of God the Father, the Son and the Holy Spirit. The Trinity has become the most important belief for many Christians.

There are three major monotheistic faiths – Judaism, Christianity, and Islam. Belief in the Trinity is a key point of difference between Christianity and the other two. In Christianity, the Trinity is a constant reference, and most Christians say that only those who believe in it can call themselves Christian.

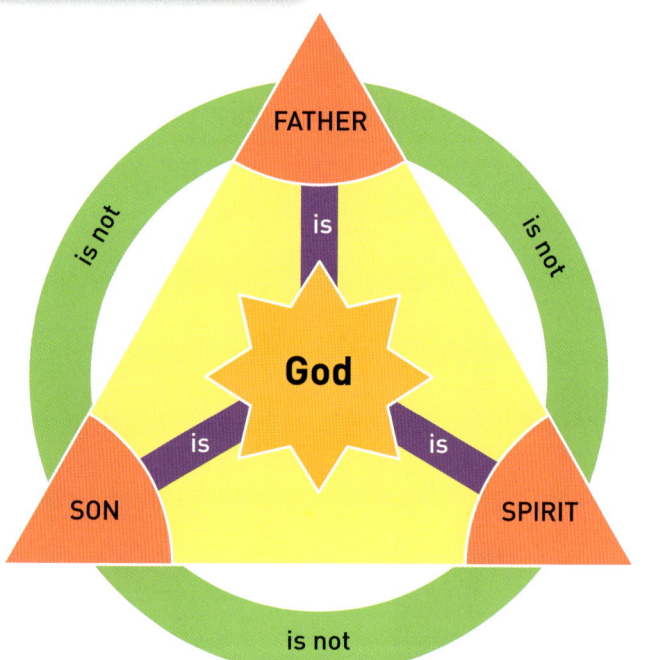

▲ This image represents what the Trinity is and also what it is not: God is all three persons, but each person of God is not the same as the other two

▶ What is the Trinity?

The Apostles' Creed, which is a statement of Christian belief, describes the three persons of God in this way:

- God the Father created heaven and Earth and sustains it (keeps it going). God is all-powerful, all-knowing and all-loving. God is eternal (has always existed) and ever-present. Some would say God the Father is beyond human understanding.
- God the Son is Jesus. He was incarnated (born) as a human to bring God's message and to be sacrificed for humans. His death as a sacrifice broke down a barrier between God and humans which had been caused by the sins of humans. He was resurrected (brought back to life) to show that death can be conquered and people can go to heaven. Humans can relate to God the Son as he was a human like us.
- God the Holy Spirit is the presence of God on Earth. After Jesus went to heaven, he left behind the Spirit as a comforter and guide. This means God is always with us.

How Christians express their belief in the Trinity

Christians express their belief in the Trinity in many ways. The following are some of the more obvious.

Repeating the belief

As it is a central belief, often Christians say 'in the name of God the Father, God the Son and God the Holy Spirit'. These words are in the important creeds, or statements of belief. They might say the phrase in times of need, or times of reflection. Some will say it when they wake up and before they go to sleep. It helps them to stay aware of God, and their own beliefs. By staying aware of God, they are less likely to behave in ways they shouldn't as a Christian.

Making the sign of the belief

Believing Jesus died on the cross as a sacrifice, then rose from the dead is key to being a Christian. You might have seen Christians make the sign of the cross. They tap their forehead, then their heart, and then their shoulders, one after the other. These physical actions help them remember the words: Father, Son and Holy Spirit. Many Christians make this sign when they enter or leave church; church leaders use it when blessing people. You may also see footballers do this before they start to play, or when they score a goal.

Displaying the belief

In most churches the Trinity is symbolised, either in paintings or in other forms of art that represent the concept of three-in-one. Some Christians also have the symbolism of the Trinity in their home. Some Christians wear jewellery that represents the Trinity. Because it is such an important belief, Christians use it as a focus for their prayer and worship.

▲ Symbolism of the Trinity carved into stone in a churchyard.

▲ It is common to see the idea of three represented in Christian buildings, for example, the three windows together over the entrance to the Tabernacle Baptist Church in Llandudno

Activities

1. What does the term 'Trinity' mean?
2. Draw a symbol for the Trinity, and label the three parts with the names of the persons of the Trinity. Add two pieces of information about each.
3. Explain why many Christians might repeat the description of the Trinity every day.
4. What evidence is there that the idea of the Trinity is very important to Christians?
5. 'God the Son is the most important part of the Trinity.' Do you agree with this statement? Give some reasons for your opinion, and some arguments which could be used to oppose your opinion.

The major world faiths

4.2 Key Christian beliefs – moral behaviour and the afterlife

Learning objectives

- To learn key basic Christian beliefs concerning moral behaviour and life after death
- To understand the importance of Jesus in each of these beliefs
- To reflect on belief in the afterlife as an influence on behaviour

Big question

Do people behave in this life for fear of what might happen in the next?

Talk it out

How many rules do you think we need as a society to live in harmony?

What might be the key rules that everyone should have to obey?

Can you think of any rules which would cover a wide range of issues?

The Book of Matthew records Jesus as having given a series of teachings to help people understand the religion. Jesus was a Jewish man, and so bound by the 613 mitzvot, or commands. These were rules given by God to Moses on Mount Sinai, and were part of a covenant between God and the Israelites. They covered all aspects of life, and are still kept today by those of the Jewish faith.

Of course, it is very difficult to remember so many rules, and so to always abide by them. Each person was expected to try their best to follow these rules given by God – and if any were broken, to make up for that.

Jesus was asked the question of what the greatest commandment was. It was a very difficult question - how do you choose between so many? Doesn't it depend on the situation, for example? In giving an answer, Jesus very cleverly boiled the whole lot down into what he called the 'great commandments', and there were two of them.

First and foremost, Jesus said 'Love God with all your heart, soul and mind'. In other words, absolutely and truly love God. Second, he said 'Love your neighbour as yourself'.

Jesus' point was that by always observing these two commandments, then any other rule would also be followed.

Think about it – if you love God, you follow all his rules; if you love each other, you live in a kind and compassionate way, helping others and not hurting them. The second commandment is really about living a life which is unselfish, and which seeks to be a benefit to others and the world. It tells us to consider everyone else as we would like them to consider us - we all want people to be kind and good to us, and not to be cruel or horrible. Every religion has a version of this. In Luke's Gospel (6:31) it says 'Do to others as you would have them do to you' – another one of the many versions Jesus gave.

The second Great Commandment can be followed by everyone – Christian or not – and is called the Golden Rule. Essentially it is that we should try to be decent human beings. No one can really argue with that as a principle, whatever they do or don't believe. If everyone lived by this principle, what a world it would be!

> '"Teacher, which is the greatest commandment in the Law?"'
>
> Jesus replied: "Love the Lord your God with all your heart and with all your soul and with all your mind." This is the first and greatest commandment. And the second is like it: "Love your neighbour as yourself." All the Law and the Prophets hang on these two commandments.' (*Matthew 22:36–40*)

▶ What Christians believe about life after death

Christians believe in the resurrection, that after death, people are raised from the dead, as Jesus was. Some Christians believe this will be a physical resurrection – that we will get a real body. Others believe it will be a spiritual resurrection – that our soul will be in a new spiritual form. We will then be judged by God.

Christians believe that God makes a judgement on each person for their actions and beliefs. Sins are actions that go against God, and that may or may not be hurtful to others. It is important for Christians to be truly sorry for any sins they have committed, and to ask God's forgiveness. This is part of the judgement on Judgement Day.

Roman Catholics believe that after death our soul is immediately judged. They believe that the judgement will be based on the strength of our faith, how we practised our faith, and how we acted on it. Then at the end of time there will be a Judgement Day when God reveals all the judgements.

After Judgement Day, everyone is sent to either heaven or hell.

- Hell is the place where sinners – those who were not truly sorry for the things they did – go. Hell is a terrible place of suffering and torture. This suffering might be forever – eternal damnation.
- Heaven is a place of everlasting life with God. It is for those who have been good in this life, and demonstrated their faith. It is a place of peace, contentment and happiness.

Roman Catholics also believe that souls might be sent to purgatory. Purgatory is a state in which our soul can be prepared for heaven. Imagine the soul becoming dirty through sins; purgatory is the place where the soul is cleaned.

Most modern Christians believe that the most important thing is to live a good life, helping others. Many believe that people who are not Christian but have lived morally good lives would also be able to get to heaven.

▲ Graveyards are full of gravestones on which are statements testifying to the belief that there will be a life after this one.

"Whosoever believes in me shall have everlasting life." (*Jesus*)

"For we must all appear before the judgement seat of Christ; so that everyone may receive what is owed to him – good or bad – according to what he has done." (*St Paul*)

"What good does it do a man if he only has faith? Faith without actions is pointless." (*St James*)

Activities

1. What are the two Great Commandments?
2. Do you think that anyone can follow the two Great Commandments? Explain your ideas.
3. Explain what Christians believe about life after death. Include the following words in your answer: soul, Judgement Day, purgatory, heaven and hell.
4. Is it more important to believe in God, or to be a good person? Explain your own ideas, then explain ideas from a different point of view.

The major world faiths

4.3 The life of Jesus – the Incarnation

Learning objectives
- To know the stories of Jesus' birth (found in Matthew and Luke)
- To explore the way these stories show Jesus to have been special from birth
- To reflect on the importance of Jesus' birth

Big question
Is every child special when they are born?

Key beliefs
Christians believe Jesus is the Son of God, one of the three parts of the Trinity. They call his birth as a human the Incarnation. The story of his birth is called the **Nativity**.

Talk it out
Quiz three classmates about the birth of Jesus.

Pool your knowledge and try to come up with the full story before reading it below.

An angel came to Mary, a young Jewish woman. She was told God had chosen her to be the mother of God's child even though she was a virgin.

Mary's husband Joseph had to go to Bethlehem for a census. He took his heavily pregnant wife with him.

All the inns in town were full. A kindly inn-keeper allowed the couple to stay in a stable. Mary gave birth in the stable.

An angel visited shepherds and told them to go and pay respect to Jesus, which they did.

Wise men had heard a king had been born, so they. They followed a star. They visited Herod's palace expecting to find the new king. When they didn't find a king there, they left to find Jesus. When they found him they gave him special gifts.

The angel told the wise men not to return to Herod. Herod felt threatened by this new 'king' and ordered his soldiers to kill all male babies.

Mary and Joseph fled to Egypt to escape Herod's murderous search.

4 Christianity

The Bible has two accounts of Jesus' birth: Matthew 2:1–11, and Luke 2:1–20. Generally, the story is the same in both: Mary and Joseph go to Bethlehem for a census, Jesus is born in a manger because there is no room at the inns. There are important differences though: Matthew mentions the wise men and the threat from Herod; Luke does not. Luke mentions the shepherds; Matthew does not. These two Gospel writers were not Jesus' disciples; they were Christians who lived after his death. They were not eye-witnesses, but learned the stories sometime after the events took place. Scholars say that where two Gospel writers say the same, they used the same source of information; where they differ, they used their own sources.

▶ Prophecies about Jesus

A 'prophecy' is a foretelling or prediction about the future. Christians believe that Jesus' birth had been predicted by prophecies in the Jewish holy book, which Christians call the Old Testament:

- In the book of Isaiah, it says a virgin will give birth to a child. When Mary, a virgin, was told she was to have a baby, the angel said it would be the Son of God.
- In Hosea, it says 'When Israel was a child … out of Egypt I called my son'. Joseph had to take his family to Egypt to keep them safe from King Herod. After Herod died, they returned to their home in Palestine.
- In Micah, it says that a person who will rule over all Israel (the **Messiah**) will come from Bethlehem. Jesus was born there.

▶ Significant visitors

Jesus was visited by three groups of people: angels, shepherds and wise men from the East.

- The angels obey and worship God. Christians believe that the fact that angels came and worshipped Jesus shows that he is God.
- Angels told the shepherds to visit and pay their respects to the baby Jesus. Shepherds were very poor in Jesus' day – they represent the ordinary person.
- The wise men, or kings, from the East are presented as wealthy and educated. They represent the rich and wise visiting Jesus.
- Animals were already in the stable – they represent the rest of God's creation.

▶ Special gifts for a special child

The wise men brought three gifts: gold, frankincense and myrrh. These were strange gifts for a baby.

- Gold has been valuable throughout history, a symbol of wealth and power. As a gift, it indicates that Jesus would be powerful and a leader.
- Frankincense is a perfume which was used to anoint priests. This gift suggests Jesus would give important religious messages.
- Myrrh is an expensive perfume which was used on dead bodies as part of the burial process. It indicates that Jesus was destined to die, so is a prophecy of his end.

Activities

1. Copy and complete the following sentences:
   Jesus was born in _____. An angel told his mother, called ____, that she would give birth to the _____ of _____. He was visited by _____ and by _____. They brought gifts of _____, _____ and _____.
2. Give two Old Testament prophecies about Jesus.
3. Why do you think it is important that in the story Jesus is visited by angels, rich people and poor people, and that there are animals in the stable?
4. Imagine you work for a film company that is about to make a film about the Nativity. Draw and/or write the storyboard for the film's eight main scenes.
6. 'Jesus' birth shows us he was very special.' Do you agree with this statement? Try to think of at least two reasons to agree, and two reasons to disagree with the statement.

4.4 The importance of Christmas

Learning objectives
- To know how Christians celebrate Christmas
- To recall the background to the Christmas celebrations
- To reflect on the influence Christianity has had on our celebrations

Big question

Should only Christians celebrate Christmas?

Christmas is an important festival in the UK. Most schools close for a fortnight, businesses close and few shops open on Christmas Day. Shops start selling Christmas cards, wrapping paper and gifts months ahead of the day. There is special Christmas food, special TV programming, people go out for Christmas meals and exchange cards and gifts. The large majority of people in the UK celebrate this festival, even those who are not Christian or religious. Christmas does, however, have a deeply religious origin, and has important religious meaning for Christians.

Christmas is a festival that celebrates the birth of Jesus (see pages 46 and 47). Christians believe Jesus was the Son of God, born as a man to eventually die and be raised from the dead. He brought a new message to guide people on how to live, based on love for God and each other. Christians also believe Jesus will come again (the Second Coming) at the end of time to judge everyone and decide if they go to heaven or hell. Christmas reminds Christians that they must be ready for that Second Coming.

There are many religious aspects to the celebration of Christmas, including the following:

- Advent
- Christingle
- Nativity scenes and plays
- Christmas carols
- Midnight Mass.

Advent is the period starting the fourth Sunday before Christmas Day and leading up to Christmas Day itself. It is about remembering the **First Coming** of Jesus (his birth) and preparing for his **Second Coming**. In some denominations, it is traditional for the clergy (qualified and ordained religious leaders) to wear some robes which are purple during Advent. Each week there are special readings in church. Many families have an Advent wreath at home, which carries four candles, one of which is lit each week of Advent.

Midnight Mass is an act of worship traditionally held late on Christmas Eve to welcome in Christmas Day. The fourth candle on the Advent wreath is lit. There are prayers, hymns and a short sermon about Christmas Day. It is a joyful time, when Christians come together in church to remember God's gift of Jesus to the world. (This is where the tradition of giving gifts comes from.) The candles represent Jesus as the 'light of the world'. Some churches ring their bells at midnight to signal the arrival of Christmas Day.

4 Christianity

The orange represents the world.

It has a red ribbon around it – representing God's love of the whole world, and the blood of Jesus who was sacrificed on the cross.

A lit candle in the top of the orange represents Jesus as the light of the world, bringing hope in the darkness.

Four dried fruits are stuck to the orange symbolising God's creation and the four seasons.

A Christingle is a children's service during Advent or Christmas. The service takes different forms in different churches, and may include hymns and prayers, but always centres around the making of a decorated orange. Each decoration is symbolic.

During Advent, models of Jesus in the manger in a stable are displayed in towns, churches and schools. This model is called a Nativity scene. Many Christians set up a Nativity scene at home as part of their Christmas decorations. In primary schools, it is common at the end of term for the children to do a Nativity play that retells the story of Christ's birth. Both of these are used to teach children the Christmas story.

Christmas carols are hymns for Christmas. They focus on Jesus' birth, and the importance of the Incarnation. Singing hymns is a joyful experience, and a good way to learn Christian beliefs about Christmas, God and Jesus.

Activities

1. What does Christmas mean to you? How does your family spend Christmas?
2. Why is Christmas important to Christians?
3. Explain what each of the following is: Advent, Christingle, Nativity, Midnight Mass.
4. Design a Christmas candle holder that includes symbols for a Christian Christmas. Add labels to explain your design and the symbols you use.
5. Do you think Christmas is only meaningful to Christians? Explain your answer
6. 'Christmas is the most important time of year for Christians.' Give two reasons to agree, and two to disagree with this statement. Check Topic 4.8 The importance of Easter (pages 56-57) for extra help with this.

The major world faiths

4.5 The life of Jesus – teacher

Learning objectives
- To learn about Jesus as a great teacher
- To understand Jesus' use of parables
- To explore charismatic leadership

Big question
Why do people tell stories?

> The best teachers make it easy to understand things, and they make you want to know more, and in more detail.

Talk it out
Have you ever been told a story that was intended to teach you something? What was it? How effective was it?

> It helps me to understand when someone explains about something using ideas I am already familiar with. I can use what knowledge I have to make sense of the new ideas.

Jesus was a teacher. He taught by using stories called **parables**. These stories helped people understand how to live as God wanted them to. People could go to the temple and listen to priests, but their words were often difficult to relate to ordinary life. Jesus' parables made things clear for ordinary people. He spoke charismatically, so people wanted to listen to him, and they gathered in huge crowds to hear him. They saw him as their leader partly because of his skills in speaking. The Gospels relate over 30 different parables. Here are three of the best known:

The Parable of the Prodigal Son (Luke 15:11–32)

A rich man had two sons. The younger son asked for his share of the money that he would inherit when his father died. He left to travel. He had a great time, partying wherever he went; he was a prodigal (he spent money wastefully). Meanwhile his older brother kept working hard on the family farm.

Eventually, the party money ran out. Being too ashamed to go home, the younger son found a job looking after pigs, but it paid so little that he was forced to eat the pigs' food to survive. He realised that his father's servants had a much better life than him, and he decided to go home, beg forgiveness and ask his father for a job as a servant.

When the younger son arrived home, his father was overjoyed and threw a huge party. He even killed the calf he had been fattening for a feast. The older brother was angry and jealous – after all, his brother had wasted all that money, whereas he had been loyal. It seemed that his father was not bothered about his younger son's selfishness. His father took him aside and reminded him that everything now belonged to him, and his brother had nothing, but that because everyone had thought his brother had gone forever, it was right to celebrate his return.

The message: Everyone (no exceptions) is welcomed and forgiven by God – if they are sorry.

> I can listen to some people for ages. The way they speak and explain makes so much sense. They are charismatic, and just make me want to hear more.

> Sometimes what a person says really rings true for that time because of how they say it, and what they link it to. Then it inspires.

4 Christianity

The Parable of the Sower and Seed (Mark 4:1–20)

A farmer went out to plant seed. As he scattered it, some fell on the path and was eaten by the birds. Some fell on rocky soil and sprouted quickly but also died quickly, having nowhere to send its roots. Some fell among the weeds, and were choked before they could grow properly. Some fell on good soil. These seeds put down strong roots, and were well nourished by the soil. They grew into fine plants.

The message: The Christian teachings are given to everyone, but not everyone takes notice of them and lives by them. The good soil represents those who do – within whom the Christian message takes root and flourishes.

The Parable of the Wheat and Tares (Matthew 13:24–30)

A man sowed his fields with good seed. In the night, an enemy came and sowed tares (weeds) among the good seed. When the plants came up, it was clear that there were grain crops and weeds. A servant asked the sower if they should pull up the weeds. The sower said to leave them, as pulling up the weeds would also pull up the grain crop. All the plants were to be left until harvest, when the servants would pull up the weeds first and burn them, and then collect the grain for the barns.

The message: At the end of time, those people who have listened to Jesus' message will be collected up by God and taken to heaven; the others will be thrown to the fires of hell.

Activities

1. What is a parable? Why were they told?
2. Write out this table so that the two halves match up correctly.

The Parable of the Prodigal Son	At the end of time, those who have not followed the right message will not be rewarded by God, but will be punished.
The Parable of the Sower and Seed	People can change and should be praised for positive change.
	We should never be afraid to ask for help when we need it.
The Parable of the Wheat and Tares	People respond differently to the same teaching – some ignore it, some seize on it but lose interest, some are influenced by others to forget it, some listen and do well because of it.

3. Choose one parable. Retell it in your own words, or as a cartoon strip or storyboard. Explain the meaning of the parable you chose.
4. 'People use parables (stories) all the time to explain things.' Do you think this is true? Explain your answer.
5. 'Parables have messages for everyone who hears them, not just Christians.' Do you agree with this statement? Explain why, giving at least two reasons. Can you think of a different point of view? Give reasons to support that view.

The major world faiths

4.6 The life of Jesus – miracle worker

Learning objectives
- To learn about some of the miracles that Jesus is said to have performed
- To explore why Jesus performed miracles
- To think about the idea of miracles, and the messages they give

Big question
Can anyone perform a miracle?

Key terms
Miracle – event contrary to the laws of nature, which brings a good outcome; often believed to be an act of God by religious people

Christians believe Jesus was the Son of God, so had special powers and could do impossible things. They see these **miracles** as proof that he was the Son of God, and that God is active in the world.

The first four books of the New Testament of the Bible record Jesus' life and teachings. They are called the four Gospels. The Gospels give accounts of thirty-seven miracles by Jesus; here are three examples.

Power of healing

At the pool at Bethesda, it was said that an angel occasionally came to touch the water, making it ripple. The first person who went into the pool after the water rippled would be cured of any illness. Many people went every day to try to be the first one into the pool. One man had been paralysed for 38 years, so could never be the first into the pool. On the Sabbath, Jesus asked him if he wanted to be well. The man said he was too slow to reach the water. Jesus instructed him to pick up his bed and walk. Miraculously, the man did as he was told, and he was cured. Later he was challenged for carrying his bed on the Sabbath – the day of no work. He explained that his healer had told him to, but that he did not know his healer's name. Still later, Jesus approached him in the temple, and told him that as he had been made well, he should not **sin** any more. It was after this that the man told people that Jesus had healed him.

▲ Jesus healing the man at Bethesda

Power over nature

Thousands had come to hear Jesus' words and be healed. Showing loving kindness, he wanted to feed them. Having been told by Jesus to collect up food from the crowds, the disciples found only five loaves and two fishes. Jesus blessed the food and broke it into pieces. The disciples then distributed it to the crowd. It fed everyone who was hungry, *and* afterward, the disciples collected twelve basketfuls of leftover food.

◀ Jesus blessed the food

Power over life and death

Jesus heard that his friend Lazarus was very ill. Instead of going to him, Jesus stayed where he was for a few days. He told his disciples that Lazarus was suffering so that God's power to send miracles could be shown. When Jesus finally arrived, Lazarus had been dead for four days, so was in a tomb. Lazarus' sister was very sad and angry that Jesus had not come earlier – she said that if he had come earlier, her brother would have been saved, but now it was too late. Lazarus' body had been placed into a tomb and the tomb sealed. Jesus asked if she believed in him, and she said she did. Jesus went to the tomb, where crowds saw that he himself was upset. He demanded the stone be removed from the entrance to the tomb. Following its removal, he then called for Lazarus to come out. Lazarus walked out, still covered in the grave cloths, but alive. Jesus had raised him from the dead.

▲ A wood-cutting showing Jesus raising Lazarus from the dead

▶ Why did Jesus perform miracles?

- He was doing the right thing and showing compassion (loving kindness) for others. Someone like the man at Bethesda would have had to beg for his whole life – there was no system of benefits from the government. After being healed, he would be able to work.
- We are told that Jesus' miracles made people praise God. In other words, the miracles demonstrated God's power and love to everyone.
- People's faith made miracles possible. Lazarus' sister believed Jesus could still help her brother, even though Lazarus was dead.

Activities

1. List some of the kinds of miracles Jesus did.
2. Why did Jesus perform miracles?
3. What do the miracles Jesus performed tell us about his character?
4. Look up these miracles in the Bible:
   - Blind Bartimaeus (Mark 10:46–52)
   - Calming the storm (Mark 4:35–41)
   - Girl restored to life; woman healed (Luke 8:40–56)

   Choose one of these. Write a front-page newspaper report about this miracle. In your report, you should describe what happened and include an eye-witness account and an image.
5. 'Jesus only performed miracles to help people.' Do you think that is true? What might have been his other motives? Explain your arguments.

4.7 Jesus – his death and resurrection

Learning objectives
- To know the events that happened before the death of Jesus
- To learn about how the Gospels describe the death and resurrection of Jesus
- To reflect on the importance of different parts of a person's life

Big question
What is the most important part of a person's life?

Key beliefs
Christians believe Jesus was the **Son of God**, one of the persons of the Trinity which is God. However, they also believe he was born and died as a human. His death was necessary as an **atonement** (to make up) for the sins of people. These sins had created a barrier between humans and God, preventing them from having a relationship with God in this life and being with God in heaven.

Jesus was seen as a threat to the religious and political leaders. They had heard he was being called the Son of God and this challenged their authority. Eventually he was arrested and sentenced to death.

▶ The Last Supper
On the evening of Jesus' arrest, he shared one last meal with his disciples – the Last Supper. He shared bread and wine, and told his disciples to copy this act as a way of remembering him. He knew that he would be arrested and killed. He told them the bread was his body and the wine his blood – both of which were to be shed (given away) for them. Christians today remember this at the Eucharist or Holy Communion (see Topic 4.12, page 64).

▶ The arrest and trials
After the Last Supper, Jesus went to pray in the Garden of Gethsemane. He was upset and asked God not to make him follow this difficult path – but he realised there was no choice and that he had to go through with it. While the other disciples slept, one of them, Judas, brought soldiers to the garden who arrested Jesus.

During the night, Jesus faced three trials. The first two were with religious leaders. They demanded he admit claiming to be the Son of God, which was blasphemy (disrespecting God) and punishable by death. Jesus did not try to defend himself, and in the third trial, the Roman governor Pilate sentenced him to death by crucifixion – even though he could not find that Jesus had done anything wrong.

▲ The image of the crucifix is very important to most Christians as it symbolises the death of Jesus as a sacrifice for the sins of humans

▶ The crucifixion
Jesus had to carry his cross to Golgotha, the execution site. At Golgotha, he was crucified between two thieves. He was stabbed in the side with a spear as he hung from the cross. Before he died, he asked God to forgive the executioners 'for they know not what they have done'. It is said the sky went black, and the cloth in the temple which hid its holiest part from view was torn in two. One soldier proclaimed, 'Surely this was the Son of God'.

▶ The burial

Jesus' family would not have had a tomb for his body, so Joseph of Arimathea – a believer in Jesus' message – had given his own tomb for Jesus to be buried in. The body was taken there on Friday afternoon and a stone was rolled across the entrance. The Sabbath had begun – the day of rest – so nothing else could be done until Sunday.

▶ The empty tomb

When Jesus' female followers arrived at the tomb on Sunday, they saw that the stone had been rolled back and the tomb was empty. They thought Jesus' body had been stolen. Two men were there, who told them that Jesus had risen from the dead. Jesus himself appeared to Mary Magdalene, who – upset and confused – thought he was a gardener.

▲ On arrival at the tomb, Jesus' followers found the stone rolled away and his body gone. An angel told them Jesus had risen.

▶ The resurrection

Jesus had risen from the dead – as he had said he would. His first appearance to his disciples after his resurrection happened when they were hiding, afraid to come out because of Jesus' arrest and execution. Jesus visited them. One disciple, Thomas, was not there when this happened, so did not believe their stories. Jesus then appeared to him and let him touch the spear mark in his side – to prove it was really him. On the fortieth day after his crucifixion, Jesus rose up to heaven (the Ascension).

Activities

1. Write out this table so that the two halves match up correctly.

Jesus shared bread and wine with his disciples at the Last Supper.	Jesus accepted his fate.
Jesus was arrested after Judas betrayed him.	The women found the tomb empty and believed his body to have been stolen.
Jesus was crucified and died on Friday before the Sabbath had begun.	Christians do this today as Holy Communion in remembrance of Jesus.
Jesus rose from the dead on Sunday.	His body could not be prepared properly because it was the Sabbath.

2. Who sentenced Jesus to death?
3. Create a timeline for the final events of Jesus' life. You could do some research of the Gospel stories to help provide details (Matthew 26–8; Mark 14–16; Luke 22–4; John 18–20).
4. How do you think the disciples would have felt at the different stages: Last Supper, Jesus' arrest, crucifixion, resurrection? Create a living graph of their emotions as events happened.
5. 'Jesus could have chosen not to be killed.' Do you think this is a fair statement? Give reasons to agree and to disagree with it. Use examples and explanations to strengthen the points you make.

4.8 The importance of Easter

Learning objectives
- To learn how Christians celebrate Easter
- To understand the importance and symbolism of Easter
- To reflect on the ideas of sacrifice and atonement

Big question
Why do people make sacrifices?

For most Christians, Easter is the most important part of the Christian calendar as it is a time for remembering Jesus' death and resurrection. Christians believe Jesus had to be sacrificed so that the sins of all people could be forgiven. His death was an atonement for those sins (it made up for those sins). They believe that the barrier between God and humans was too great to be broken in any other way. While Easter has a very sad element to it – that Jesus had to die – it also has a joyful one: Jesus rose from the dead, humans were reconciled with God, and now heaven is open to them after death. Look back at pages 54–5 to find out more about the events that Easter recalls.

During the Easter period, the sadness and the joy are both reflected in how churches are decorated, how Christians worship and how the clergy dress.

The following are the key elements of the festival.

▶ Palm Sunday

Palm Sunday is the Sunday before Easter Sunday, and the start of Holy Week. The service on Palm Sunday often includes processions, as a representation of Jesus' entry to Jerusalem before his arrest. Palm crosses are given out to everyone who attends to remind them that the people of Jerusalem waved palm branches in honour of Jesus. They were greeting him as a king. In Wales, it is traditional to lay flowers at graves on Palm Sunday.

▲ A palm cross

▶ Good Friday

In many churches there is a special evening service on Maundy Thursday, which is the day before Good Friday. This service recalls the Last Supper, Jesus' last night of freedom with his disciples, when he was very sad about what was to come. During the service, the altar will be stripped of almost everything, and a black cloth is laid over it.

The service on Good Friday is sad and thoughtful. All the hymns, readings and the sermon are about what happened to Jesus, and that this made God's forgiveness of human sin possible.

Christians think a lot about how they can be better people, and the sacrifices they could make for their faith. In some churches, there is a procession with someone carrying a cross, to remind people of what Jesus was made to do.

▲ Good Friday focuses on the crucifixion of Jesus

4 Christianity

▶ The Easter vigil

The Easter vigil is a service that takes places very late on Easter Saturday. It is about waiting for the day when Jesus rose from the dead (Easter Sunday). In many churches, the service finishes before midnight, everyone leaves and the church lights are turned out. There may be a procession round the church or hymns may be sung outside the church, with everyone holding candles that have been lit from the Paschal (Easter) candle. This represents Jesus as the 'light of the world'. At midnight, the church is opened again in a blaze of light. The altar will be newly dressed, the black cloth replaced with a white one, and flowers decorate the church. Traditionally, this was a day used for Confirmation – when a person is confirmed a Christian by being blessed – and in Roman Catholic and Anglican traditions this is still very common. This is a joyful service because it celebrates that 'Christ is risen'.

▲ Chocolate eggs, painted eggs and Easter cards are all exchanged at Easter

▶ Easter Sunday

The service on Easter Sunday is a happy one, and the sermon, hymns, readings and prayers focus on Jesus rising from the dead, and heaven being open to all. God's mercy and forgiveness are celebrated. After the service, many churches have a congregational meal, so that everyone can eat together like one big family.

▶ Celebrating Easter outside church

Like lots of other people in the UK, many Christians give chocolate eggs as gifts. The egg represents life, and the stone that covered Jesus' tomb. Easter is also a holiday in the UK so many people enjoy the days off school or work. Some people send cards – Easter greetings with religious images or symbolism. People may paint eggs, and roll hard-boiled eggs, in races downhill whether they are Christian or not.

▲ Easter vigil

Activities

1 Copy and complete this table:

Day	What is remembered?	How is it celebrated?
Palm Sunday		
Maundy Thursday		
Good Friday		
Easter Saturday		
Easter Sunday		

2 Explain why Easter is the most important event in the Christian calendar.

3 Find the dates for Easter this year. Use them to create an advert for events for a church – you need to include the day, date and time of each service, and a brief explanation of what people can expect.

4 Do you agree that Jesus' sacrifice is why Easter is the most important festival for Christians? Explain your opinion.

The major world faiths

4.9 Where Christians worship

Learning objectives
- To know the basic elements of a church building
- To explore some Welsh churches and their different styles
- To explore how beliefs influence church architecture

Big question
Do all churches look the same?

Talk it out
Identify the churches in your community. List the features that help you to recognise a church.

▶ Church-spotting

Christians worship in a church. In Wales, many are called chapels. They might also be called a cathedral or meeting house. The people who go to church are also known as the church, or congregation.

For Christians, most acts of worship take place in a **church**. Churches have different styles depending on what denomination they were built by, and when they were built. Wales has a long history of Christianity, so many churches are quite old. The period of time from the seventeenth to the nineteenth century saw many more Nonconformist churches and chapels built, which have a different style to those that were built earlier. Modern churches are different again. Despite the differences, many churches have certain features in common which make them easy to recognise.

Many churches have bell-towers. The bell was used to alert people that worship was due to begin, to mark the time (before people had watches) and for special occasions like festivals.

Many Nonconformist chapels have simple architecture. They are like big houses because the decoration and splendour of traditional churches was rejected as a distraction from worship (rather than a way to aid worship).

◀ Providence Baptist Chapel, Cwmdu

Churches usually have big doors – this shows that all are welcome. Some Nonconformist chapels have two doors. Historically, one was for men and one was for women.

▶ Church of St David, Llanddewi'r-Cwm

Many churches have their own churchyard. The graves are positioned inside the wall, which is the border for the sacred land of the church. Historically, the wall was the border of the consecrated land (land that is blessed by being dedicated to God). The church building itself was a place of sanctuary where anyone could seek protection from persecution or the law.

▲ New Life Church, Llandrindod Wells

4 Christianity

Stained glass windows let light in, which is symbolic of the light of Jesus' teachings. They also help to remind church-goers of the Christian message and to teach them, by showing famous saints, people and events. They can also be impressive and awe-inspiring.

The font is found at the entrance to many churches. It is a standing bowl for the baptism of babies. Being at the entrance, it symbolises a welcome into the Christian faith for the child. Some churches, for example Baptist churches, have a baptism pool for adult baptism.

The altar is the focal point of most churches and is located at the front. It represents the holiest part of the church, so often has a barrier, such as a communion rail around it, separating it from the rest of the church. There is usually a cross or crucifix on the altar, as a reminder of Jesus' sacrifice as an atonement for human sin. The communion service, with its bread and wine, is usually done around the altar.

The organ is a common feature of churches. Music is very important in Welsh Christianity – hymns praising God are a feature of worship. The Bible tells Christians to 'raise a joyful sound' to God.

Pews are seats or benches. Pews in a church are mostly all the same, symbolising the equality of all people before God. Many churches use chairs instead of pews, but they will still all be the same.

The pulpit is a special raised stand for the vicar or minister to speak from when reading the sermon. It may have Christian symbols on it and can be simple or decorated. It is a central feature of Nonconformist chapels. The lectern is a stand which holds the Bible for people to read from. Sometimes these are decorated with Christian symbols like the eagle you can see here.

Activities

1. What different names are given to a Christian place of worship?
2. List the ways in which it is possible to recognise a building as a church from the outside.
3. Write about each of the following: altar, font, stained glass window, pulpit.
4. What is the most important feature of a church? Explain your answer.
5. 'Church buildings give us a good idea of Christian beliefs.' Do you agree with this statement? Explain your ideas.

The major world faiths

4.10 How Christians worship

Learning objectives

- To know the elements of a Christian act of worship
- To understand how Christians use aids to worship
- To reflect on whether worship should be private or public

Big question
What counts as 'worship'?

Key terms
Orthodox – a Christian denomination which is the oldest form of Christianity; based mainly in the region from Greece to Russia today

Blessed – granted grace or good will from God

Prayer – communicating with God; speaking to God

All Christians attend public acts of worship; they join with others in worshipping God. Group worship takes place in a church on Sunday each week. Many churches have more than one act of worship (service) on Sunday, and many have additional ones in the week.

Christian acts of worship have some common features, as explained in the diagram below:

Bible readings – Christianity is based on the message of Jesus which is in the Bible, so there will always be at least one reading from it. The reader stands at a lectern so that they can be seen and heard. In many churches, it is common for there to be a reading from the Old Testament and the New Testament.

Sermon – the lesson of the service. This is the message that the person leading the service wants to get across that day. The Bible reading, prayers and hymns will reflect it. The subject might be decided by the time of year, such as a Christmas sermon about giving; or events in the world, for example, a sermon about helping others after a natural disaster.

Prayers – talking to God. The Lord's Prayer will always be said since it is the prayer Jesus taught his disciples, as recorded in the New Testament. Some prayers are said only by whoever leads the service, while others are spoken together by everyone. There may also be time for people to pray silently.

Hymns – songs of praise for God. In the Bible, it says 'make a joyful noise unto the Lord' so it is traditional for Christians to use music in their worship, especially in Wales. Many churches have choirs that lead the singing.

Liturgical and non-liturgical worship

Roman Catholics, **Orthodox** and Anglican churches use a set format and wording for their services – this is called liturgical worship. In the Anglican church (called the Church in Wales since 1920), this is in the *Book of Common Prayer*, which was originally published in 1549. The first version in Welsh was written in 1567, though a definitive version was only published in 1664 (after an Act of Parliament). This was the official and lawful version to be used by all. As this is used in all liturgical services, a person going to such a service anywhere can join in, and feel part of the service.

In Wales, the Nonconformists rejected liturgical worship, as do the modern Evangelical and Pentecostal movements. Though very different forms of Christianity, Nonconformists, Evangelical and Pentecostal Christians all believe that the act of worship should come from inspiration, and not be fixed by a book. They also believe that those leading the service will have been guided by God to focus on a message specific to that time. This is called non-liturgical worship. Evangelical and Pentecostal Christians also believe worship to be open to the Holy Spirit, so people can be overcome by that and respond in whatever way they are moved to respond by the Spirit.

> **Key beliefs**
>
> Christians believe God is always with them in the form of the Holy Spirit. God guides, protects and comforts them. This means they can talk to God or worship God at any time. For some Christians, everything they do can be done as an act of worship – they just need to dedicate it to God.

Private worship

Most Christians do not just worship with others in church on Sunday – they worship at other times in many ways. They believe God wants people to worship him, and that by worshipping God, they can forge a close relationship with him. They feel comforted and energised by their worship; it gives them a sense of well-being. By worshipping, they gain a deeper understanding of their faith, and they feel **blessed** by it – it is a very personal thing.

Christians feel closer to God when they pray to him. This does not have to involve kneeling down, putting their hands together and bowing their head. Many Christians just talk to God in their heads as a form of **prayer**. They could be doing something else and thinking of God. This makes them feel connected to, and at peace with God.

Many Christians set aside time specifically for God in their daily life. They might sit and pray to God, using rosary beads or an image to help them focus. They might read a section of the Bible or another text which helps them understand its words. Others might paint. Some might do something to help others, or help at church. The point is that they are giving this time to God in their thoughts or actions, so it is seen as an act of worship.

Aids to worship

The Bible is used by all Christians. Many read a small section of the Bible each day. It contains the history and teachings of the religion, so it helps them to understand their religion. Many read then reflect or pray.

Prayers are important in any worship. Some people repeat the same prayers over and over, in a kind of prayer-meditation. **Rosary** beads are used when the same prayer is being said a set number of times; each bead is held in turn to enable the person to keep count. They are used mainly by Catholic and Orthodox Christians.

> **Activities**
>
> 1. Design a poster explaining the four main parts of an act of worship (as shown opposite). Illustrate your poster with images and examples of each part.
> 2. Explain the difference between liturgical and non-liturgical worship.
> 3. How might a Christian worship privately?
> 4. Explain why worship is important to Christians. Include both public and private worship in your answer.
> 5. 'Private worship is better than public worship.' Give reasons for agreeing and disagreeing with this statement.

The major world faiths

4.11 The Bible and worship

Learning objectives
- To understand the use of the Christian holy book in worship
- To understand the importance of the Bible for Welsh Christians
- To consider the different ways in which Christians interpret the Bible

Big question
How important are holy books?

The Bible is the holy book of Christianity. Different Christians will give you different reasons for its importance, including the following:

- It tells humans the qualities of God, and how God has acted in the world.
- It gives God's message for humans, including how they should live in order to go to heaven.
- It provides accounts of some key events in human history, including the story of Jesus.
- People have died because they believed in this book.
- It is the most translated, most printed and most sold book in the world ever.
- It has ensured that millions could read and write, improving their lives.

Activities
1. What is the name of the Christian holy book?
2. Give two ways in which the Bible is important to Christians.
3. Christians interpret the Bible in three different ways. Explain each way.
4. Draw a picture of a Bible. Around it, add labels explaining some of the ways in which Christians use the Bible in their worship.
5. 'Books written many years ago cannot help us in the modern world.' Do you agree? Explain your ideas.

▶ How do Christians understand the Bible?

Different Christians understand the Bible in different ways. There are three main ways in which it is understood:

- A literal understanding – this is the belief that the Bible is the absolute word of God, written down by humans exactly as God wanted. These people believe that where the Bible seems wrong, or where there are different accounts of the same story, we just don't understand it properly. Even the most recent parts of the Bible are hundreds of years old and languages have changed a lot over time. This makes understanding its full meaning difficult. These people would also say that humans are not as clever as God, so we should accept what the Bible says even if we don't quite understand it. They say that this is part of the test God has given us.
- That the Bible was directly inspired by God – this is the belief that the writers of the books of the Bible were human and used their own words, but had been inspired by God to write them. This interpretation suggests there is truth in the Bible, which people can understand and which has come from God. There may be mistakes – human errors – but the Bible is still a good source of guidance on how to live, with a strong message of faith and love.
- That the Bible has a spiritual message – this is the belief that the writers of the Bible were trying to interpret the world around them. They believed in God and believed they were seeing God at work in the world. In their writing, they are trying to help others to see that there is a God, that God is good, and that God is responsible for this amazing creation we all live in.

> I read a small part of the Bible each day. I just pick any part and read. I find that it makes me feel calm. I can then think about what I have read. It is amazing how often that random part has a relevant message for me.

> The Bible is a guide, a story book, a set of poems, history – it has all kinds of literature in it. I am reading the Gospels at the moment to have a better knowledge of Jesus' message – after all, that is what Christianity is based on.

> I read it as part of Bible study. Each week I attend a class where we discuss what the selected section means for Christians here and now in the UK. I get a deeper insight into how to live my life as God wants me to.

> When I write a sermon, I base it on the Bible readings I will use. So, my guidance and advice to the people who attend my church comes from the Bible. When I carry out ceremonies – baptism, marriage, funerals – I use specific readings that fit the occasion.

> There is always an Old Testament reading and a New Testament reading from the Bible at my church on Sunday. When someone reads it aloud, I read it to myself – you get a sense of God from reading it; it is a blessing really.

> I am in the church choir. We sing hymns, most of which come from the Bible or are inspired by it. Since I practise every day, you could say that I am always mindful of the words of the Bible and God.

4.12 The Eucharist

Learning objectives
- To understand the meaning of the central ritual in Christianity
- To explore the different ways in which Christians hold the Eucharist
- To reflect on what difference making a commitment makes to a person, and if renewing that commitment helps

Big question
How does making a commitment affect a person?

▲ Representation of the Last Supper in a stained glass windows

▶ The Last Supper

The story of the Last Supper appears in three of the Gospels (Matthew 26:17–29; Mark 14:12–25; Luke 22:7–38). The Last Supper took place on the evening of Jesus' arrest which was the day before his crucifixion. Christians remember that day on Maundy Thursday. It is also told in I Corinthians 11:23–6, where it says: 'the Lord Jesus, on the night he was betrayed, took bread, and when he had given thanks, he broke it and said, "This is my body, which is for you; do this in remembrance of me." In the same way, after supper he took the cup, saying, "This cup is the new covenant in my blood; do this, whenever you drink it, in remembrance of me." For whenever you eat this bread and drink this cup, you proclaim the Lord's death until he comes.'

▶ Why is this ritual important?

Almost all Christians copy this event through a service which has several names including Eucharist, Mass, Holy Communion and Divine Liturgy. They view this ritual as a sacrament. This is a ritual through which a person receives the grace of God. It is one of two sacraments, alongside baptism, which most Christians observe. A few Christian groups – Salvation Army, Quakers – do not, as they do not believe Jesus commanded people to do it.

The ritual symbolises commitment: Jesus was sacrificing himself for humans, to make atonement for the sins of humans. It also symbolises renewal and recommitment. Some Christians complete this ritual daily. Anyone completing the ritual sees it as a fresh start – they are atoning for sins, making themselves right again with God. Lots of Christians talk about a sense of peace and well-being that they get from taking part in the Eucharist.

4 Christianity

▶ The ritual of the Eucharist

In a liturgical service, the ritual of the Eucharist is known as a sacrament – by following this ritual, a person receives grace from God. For Nonconformists, there is a very common pattern and language to the ritual, which often consists of reading the original story from one of the Gospels.

The four main forms of the ritual are described below. Try to spot the key differences between them:

▲ In the top image, a vicar blesses the host and wine for the Eucharist. In the lower picture, a worshipper holds the bread and non-alcoholic juice for their service.

In a Roman Catholic Mass, only those who have been confirmed may take part in the ritual of the Eucharist. There are Bible readings, prayers and a sermon, and the Nicene Creed is recited (reminding everyone what a Catholic must believe). The bread (unleavened wafers) and a chalice (large cup) of wine are brought to the altar, where the Eucharist prayer is said to bless them. Catholics believe the bread and wine then become the body and blood of Christ. Each person goes to stand in front of the priest, open-mouthed. He places a wafer onto their tongue and blesses them. The priest drinks the wine. The Mass ends with the reciting of the post-Eucharist prayer.

Orthodox Christians follow the Divine Liturgy. The bread and wine are prepared on the altar, which is hidden from view behind the iconostasis (a wall of images behind which only priests may go). The bread (made with yeast to represent life) is divided into four parts, three of which are blessed by the saying of the Eucharistic prayer. Orthodox Christians believe that Jesus is then present in some way in the bread and wine, but they do not become Jesus' actual body and blood. After Bible readings, prayers and a sermon, first the Bible and then the bread and wine (mixed together in a single chalice) are brought out. Everyone is invited to receive a spoonful of the mixture. The fourth portion of bread is given out to be taken to people who were not able to attend the service.

For the Church in Wales the service follows a liturgy, or set pattern. Worshippers first receive the bread or wafer, taking it in their hands. They each drink wine from a single chalice. They say the Eucharistic prayer.

Protestants and Nonconformists have a simpler service which still includes prayer, hymns and readings. Anyone may participate. It can take place at the front of the church, or be brought to them in their seat. They often have individual cups which are filled with a non-alcoholic drink, and pieces of ordinary bread, symbolising the body and blood. They remember Jesus' sacrifice but also that he gave new life.

Activities

1. Using one of the Gospel versions, outline what happened at the original Last Supper.
2. Explain why this is an important ritual for Christians.
3. Choose two of the Christian groups whose ritual is outlined. Write in your own words how they keep this ritual.
4. Christians do not all hold the same ritual. Find three differences between the groups and explain them.
5. 'In the same religion, everyone should keep religious rituals in the same way.' Give some reasons for agreeing and some for disagreeing with this statement.

4.13 Baptism – joining the faith as an infant

Learning objectives
- To explore what happens at infant baptism
- To explore the ideas of initiation and belonging
- To consider why parents make choices for their children

Big question

Does it make a difference to have an initiation when you join something?

▶ Initiations

An initiation is usually a ritual that formally admits someone to a group. Many groups have initiation rituals – some are fixed in form, others are not. You will probably know some, or may have taken part in some. Many societies have a ritual for when a person becomes an adult, for example. Initiations mark a significant point in someone's life – what is a called a 'rite of passage'.

Once initiated, a person 'belongs' to the group. The group will expect the initiate (the person who has been initiated) to follow that group's codes and rules, to behave in a certain way and to complete certain tasks. The group has gained a new member, and the initiate has gained a new 'family' which will guide and protect them. Humans are 'social animals'; belonging is very important to them. Lots of scientific research has shown that people need other people for their health and well-being.

All religions have some kind of ceremony to welcome new-born or young children. Children are the future of any religion. Religious believers are following a spiritual path. They believe it is the best for them and that it will lead to happiness or contentment on a level which is not achievable in this life. For Christians, that is an eternal afterlife with God in heaven. They want their children to have the best possible future, including after death, so it is natural for them to want their child to be in the same religion. The parents live their lives following religious beliefs and teachings, so they will bring up their child to follow them too.

Most Christians have at least a naming and welcoming ceremony for their new baby. This allows their church community to know their baby, and welcome him or her. Most also have a baptism for the baby, which formally welcomes it into the religion, making the decision for it that it will be a Christian.

▶ What happens at infant baptism?

▲ The font at Brecon Cathedral dates back to its Celtic church period

The service for baptism takes place at a font. This is a large stand with a bowl for water on the top. The water has been blessed for use in the ceremony. Many churches have their font near the main door, which indicates that the baby is welcome into the Church.

The baby is held by the vicar, with both the parents and the godparents present. The parents make promises on behalf of the child, and the godparents agree to support this and take care of the child if need be. They all agree to bring the child up in the faith. The three promises are:

- To turn to Christ
- To repent sin
- To renounce evil

The vicar makes the sign of the cross on the baby's forehead, the cross being the symbol for Christianity and Jesus' sacrifice and resurrection. The vicar then pours water over the baby's forehead three times and says, 'In the name of the Father, the Son and the Holy Spirit'. In the Catholic Church, the water represents being absolved (made free) of sin. In the Orthodox Church, the baby is fully dipped in the font three times. Water is a symbol of rebirth, of the new start that they are making as they join the religion.

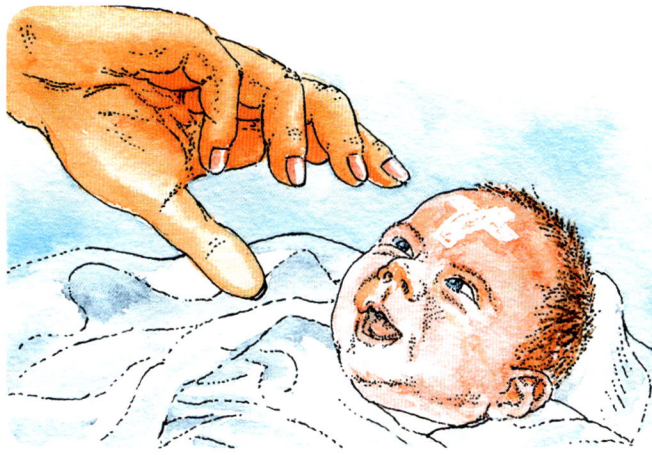

The baby is dressed in white – a symbol of purity. Many churches give the parents a baptismal candle. Christianity calls Jesus 'the light of the world', so this candle is a reminder of that name. It reminds Christians of the belief that Jesus' teachings bring light and hope to his followers, as well as showing the way to God (and heaven). For the parents, the candle is also a reminder of the promises they are making on behalf of their child, and to bring the child up in the faith.

Activities

1. Why are initiation ceremonies important?
2. Why do Christian parents have ceremonies for babies?
3. Describe a Church baptism, including explaining the symbolism. You could present this as a cartoon strip with notes and explanations.
4. Do you think that parents should have their babies baptised? Explain your reasoning.

The major world faiths

4.14 Baptism – joining the faith as an adult

Learning objectives
- To explore what happens at an adult baptism
- To explore some different forms of adult baptism used in Wales
- To reflect on the ideas of self-determination and devotion

Big question
Who should make decisions for a person?

Key terms
Baptistry – a pool in a church, used for adult baptism

Welsh Christianity has a very strong Nonconformist tradition. Nonconformists are protestants who do not follow the doctrines and rituals of the established Church of England. The Church in Wales came originally from the Anglican tradition. In 1920, the Welsh Churches separated themselves for the purpose of governance from the Church of England. The Nonconformist groups began in Wales before the nineteenth century, and include Methodists, Independents (Congregationalists), Baptists, Wesleyans, Unitarians and Quakers. Many of these denominations practise adult baptism.

Adult baptism is the baptism of a person who is old enough to have made the decision to join the religion for themselves. They are old enough to have thought about what it means to be baptised and to show this new level of devotion to God. They are old enough to decide to change their life to fit their new beliefs, and to stick to these changes. In other words, they are old enough to understand the commitment they are making and the responsibilities it brings. The denominations that use adult baptism see that in infant baptism, children are not making decisions for themselves and believe that the children are too young to make this serious decision.

▲ An impression of the baptism of Jesus

In Wales, some churches have a **baptistry**, which is a pool for baptism inside the church. Some Welsh churches complete the ritual of adult baptism in flowing water – a stream or river – following the example of Jesus being baptised in the River Jordan (Mark 1:9–13).

68

What happens at an adult baptism?

The candidate for baptism wears white clothes, as a sign of their genuine commitment to 'begin a new life in Christ'. The service might include hymns and prayers, and a short sermon by the person leading the service.

There are two focal points to the service. The first is a testimony (formal statement) by the candidate for baptism. They explain to the congregation what brought them to the decision to commit to a 'life in Christ'. This ceremony is a symbol of that commitment; it shows they are willing to devote themselves to a spiritual life. The testimony might also include a description of their life before, and the responsibilities they will observe from now on. The candidate will say sorry for their past sins and misdeeds. They will affirm their faith in Jesus, and their intention to give lifelong service. This is their decision and a more serious commitment than the commitment made by parents at an infant baptism.

 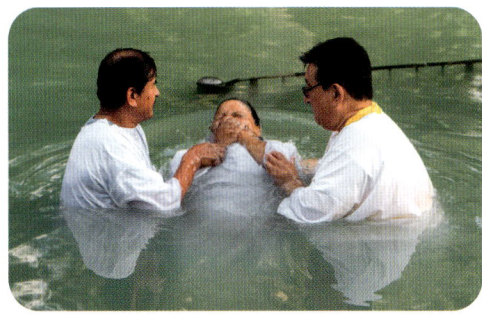

▲ Adult baptism can happen in a baptistry in a church (left) or outside in a natural body of water (right)

The second focal point is the baptism itself. This involves the person stepping down into the waist-deep baptistry water from one side of the baptistry. They are leaving behind their old life of sin and separation from God. In the water, someone waits to hold them as they drop back to immerse themselves fully in the water, washing away sins. As this happens, the person who is holding them says, 'I baptise you in the name of the Father, the Son and the Holy Spirit. Amen'. Rising from the water symbolises resurrection – the person is starting a new life with Christ. The newly baptised person steps out of the baptistry, often at the opposite end to where they entered it – the new steps symbolising the new life. They will go to get dried off before re-joining the congregation.

It is very common for the service to be ended with a show of fellowship from the minister on behalf of the congregation. As this is such a joyful occasion, many people who have attended want to give their own personal congratulations to the baptised.

Activities

1. Why do some Christians think people should be baptised as adults?
2. Using pictures and text, describe the process of adult baptism.
3. In your opinion, which is the most important part of the process of adult baptism – the testimony, the actual baptism or the welcome by the congregation? Explain your ideas.
4. 'People who are baptised as adults will be more devoted to worshipping God and giving service to others.' Do you agree? Explain your reasons.

I felt very humble when I did my testimony – it was really hard to talk about myself and my faults like that. I was nervous stepping into the baptistry, but when I broke up through the water – such joy and elation. Afterwards, everyone was laughing and smiling and hugging me. I know they will make this difficult life journey easier for me. Jenny

I was baptised as a baby – but that meant nothing, I was too young. As a young man, I learned what faith in Jesus could really mean in my life. I decided to be baptised again – my decision, my promises to keep. Dewi

Our church baptises in flowing water. Just as Jesus was baptised, so are we. The water literally washes us (and washes away our sins). It is a connection with God's creation as well as with the Holy Spirit. Gwyn

The major world faiths

4.15 Pilgrimage in Christianity

Learning objectives
- To understand why pilgrimage is important for some Christians
- To explore the North Wales Pilgrim's Way as an example of Welsh pilgrimage
- To reflect on ideas of devotion and resilience

Big question

Is it better to travel or to have reached a destination?

Unlike in some religions, there is no duty to make pilgrimages in Christianity. Many Christians will never make a pilgrimage in their lifetime. However, many Christians do visit places that are important to their religion and some will make journeys, stopping at specific holy places before reaching a final pilgrimage destination.

In Wales, there are many places for pilgrimage, some of which are linked to the many Celtic saints. There are also several 'Pilgrim's Ways' – walking routes that pass through a number of holy places. Every year, more people undertake the walk along these ways. Religious tourism is also targeted by the Welsh Tourism agency (Visit Wales) to bring money into the Welsh economy.

▶ Why is pilgrimage important to Christians?

- A visit to a place of importance in the religion enables the pilgrim to touch history.
- The journey is a way to show devotion. By walking, for example, a pilgrim has to put effort and energy into their pilgrimage. It also allows them time to reflect on their life and their faith.
- The journey through Wales is beautiful, which reminds the pilgrim of God's creative power.
- The whole visit is time devoted to faith and God, and time out from normal life.

▶ The North Wales Pilgrim's Way – Taith Pererin Gogledd Cymru

This route was first walked in 2011. It was an attempt to re-establish a pilgrimage route across North Wales from Basingwerk to Bardsey Island, which had been used centuries ago. Today it is nick-named 'the Welsh Camino' – a route linking chapels, tiny churches and places associated with many of the Celtic saints. There are thirteen parts to the route, and pilgrims collect stamps from places all along the route in their 'Pilgrim Passport'. Historically, pilgrims bought small tokens – shells, metal badges and pins – as souvenirs and proof of their visit to a place. The North Wales Pilgrim's Way is nearly 140 miles long, and takes a couple of weeks to complete if time is taken at each point on the journey.

Some of the places visited on the Way

The pilgrimage starts at the ruins of the Cistercian medieval Abbey of Basingwerk, which was closed during Henry VIII's dissolution of monasteries (see page 9).

In the seventh century, when St Winifride was beheaded, the place her head landed became a spring. This is now St Winifride's Well, Holywell. It is thought to be the oldest continually visited place of pilgrimage in the UK. The water in the well is said to have healing properties.

St Asaph's Cathedral was first established about 1,400 years ago, when it was a church built by St Kentigern. He was succeeded as bishop by St Asaph. The building that stands there today dates back to the thirteenth century. Inside is a copy of the first Welsh language Bible (see pages 10–11).

Bangor Cathedral is dedicated to St Deiniol, and was originally built on low-lying land to try to escape the notice of Viking raiders. A church has been here since the sixth century. St Deiniol was the first Bishop of Bangor.

The church of St Bueno is at Clynnog Fawr. St Bueno was the uncle of St Winifride and is credited with resurrecting her after she had been beheaded. She is one of seven people St Bueno is said to have brought back to life.

4 Christianity

◀ The North Wales Pilgrim's Way

The Welsh poet RS Thomas was vicar of St Hywyn's Church in Aberdaron from 1967 to 1978. He was a Welsh nationalist whose poetry was based on his religious faith. In 1995, he was nominated for the Nobel Prize for literature.

Bardsey Island is also known as the island of 20,000 saints. In medieval times, three pilgrimages to Bardsey Island were considered to be equal to one to Rome. It is believed that St Cadfan began building a monastery here, and the island was certainly a place where devout monks went to study and live. The remains of an Augustinian Abbey (St Mary's) are found on the island – it was abandoned during the dissolution of the monasteries in 1537.

▶ Other Welsh pilgrimages

As there are many places linked to saints in Wales, there are many places of pilgrimage: St Govan's Chapel, St David's Cathedral, St Cybi's Well, St Tudno's Church – and many, many more. There are also many village churches linked to the development of social rights, and to social reformers. A visit to any of these is a kind of pilgrimage for many.

The North Wales Pilgrim's Way is not the only pilgrim way either; others include the Welsh Cistercian Way, the Penrhys Pilgrimage Way, the Saints and Stones trails in Pembrokeshire and the Celtic Way.

Activities

1. Why is pilgrimage important for Christians?
2. Give some reasons why Wales has so many pilgrim links.
3. Write an introduction to the North Wales Pilgrim's Way.
4. Research a different Welsh pilgrim way and write an advert for it to attract visitors.
5. Do you think Wales should do more with its potential for Christian pilgrimage? Explain the reasons for your answer.

4.16 Christian beliefs into action

Learning objectives
- To understand Jesus' teaching about faith and action
- To understand the power of the motivation of Jesus' teachings on Welsh Christians today in their wider communities
- To reflect on whether Christian social action is the most important contribution Christians make to the world

Big question
What is the most important contribution religions make to the world?

> Matthew 22:39 – Jesus said the second greatest commandment is 'Love your neighbour as yourself'.

> James 2:17 – 'faith by itself, if it is not accompanied by action, is dead'– worse than pointless.

A Christian belongs to a particular church and denomination. Christians show their faith by devotion to God through acts of worship in private and in public. However, Jesus stated that worship was not enough on its own. People have to show their beliefs through their actions, and those actions have to be positive ones, which help others. This shows their beliefs are genuinely held, but also means they will receive a favourable judgement on Judgement Day.

In the Parable of the Sheep and Goats (Matthew 25:31–46), Jesus describes the end of time when the sheep and goats are judged. The ones who helped others are allowed into heaven (sheep); those who did not help others are cast into hell (goats). In explanation, Jesus says 'Truly I tell you, whatever you did not do for one of the least of these, you did not do for me.' In other words, by helping others a person helps Jesus, but not helping others is like not helping Jesus.

Many churches host groups for community learning and support; many foodbanks have strong church links in terms of the venues and the volunteers who run them. Individuals show their beliefs in many voluntary roles, such as befriending, as well as having jobs in which they can help others.

Here are some examples of how Christian groups are following Jesus' teachings about faith and action.

▶ Helping the environment – Shore to Shore

Shore to Shore was a 2021 summer initiative by the churches in the St Asaph diocese of North Wales. Four mission areas (Bryn a Môr, Aber-Morfa, Aled, Aberconwy) worked together as part of St Asaph Coastal Strategy. Along with Keep Wales Tidy (which provided litter pickers and bags), they mapped a pilgrimage route from Talacre to Llandudno. The route was split into six parts, walked over six Mondays.

The strategy had two parts. The diocese wanted to reinvigorate church life by the sea in North Wales, where many of the communities have been badly affected economically, and where church attendance has declined, with some locals unable to see the value of the Church or faith. The second strategy recognises the world as being created by God, and humans having a duty to look after it. The walkers would clean up the routes as they walked.

Church clergy, church members and members of the public walked and litter-picked. There were scheduled prayer stops at the start and end of each walk as well as along the way for anyone to join if they wished. The sight of vicars litter-picking stimulated discussion and conversation among the pickers as well as passers-by, allowing discussion of faith, but more importantly, showing that the churches care for their community and the environment.

▶ Linden Church – Red Community Project

▲ Swansea's Linden Church's Red Community Project

Over twenty years ago, Linden Church set up a place for young people, run by young people – the Red Café. It was used for all kinds of youth work, and gave young people a safe space in which to try new opportunities. The range of projects included a film-making course and café-style youth nights.

Over time, their work has expanded. Now called the Red Community Project, it includes Bloom – a support group for women refugee and asylum seekers, which connects women and their families, signposts relevant support, creates volunteering opportunities (by law they cannot have paid income) and generally helps them to settle and begin to live without fear. It hosts the Swansea foodbank once a week, providing families in crisis with three days of emergency supplies. It hosts the Musical Memories Choir which supports people living with dementia and their carers. It works with people in the prison system, helping them transition back into normal life. As is the case at many other churches, it provides parent and toddler groups and play schemes.

Linden Church sees its mission as bringing people together, recognising the value of each individual. Their community work certainly reflects those beliefs.

www.lindenchurch.com

> **Find out for yourself**
>
> What have Christian groups done in your local community?

> **Activities**
>
> 1 Explain Jesus' teachings about belief and action.
> 2 Describe some ways in which Christians are helping their local communities.
> 3 Do you think that Christians should do more in your local community? Explain your reasoning using examples. What else could they do to help the community?

5 Judaism

5.1 Key beliefs in Judaism

Learning objectives
- To know about the Jewish concept of God
- To know about the concept of the Messiah
- To reflect on how belief influences behaviour

Big question
How might having belief help a person?

▶ The Jewish idea of God

> 'Hear O Israel: the Lord is our God, the Lord is One.' (*Deuteronomy 6:4*)

These words are at the start of the Shema, a declaration of faith for Jewish people that is repeated every day. They sum up the most important idea about God in Judaism, that there is only one God. Judaism is therefore a monotheistic religion. When Judaism began, this belief separated the Jewish people from others. It was the most important teaching by Abraham, one of the Jewish founding fathers, that they were to believe in one God and that he should be the only focus for their worship.

> '… so that from the rising of the sun to the place of its setting,
>
> People may know there is none besides me. I am the Lord, and there is no other.
>
> I form the light and create darkness. I bring prosperity and create disaster;
>
> I, the Lord, do all these things.' (*Isaiah 45:6–7*)

Jewish people believe that God created the universe and everything in it. God did this without help and from nothing. Only God exists eternally; everything else is created by God from God's will. It exists because God wants it to. Humans can look at the world around them, and see evidence of God's work. This means God is all-powerful and all-knowing. God exists everywhere. Humans cannot understand God, but can have some ideas about God. For centuries, Jewish scholars and rabbis have discussed and puzzled over the idea of God, and their ideas are written in the Talmud (the book which explains the Torah, the holiest book of Judaism).

The Genesis creation story describes how God created the world in seven days (Genesis 1:1–2:3). It describes God creating first light; then the heavens; then land, sea and vegetation; then the sun, moon and stars; then fish and birds; then animals and humans; with a final day of rest.

> 'And now, Israel, what does the Lord your God require of you … to observe the Lord's commandments and his decrees that I am giving you today for your own good?' (*Deuteronomy 10:12–13*)

Jewish people believe God wants humans to live in a certain way, and that by doing this they serve God. One of the founding fathers of Judaism was Moses, who received from God the Ten Commandments and all the laws which Jewish people were to keep. There are 613 of these laws, called the mitzvot, and they are split into laws about God and worship, and laws for living. The Ten Commandments are also known as 'forever' commandments, because they can be kept by every believer anywhere and at any time. Another name for God in Judaism is 'Law-giver'.

74

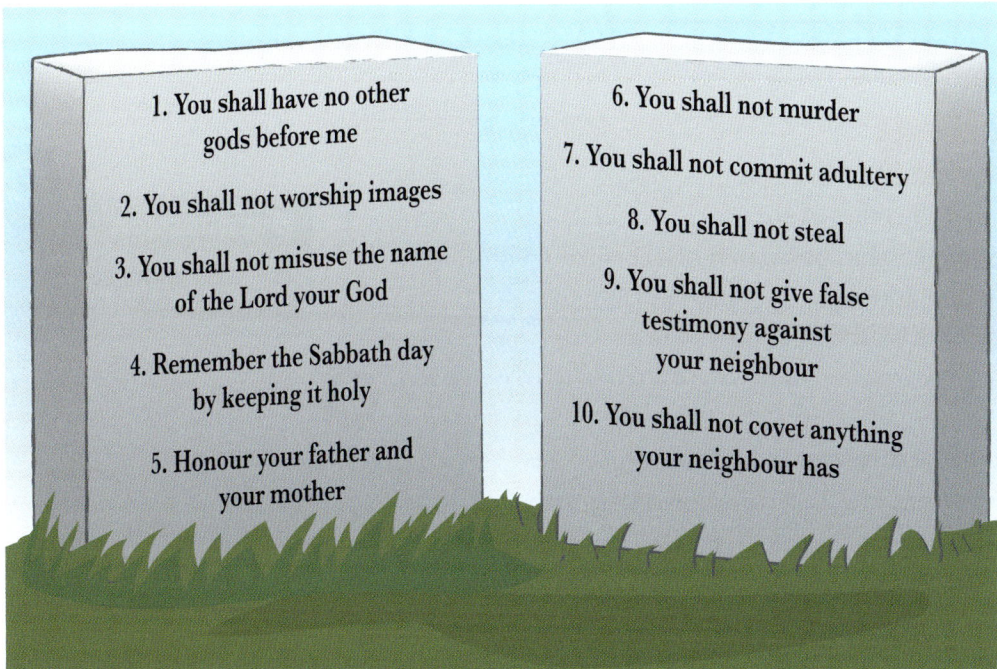

◀ The Ten Commandments (Exodus 20:1–17)

▶ The Covenant

Judaism teaches that God has made a series of covenants with the Jewish people. A covenant is an agreement between two parties. Judaism speaks of many covenants, but two stand out. God made a covenant with Abraham, one of the founding fathers of the religion. The terms were that God would give land and protection to Abraham and his descendants; in return they would worship only this one God, and would follow his path. The second is the covenant with Moses, in which God renewed the covenant made with Abraham, and gave Moses a set of laws by which everyone should live. These were the Ten Commandments and the mitzvot. The covenants are between the entire community and God – helping Jewish people focus on their duty to live as tradition tells them to.

▶ Life after death

For centuries, Jewish scholars and rabbis have suggested what might happen when a person dies, but they have always come to the same conclusion: that we really do not know. They have therefore come to the conclusion that it does not make sense to focus on a life after this one. Judaism instead focuses on getting things right, and doing things right, here and now in this lifetime. Judaism stresses the need to keep the moral and religious laws of the religion that is, to pray and worship, and to live a morally and ethically good life. Jewish people believe that whatever the next life is like – if there is one – the best way to have the best outcome is to live by God's laws.

Activities

1 Explain what Jewish people believe about God, using religious teachings in your answer.
2 Find a version of the Genesis creation story. Create a storyboard of the story with eight stages.
3 Explain what a covenant is. Describe the two key covenants between God and the Jewish people.
4 How does believing in God affect the behaviour of Jewish people?
5 'It does not make sense to believe in life after death.' Do you agree with this statement? Give reasons for agreeing and disagreeing with it, and then write your own conclusion.

The major world faiths

5.2 A faith that governs life – the mitzvot

Learning objectives
- To understand what the mitzvot are
- To understand the mitzvot as being part of a covenant with God
- To reflect on different attitudes to keeping the mitzvot

Big question

Is it ever okay to break rules?

Key terms
Covenant – a binding agreement, between God and man
Mitzvot – commandments from God (a single commandment is mitzvah)

▶ The Sinai Covenant

One of the founding fathers of Judaism was Moses. He was born in Egypt at a time when the Jewish people (Israelites) were enslaved. Guided by God, who sent ten plagues upon the Egyptians (see page 86), Moses persuaded Pharaoh (the king) to release the Jewish people. For 40 years, they wandered in the desert. During this time, having no fixed homeland, God provided food every day for them in the form of manna (bread) from heaven. The words of the Welsh hymn, Cwm Rhondda (Bread of Heaven) describe the time. After forty years of wandering, God led the Israelites to the Promised Land (a land today occupied by both Israel and Palestine). This was part of God's earlier covenant with Abraham, another of the founding fathers of Judaism.

During this time of wandering in the wilderness, Moses climbed Mount Sinai where God spoke to him. God revealed to Moses the Ten Commandments and the **mitzvot** for the Jewish people to follow. These were 613 rules for worship of God and living. They are recorded in the Torah, which is the most sacred text in Judaism. God made a covenant with the Israelites that if they kept these laws, God would make them the 'chosen people' and bless them. This **covenant** stands for all time.

▲ Moses

'What is this 'chosen people' about?'

'Well, that word is commonly used; but the Hebrew words translate as 'treasure people' or 'heritage people'. It reflects the agreement with God which only they made.'

Activities
1. What are mitzvot? Give some examples.
2. How did Jewish people come to follow the mitzvot?
3. Explain the different ways in which the mitzvot can be grouped, using examples to illustrate each group.
4. 'People should always keep rules and laws.' How far do you think that is true? Use examples to explain your reasoning.

Times   Dietary laws   Business practices   Employees   Vows   Sabbath   Court   Injuries

God   Torah   Signs and symbols   Prayers   Love and brotherhood   The poor   Gentiles   Family   Forbidden sex

▶ The mitzvot

The mitzvot are the commandments that God gave to Moses. Jewish people are required to follow these laws as a religious duty and by doing so they are keeping their side of the covenant with God.

The Talmud says there are 613 mitzvot. They cover every aspect of life – see the words and phrases around these two pages for just some of these. There are different ways to group the mitzot:

- The reason for keeping some of the laws is obvious. For example, 'Do not kill' is a law which every society has, and which makes sense to almost everyone. Whereas others are laws because God said they were, for example a law about not wearing wool and linen clothes together.
- Of the 613 laws, 365 command the believer *not* to do something, and 248 instruct the believer to *do* something.
- Some of the laws relate to the Temple in Jerusalem. This Temple was destroyed in 70 CE by the Roman occupiers, and only one wall still remains standing, so these laws can no longer be kept.
- Some laws are about the relationship between God and humans, for example the law to keep the Sabbath holy. Others are between people, for example, the law to not steal.
- Six of the mitzvot are 'constant', that is, they are valid all of the time everywhere. These are: to know there is a God, to not believe in other gods, that God is One, to love God, to fear God, and not to be misled by hearts and minds. The other mitzvot are applicable at specific times or in specific situations.

Keeping the mitzvot

Jewish people believe in free will. They believe that God has given laws for humans to follow, but they can decide what they will do. Jewish people are guided by the mitzvot to do what is morally good and what is right and to avoid what is not.

Judaism is split into different groups. Orthodox Judaism believes that the mitzvot have to be followed as written – the only choice is to follow them or not. They believe that the covenant between Moses and God committed Jewish people to keeping the mitzvot, and this commitment remains.

Reform Judaism believes that Judaism should develop over time and adapt to changes in society to be inclusive. It therefore supports equality of opportunities for women, diverse kinds of families, same-sex relationships, women rabbis. They believe that this requires the mitzvot to be understood more as principles rather than fixed rules. They use free will to interpret the laws for the benefit of society.

The majority of Jewish people believe a person can live a modern Jewish life in harmony with the Torah. It is understood that Jewish laws 'walk forward' to keep up with modern times, and Jewish rabbis are constantly updating guidance on keeping the laws as technology changes.

Wars Nazarites The King Leprosy Ritual Purity Sacrifices The Temple Tithes Priests The firstborn Clothing

Property   Criminal laws   Punishments and restitution   Prophecy   Idolatry   Agriculture

The major world faiths

5.3 The holy books of Judaism

Learning objectives

- To know what the Tenakh is
- To understand the primary importance for Jewish people of the Torah compared to other holy books
- To reflect on how holy books hold great value for believers

Big question

What is the most important book you have ever read?

▲ A girl reading the Torah scrolls

These are the Jewish holy books, split into their three sections. The name for the whole is Tenakh, which comes from the start of each section's name. You can read their Hebrew name and the name they are given in the Bible. Of course, for Jewish people, it is right to call them by their Hebrew name, but non-Jewish people are usually more familiar with them in their biblicised form (or some of them at least).

The Torah is the first and the most important part of the scriptures. It is the most sacred part of the Tenakh, because it is considered to be the word of God, which was written down by Moses. Torah means guidance. The Torah contains the stories of God's creation of the world, and the early history of the Jewish people, as well as the mitzvot and Commandments. The Torah is absolute and unchanging; Jewish people believe it is relevant everywhere all the time. Some Jewish people believe the Torah existed before even the world existed – it is part of God's eternal law.

Jewish synagogues have copies of the Torah in scroll form, called Sefer Torah, which are read aloud during acts of worship. Over a year, the Torah is split into 54 portions, which are read consecutively during the Monday, Thursday and Saturday services. This means that in a year the whole Torah is read. The scrolls are kept protected when not in use in a special cupboard at the front of the synagogue called the aron hakodesh (holy ark).

For many Jewish people, study of the Torah is a central part of their obedience to God. It fulfils the constant mitzvot of 'to know God', because they are studying God's word. Some will devote time every day, even several hours, to studying the Torah and the interpretations made by scholars and rabbis over the centuries. These interpretations are found in commentaries which make up the Talmud (the most important source of Jewish law).

5 Judaism

▲ The Torah scrolls in the Ark in the synagogue

The Nevi'im, meaning 'prophets', are the books of the prophets. They include the stories of the prophets, such as Jonah (and the whale), and their message to the people of their time. Prophets were people chosen by God to give a message to humans, either to guide or warn them. Not all the prophets wanted the role – it could be very dangerous. The story of Jonah and the whale, for example, is as much about how people cannot avoid a task God gives them, as it is God's warning about bad behaviour.

The Ketuvim, meaning 'writings', are a mix of different kinds of literature. There are poems, or Psalms, which have provided the words for many hymns. The book of Daniel is an example of a history book. The book of Job is about an argument between God and the devil about Job's strength of faith – the devil is allowed to test him to see if he will give up his belief in God. The book of Proverbs claims to give 'prudence to the simple, knowledge and discretion to the young, and to make the wise even wiser' – it is a book of guidance for daily living. For example, wise people think before they act; fools don't – and even brag about their foolishness (Proverbs 13:16).

Five of the Ketuvim are important at specific festivals. They are the shortest of the books of the Ketuvim, and have another name: Megillot, which means 'scrolls'. As they are so short, it does not take many services to read them, so becoming traditional at certain festivals. At Pesach, Song of Songs is used. Shavuot recalls the story of Ruth. Tishah B'Av uses Lamentations, which is a mournful writing about the destruction of Jerusalem and the Temple. Sukkot uses Ecclesiastes, which has been interpreted to be about the autumn harvest. The story of Esther is the focus of Purim.

Most Jewish people will learn to read Hebrew, and will have their own copy of the Tenakh in Hebrew. The Christian Bible in Welsh or English is a translation of most books in the Tenakh.

Activities

1. Write out this table so that the two halves match up correctly.

The Tenakh is	the writings; a mix of different kinds of Jewish literature.
The Torah is	the whole of the Jewish scriptures.
The Nevi'im is	the most important part of the Jewish scriptures, believed to be the word of God.
The Ketuvim is	the prophets. These tell the stories of the prophets, and the messages God chose them to deliver.

2. Explain the importance of the Torah for Jewish people.
3. What was the role of the prophets? Why do you think they were important?
4. Find out the story of Esther, and write your own version of it.
5. Do you think that holy books are valuable to everyone or just to believers? Explain the reasons for your answer.

The major world faiths

5.4 The Jewish place of worship – the synagogue

Learning objectives
- To know the key features of a Jewish place of worship
- To understand that different groups within Judaism express their beliefs differently through the synagogue
- To reflect on the importance of places of worship to believers and non-believers

Big question

Are buildings important?

In the tenth century BCE, the Jewish people had a temple, built by King Solomon. When it was destroyed in 70 CE by the Roman occupiers, it was never rebuilt. However, from the sixth century BCE, there are mentions of synagogues in historical documents. Not all Jewish people could get to the temple, so the synagogues were built. 'Synagogue' means 'bringing together' – it is the place where Jewish people meet to share worship and discuss their religion. Many Jewish people call the synagogue 'shul', meaning 'school', because it is where the Torah is studied.

▶ Why are synagogues important?

- Synagogues are a place of worship; worship is a duty for Jewish people. Another name for the synagogue is Bet Tefilah – house of prayer.
- For worship, Judaism requires a minyan, a group of ten. For ten people to worship together, they need a place, which is the synagogue.
- Synagogues are places to study the Torah and Jewish law. People can study alone or discuss with others there, and many synagogues have books to help with that study, such as the Talmud.
- Most synagogues have community rooms, so can provide a space for celebrations such as weddings, and for community meetings and events.
- For non-believers, visiting a synagogue is a chance to learn about the religion, and appreciate the faith people show. This helps bring greater harmony to society. Also, the buildings and their interiors are often very beautiful, and are places of calm, which anyone can appreciate and benefit from.

▲ Jewish synagogues from the outside

▲ The interiors of different synagogues

Key features of a synagogue

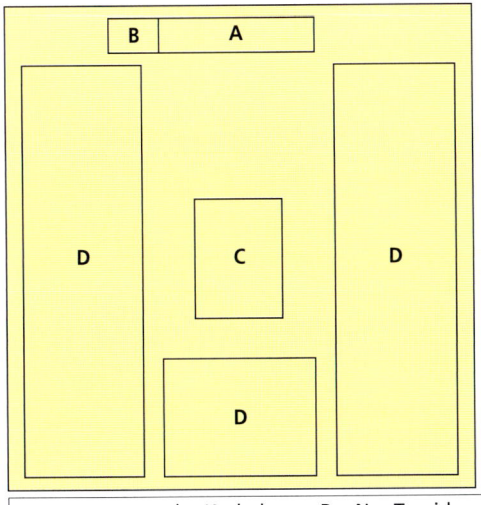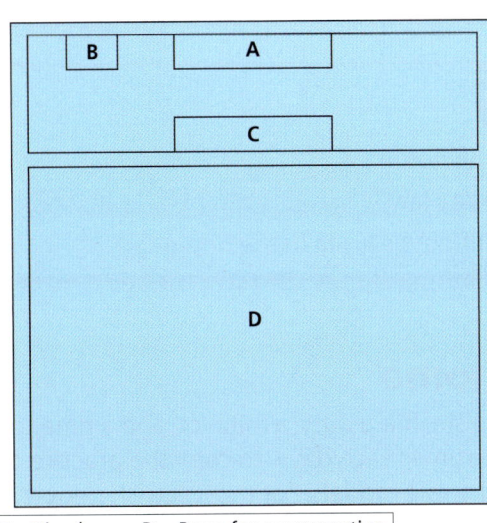

Simple plans of an Orthodox synagogue (left) and of a Reform synagogue (right)

| Key | A = Aron ha-Kodesh | B = Ner Tamid | C = Bimah | D = Pews for congregation |

The plans above are very simple versions of Orthodox and Reform synagogues. The differences between them indicate some of the differences in Orthodox and Reform beliefs.

A Aron ha-Kodesh – the ark (special cupboard) for the Torah scrolls which are read at services. The Torah is the word of God, and is sacred. In ancient times, the Jewish people had a special case made for the Torah, which they carried with them on their travels until they reached the Promised Land, when it was placed in the temple. The Aron ha-Kodesh reminds Jewish people of the temple, as well as God's covenant. It is always at the front of the synagogue, built into or set against the middle of the wall.

B Ner Tamid – the everlasting light. This reminds visitors to the synagogue of God – eternal and constant. In the temple, a light was kept burning all the time to represent God always looking over his people. For the same reason, the synagogue has a lamp which is kept lit at all times. It usually hangs from the ceiling, and is always at the front of the synagogue.

C Bimah – a reading desk. At each service, the Torah scrolls are brought from the Aron ha-Kodesh to the bimah, where that day's section of scripture is read aloud. The bimah is a raised platform, which means everyone must look up towards the Torah, which shows respect. In Orthodox synagogues, the bimah is in the centre of the room, showing that the Torah is central to everyone's life and faith. In Reform synagogues, it is at the front, but still central. This is so that the congregation is looking toward the ark as well as the Torah when it is read.

D Pews for the congregation. In Orthodox synagogues, the pews are traditionally down the sides and at the back. The congregation faces inwards to the bimah in the centre. Often there are separate sections for women, sometimes an upstairs balcony, but these never directly face the men's sections. The idea is that people then focus on their worship, and do not get distracted by the opposite gender. In Reform synagogues, families sit together, so the genders are mixed in one large group.

Activities

1. Why are synagogues important for Jewish people?
2. List the key features of a synagogue. Explain what each is, and what it symbolises.
3. Find an image of the inside of a synagogue. Add labels to explain the key features.
4. 'Religious buildings are only important to those who worship at them.' Give some reasons to agree with this statement, then some to disagree with it, before writing a conclusion to say which point of view you think is stronger.

The major world faiths

5.5 A Jewish home and daily life

> **Learning objectives**
> - To learn about prayer in the home
> - To learn about Jewish dietary law
> - To reflect on how beliefs affect daily life in the home

Big question
Do you have any rules around food?

▶ Prayer in the home

Prayer is very important in Judaism. It is a duty, a mitzvot, and a time to focus on God alone. Jewish people pray three times each day – to copy the practice of three key historical Jewish figures, who are role models. For most Jewish people, these prayers are said at home.

Morning prayer – sunrise, early morning	Afternoon prayer – after midday, before sunset	Evening prayer – after sunset
The time Abraham prayed – starting the day with God	The time Isaac prayed – interrupting one's day for God	The time Jacob prayed – so that God is the last thing on your mind before sleep
Prayer is compulsory, and the times – though set within several hours – are fixed.		

A Jewish person will wear particular items for prayer.

Tallit and tzitzit – a tallit is a prayer shawl. It is usually white with blue stripes near the sides but can be plain white as here. It has a hole in each corner through which are tied tzitzit (fringes). The blue represents God. The fringes are twisted strands which hang loose to represent the mitzvot. They are in the four corners to represent the whole world, and to show that God's commandments are relevant everywhere. When reciting some prayers, the tzitzit have to be held.

Kippah or yarmulke – this is small cap that sits on the back of the head. This is to show respect to God.

Tefillin – these are little boxes threaded onto two leather straps. Each box contains parchment with passages from the Torah written on them. One tefillin sits against the forehead – to show the wearer thinks about God; the other is on the upper arm turned inward – to show that the wearer loves God. The strap for the arm tefillin is long, and winds round the biceps, forearm, hand and fingers in a specific way.

Putting these items on is considered part of the prayer because by concentrating on being properly dressed for God, the person is preparing their mind for prayer. Many Jewish people say prayers while putting on these items.

The prayers might be recited from memory, but most Jewish people will use a Siddur (a prayer book) to make sure they say the right prayers at the right time.

82

5 Judaism

▶ Jewish dietary law

There are many laws in the Torah about food. This makes Jewish cuisine and cooking unique. To keep the laws, which are mitzvot, many Jewish families have their kitchens arranged specially. You might recognise the word 'kosher', which is used by people generally to mean that something is okay or legitimate or legal. Kosher comes from 'kashrut', a word that covers anything that is acceptable under Jewish laws. Jewish people must eat kosher food, and keep a kosher kitchen.

- Only certain animals are kosher. These are animals that eat grass and have split hooves. This includes sheep, cows and deer; but not rabbits or pigs. Any fish that has scales, a backbone and fins are kosher. Birds such as hens, geese and ducks are kosher, but birds of prey are not. All insects are treyfah – forbidden.
- Animals must be ritually slaughtered to be kosher. Ritual slaughter is done by a shochet, a qualified kosher slaughterer, by slitting the throat to drain the blood. No blood may be consumed, as blood is considered the life of the animal.
- Even for kosher animals that have been kosher butchered, certain parts are treyfah, so cannot be eaten. This includes the internal fat, the sciatic sinew (a nerve running from the spine down the leg), and certain organs.
- Meat and milk may not be consumed in the same meal, or within a set time of each other.

In Jewish communities, it is easy to get kosher food as there are Jewish food shops and butchers available. Many Jews do not live in big Jewish communities, however; for example, there is no kosher shop in Cardiff, though many shops do sell kosher items. The community therefore uses a twice-monthly delivery service from London-based kosher butchers and other stores. The North Wales Jewish community is supported by Manchester-based kosher companies.

The rules about meat and milk mean that many Jewish families organise their kitchens to make sure meat and milk do not get put together or mixed. Meals will not include both, so for example, a milk-based pudding will not follow a meat-based meal. Jewish people use non-dairy milk alternatives to allow for dishes like meat lasagne to be made and eaten. The meat and milk rule also applies to preparing food, so most families have two sets of equipment – one for meat and one for milk. They could use the same equipment for both, but the cleaning required after either is very complicated to be absolutely sure that there is no mixing so this is rare.

Activity

With a partner, discuss which of the animals shown above could be used for food for Jewish people.

Activities

1. Draw a Jewish person wearing items for prayer. Add detailed information for each of the items.
2. Why is prayer important for Jewish people?
3. Find out why Abraham, Isaac and Jacob are important figures in Judaism.
4. Research the symbols which are used in food packaging to show that it is kosher. Find some examples to use in the next task.
5. Imagine you have to explain Jewish food laws to a classmate who has been absent from class. Design an information sheet that uses text and pictures to explain the laws.
6. How much do beliefs shape a Jewish person's daily life? Explain your answer.

The major world faiths

5.6 Jewish life – observing Shabbat

Learning objectives
- To learn how Jewish people observe Shabbat
- To understand the religious and spiritual significance of Shabbat
- To reflect on the need for a day off in the modern world

Big question

Is it important to have a day off?

Talk it out
What would it be like to be in school seven days a week?

Can you think of any job that is seven days a week?

Think about the positives and negatives of such a job.

> 'Remember the Sabbath Day by keeping it holy … For in six days the Lord made the heavens and the earth, the sea, and all that is in them, but he rested on the seventh day.' (*Exodus 20:8 and 11*)

A few people might work seven days a week. They probably only work that way for a certain period of time or on a certain project, and then get a break. If people work seven days a week without any rest, they soon burn out and become ineffective in their role or job. Humans need to rest. In the Genesis creation story, God rested after creating the world. In the Ten Commandments, God commands humans to rest on the Sabbath.

Jewish people keep the Sabbath holy, as a day of rest. The Sabbath starts at sundown on Friday, and ends at sundown on Saturday. There is a series of preparations to make before the Sabbath, and rituals that take place on the Sabbath.

▶ Getting ready

No work is to be done during Shabbat; though if anyone falls ill or is in danger, then this rule is set aside. Work – melacha – is not what you might think. The Torah lists 39 types of activity which are forbidden, involving constructive or creative efforts, such as carrying and baking. It is only in the event of risk to life that this rule of no work can be broken, as saving a life takes precedence. Meals that will be eaten during Shabbat are prepared ahead of time and the table is laid. The house is tidied and everything is made ready so that all energies can be focused on God on the day. Many families switch off their phones, so there is no interruption allowed from anyone.

> Getting ready for Shabbat is important. First it puts me in the right mind for Shabbat itself. Secondly, it ensures Shabbat goes without issue.

> Times change. When I was a child, my mother welcomed Shabbat, my father led the meal. Today, we do things differently – my wife and I take turns for these tasks; my brother lives alone, but keeps Shabbat, so does them all himself. My sister and her wife share the rituals. We change with the times.

Activities
1. Give some reasons why Jewish people keep Shabbat.
2. Describe the key rituals of Shabbat in the order in which they happen.
3. Explain the symbolism of Havdalah.
4. 'Everybody – religious or not – needs something like Shabbat.' Do you agree with this statement? Give reasons for agreeing and disagreeing before deciding which point of view you think is stronger.

5 Judaism

▶ The rituals

No later than eighteen minutes before sunset, before the family meal, two Shabbat candles are lit. Traditionally by a woman, but in modern times the ritual is shared by men and women. The one lighting the candle passes their hands over their eyes and recites a Shabbat blessing. Shabbat has begun.

The family attends the evening service at the synagogue and then returns home for a meal. Traditionally, the meal is led by the man of the house – he blesses the children, recites Kiddush (a prayer over wine) and blesses two loaves (challah). During the meal, Shabbat songs are sung. The meal ends with a further blessing.

Saturday begins with breakfast. The same Kiddush and challah rituals are observed. The whole family goes to the synagogue for the service which focuses on the Torah. The Torah scrolls are carried from the ark to be processed around the synagogue for people to try to touch with their tallit, before being taken to the bimah to be read. After the service, it is usual for the congregation to share Kiddush – traditionally wine and cake – reinforcing the sense of community.

Many Orthodox Jewish people stay at the synagogue to study Torah for the afternoon. However, most spend the time as a family. Many do study Torah at this time, and they catch up on events and conversations of the week. Some will visit friends and family. It is a time to not work, a time to refresh and recharge.

The ritual of Havdalah (separation) shows that Shabbat has ended. It can take place anytime from three stars being visible on Shabbat until the Tuesday after it. Blessings are recited over wine, spices and candles. The candle used has several wicks entwined to represent torchlight, passing the light of Shabbat into the week. The spices are in a box; their smell is sweet to show that Shabbat is the sweetest part, or the highlight, of the week. Shabbat is the day to look forward to; in fact, many say the week leads up to it. In the past, rabbis called Shabbat a 'queen' to show how special the day is.

> Shabbat gives me a chance to be present in the moment. I focus on now, not on what I need to do later. It refreshes me.

> Shabbat is time with my family in my faith. Everything at Shabbat is about our faith. We don't let everyday worries in.

> My family use Shabbat afternoon to visit relatives. Some are in care homes, so we visit with cake we have made – sharing Shabbat and showing our love.

> For me, Shabbat is a time to give to studying the Torah. Everything else, I can ignore. What I learn I use in the rest of the week. I prepare for Shabbat, but Shabbat prepares me for life.

5.7 Jewish celebrations – Pesach (Passover)

Learning objectives
- To learn about the origins of Pesach
- To explore some of the key ways in which Jewish people celebrate Pesach
- To reflect on the importance of celebrations of past events

Big question
For you, what is the best celebration – and why?

Pesach (Passover) recalls an event from the time of the Pharaohs, 3,000 years ago. The Jewish people (**Israelites**) were enslaved in Egypt, and lived very difficult lives. At one point, Pharaoh had all of the new-born sons of the Israelites drowned at birth to prevent the slaves gaining too much strength. It was not unusual for slaves to be beaten or worked to death. Moses was born an Israelite but was brought up an Egyptian. He fled Egypt after killing a man who was beating a slave. Years later, God spoke to Moses via a burning bush, and told him he had to go back to Pharaoh to demand the release of the Israelites. Moses did as he was instructed and, with God's help, freed them.

The story in Exodus says that Pharaoh initially refused Moses' request to release the slaves. In fact, he ordered his sorcerers (people believed to have magic powers) to demonstrate their powers to frighten Moses away. When Moses told Pharaoh what God would do to force him to release them, Pharaoh's response was 'Do your worst!' He believed his sorcerers could fix anything.

God then sent ten plagues. After each one, Pharaoh had a chance to change his mind and release the Israelites, but he ignored each opportunity and so the Egyptian people continued to suffer. The final plague was the death of the first-born son. On the given day, Moses told the Israelites to paint the blood of a sacrificed lamb onto the door posts of their home before sunset. If they did not leave their home before dawn, this gave protection to first-born sons. That night the angel of death flew over all the homes, and took the life of the first-born son in any unprotected home.

The son of Pharaoh – the heir to the throne – died. Pharaoh finally agreed to the release of the Israelites.

Key terms
Israelites – the twelve tribes of Israel, the ancestors of the Jewish people

Leavened – food that has used a raising agent, such as yeast, in its preparation

Matzah – unleavened bread used specifically at Pesach

Unleavened – food that has not used a raising agent in its preparation

Talk it out
Look at this list of the Ten Plagues sent by God to make the Pharaoh release the Israelites. The Plagues were instant, or for a short time –

- water turned to blood;
- frogs;
- gnats;
- flies;
- death of livestock;
- boils;
- storms of hail and fire;
- locusts;
- darkness;
- death of firstborn son.

The Pharaoh released the Israelites after the final Plague.
What would you have done, if it had been your decision? Explain your ideas.

Activities
1. Retell the story of the first Passover.
2. Draw a seder plate in your book, and add labels for each item.
3. Why do you think that this festival is so important in Judaism today?
4. Do you think it is important to remember past events – good and bad? Explain your answer.

Pesach is a festival of joy, as it focuses on the end of a difficult time in history. It lasts for eight days, the first two of which include seder meals (meals attended by the extended family).

▶ Before Pesach begins

The night before Pesach, many traditions take place. In one, the mother hides ten pieces of bread around the house, which the children go and find. Once found, the bread is wrapped in cloth, and then burned in the morning. Any other chametz (**leavened** food) is also cleared from the house before 10 am.

This reminds Jewish people that the Israelites did not have time to make leavened bread when they fled Egypt, so they could only take **unleavened** bread, which baked in their backpacks in the sun.

After morning prayer on the Saturday before Peasch, synagogues deliver a study session for first-born sons, which covers part of the Talmud.

▶ The seder meal

The seder meal follows a service which is written in the Passover Haggadah (a service book), and has many traditions. The wider family share the meal, remembering the Israelite families who huddled together on the night when the first-born sons were killed. The table is set as if for a normal meal, but with three **matzots**, wine and a seder plate in a central place on the table.

Children ask four set questions which lead to the story of how the Israelites were freed being retold. The answers also explain the items on the seder plate:

- Maror (bitter herbs) – representing the enslavement of the Israelites
- Karpas (usually parsley or celery) – dipped in salt water before eating – representing the tears of the slaves
- Charazet (usually lettuce) – another bitter herb, because the Torah suggests more than one bitter herb
- Charoset (a mix of chopped fruit and nuts, mixed into a paste with wine) – representing the mortar used by the Israelites when working as slaves to build structures for their Egyptian masters
- Zeroa (a lamb shankbone) – symbolising the mighty arm of God, and the Lamb sacrificed at the first Pesach
- Baytza (a roasted, hard-boiled egg) – symbolising the regular temple sacrifice

Some Jewish people place an orange on the Seder plate. It represents the fruitfulness of the Jewish community when LGBTQ+ people are included. The orange has pips which need to be spat out – the rejection of homophobia. During the meal, ten drops of wine are spilled – for the ten plagues. An extra cup sits in place for Elijah – one of the prophets – as there is a belief that Elijah will come one day. Some families also add a cup for Ruth – she was a Moabite who married into the faith. The cup shows the welcoming of new people to the Jewish faith and community, and making the Jewish community more diverse. The door of the house is opened twice at the end of the meal in case Elijah has come, and to show that the household is protected by God from harmful forces.

The major world faiths

5.8 Judaism in the Welsh community

Learning objectives
- To explore the role of a religious community in their wider society
- To learn about examples of social action led by Jewish people in Wales
- To show how beliefs influence social action

Big question
What is the most important principle to live by?

▶ Jewish moral principles

Moral principles are ideas that shape the way a person lives their life. They guide a person's behaviour, and are often what motivates a person to do things for others.

Tzedakah – this is a combination of justice and charity. Giving charity can help to bring justice, as it helps to level things up. For example, a charity that supports Fairtrade allows farmers to earn more for their crops; by earning more, their lives improve.

Chesed – loving kindness. If everybody showed loving kindness to other people, they would always help them. That might not always mean giving what is asked for, however, as that is not always the best thing. You might have heard the phrase 'Give a man a fish, feed him for a day; teach him to fish, feed him for life'. Chesed can be shown in many different ways, directly and indirectly. Everyone can show chesed in their attitude to others, by trying to be more understanding, calmer and friendlier, for example. Psalms says 'The world is built on chesed.' Imagine what it would be like if this really was the case.

Pikuach nefesh – saving a life. This principle is more important than everything else in Judaism. For example, the Shabbat laws can be set aside if there is any concern over life. Jewish people are encouraged to use this principle proactively, which means they should do things to prevent danger to life. Many social issues can be approached with the attitude of pikuach nefesh as a motivator, for example, helping the homeless.

Tikkun Olam – healing the world. This can refer to helping people, or looking after the world itself. Jewish people believe God created the world, and made humans the stewards of it. While humans can make use of the world for their benefit, they still have the responsibility not to abuse it and not to over-use its resources. This is about an environmentally responsible attitude to living.

▶ Why do Jewish communities do things in their wider community?

> I know I should show chesed; whenever I do something for others, whether it is litter-picking for the community, or dropping off groceries for an elderly person or whatever, I am sticking to that principle. It makes life better for them, and I feel good because of it as well.

> I want to be a role model for my religion. Non-Jewish people see me, know I am Jewish, see the help I am giving, and think how good it is that Jewish people help others, that we are an important part of their society.

> My religious principles motivate me to get up and do something. I have friends whose humanist principles motivate them to do some of the same things. Together we are stronger.

> I might be part of a religious community, but I am also part of many communities – one of which is based on the place I live. I have to do my part to make this community a good place for everyone, not just me.

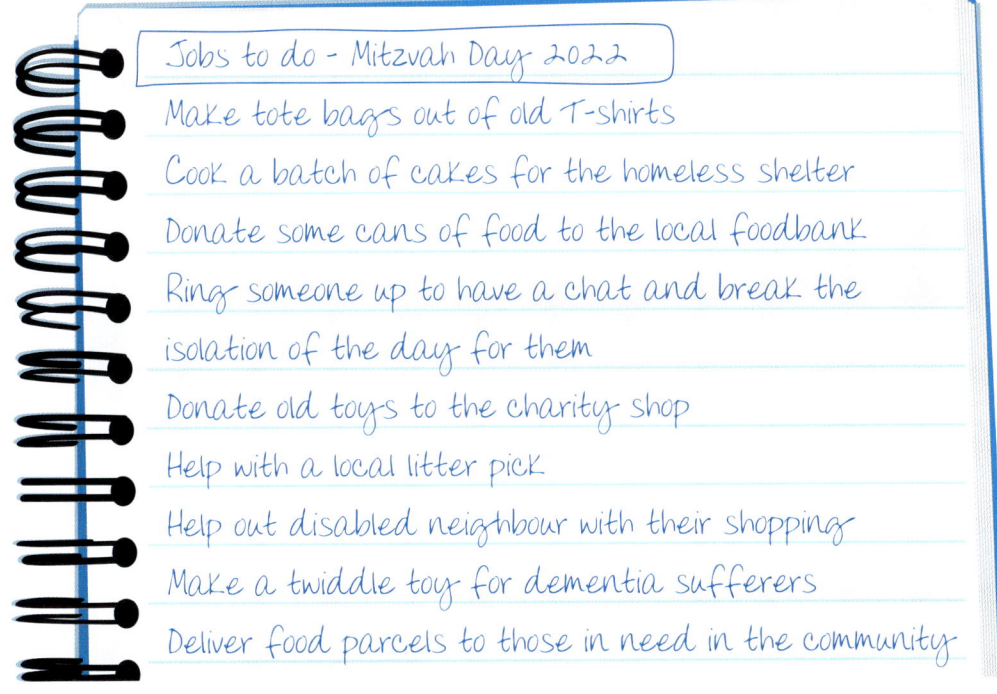

▶ Mitzvah Day

Mitzvah Day began in 2008 with 65 organisations involved. By 2017, that had increased to 731. It helped launch Sewa Day (for Hindus) in 2010, and Sadaqa Day (for Muslims) in 2015, and is deliberately placed on the last day of Inter-Faith Week in November so that different faiths are working together. It brings people together so that they connect, share and support each other, which helps them to understand their differences. This is important for creating mutual understanding between religious and non-religious groups.

Mitzvah Day combines all the principles of chesed, tikkun olam, tzedakah and pikuach nefesh. It allows people of any age, religion, gender or ability to be involved with hands-on social action without necessarily costing them anything. Mitzvah Day is something a person can do on their own, with their family or with their (religious) community – so every Jewish person can volunteer, whether they are part of the Jewish community based in Cardiff, or are one of the Jewish people who live all across Wales.

In 2020, the pandemic made Mitzvah Day more difficult, so it became Mitzvah month. Volunteers were encouraged to commit to a small act of kindness each day. Food poverty and combatting loneliness were two big issues for people in every community across the UK. Both Cardiff Reform Synagogue and Cardiff United Synagogue signed up to Mitzvah Day, with members of each synagogue being involved in individual and group actions. Cardiff Reform Synagogue runs 'community angels' – people who help the sick, taking them to and from appointments, shopping for them, dropping by for a chat, and so on. Cardiff University students arranged a day to clean up Bute Park.

Activities

1. Explain the principles that encourage Jewish people to do things to help their local community and environment.
2. For each principle, give an example of how a Jewish person might be able to keep it in their wider community.
3. Describe Mitzvah Day. Explain why this initiative is important. What kinds of things might volunteers in your local community be involved in?
4. Which is the biggest motivator: principles or self-interest or need? Or does it depend? Explain the reasons for your answer.

6 Islam

6.1 Key beliefs in Islam

Learning objectives
- To know the three key beliefs of Islam
- To understand some of the detail of each belief
- To reflect on how important it is to have religious beliefs today

Big question
What is the most important belief to hold?

Talk it out
What sort of things do we believe in in everyday life? Do we need to 'believe' things?

The census figures for Wales for 2001 and 2011 show a decline in the number of people claiming to be religious in any way. The figures also show that in Wales, the number of Muslims is increasing. In fact, Islam is the fastest growing religion in Wales – numbers doubled between 2001 and 2011, and the Government estimates a 20 per cent increase from 2011 to 2020. In 2020, there were an estimated 55,500 Muslims in Wales, according to the Welsh Government.

Key beliefs
Muslims use the word Allah which is the Arabic word for God. Allah means 'The God'. This signifies only one God, who is supreme.

▶ Belief in Tawhid

This belief is the basis of the religion of Islam. It means 'the oneness of God'.

Look at the spidergram below which describes Allah (God).

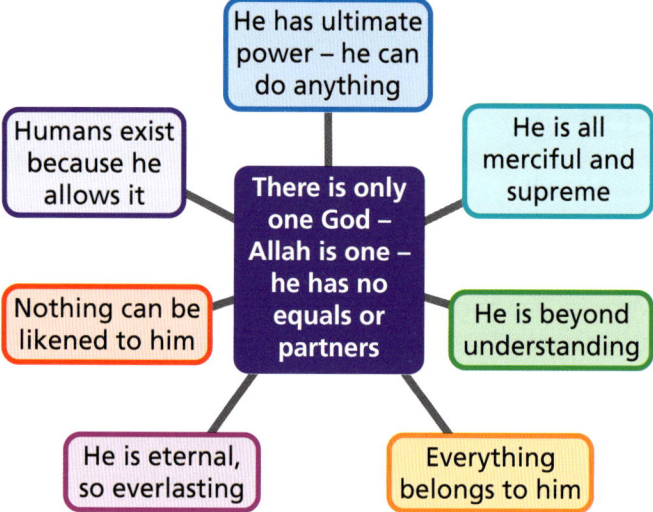

Having read these descriptions, can you imagine what Allah is like? It isn't easy because how could anything be *all* these things? For a Muslim – no matter how difficult it is to imagine or explain – Allah is all those things. Muslims say there are 99 names for Allah, and these names tell us Allah's qualities, but even so, we still can't properly understand everything about Allah.

Muslims believe that Allah knows everything about each of us. Allah knows every aspect of our characters, including how we will behave even before we do something. Allah knows the future of everything and has the power to control it. This is called Al-Qadr.

Muslims believe all this about Allah. Their beliefs about Allah are the reason they follow the rules of the Qur'an and Shariah law – Allah has given both. Their beliefs about Allah are the basis of their religious faith and religious practices.

6 Islam

▶ Belief in Risalah

Risalah is prophethood or messengership. It means communication between Allah and all people by way of angels, prophets and books. Allah is guiding humans to know the right way to live. This takes place in three ways:

- Books – Allah sends books to teach humans, but only one remains in its original state. This book, which is believed to be the word of Allah, is called the Qur'an.
- Angels – these are not like humans. Angels always obey Allah, and one of their jobs is to bring Allah's guidance to humans. Jibril is one of these angels.
- Prophets – these are humans specially chosen by Allah to tell people what they should believe, and how they should live and behave. Muslims believe there have been 124,000 Prophets, the last being Prophet Muhammad.

▶ Belief in Akhirah

Akhirah is the belief in the afterlife in either paradise or hell.
This includes belief in:

- Judgement Day – when each person is judged to decide if they are worthy to go to paradise or not, depending on how they lived their lives
- paradise and hell – paradise being a place of reward and pleasure, hell a place of suffering and punishment.

To be placed in Paradise by Allah requires effort, discipline and always trying to do the right thing. Doing the wrong things in life can seem the easy option at times but Muslims should always try and follow Allah's teachings. The bridge to paradise is described as being as thin as a human hair. Obviously, people would prefer to go to paradise rather than hell, because paradise is beautiful beyond description whereas hell is torture and suffering.

> I pray every day, and keep all my duties as a Muslim. Allah will reward me for this in the next life. Jamal

> The next life is eternal. I don't want to suffer, so I am a good person for my family and to others. Rebekkah

> I can only do what is right now. My religion tells me how to live. By following this, the next life is taken care of. Kane

Activities

1. Write out this table so that the two halves match up correctly.

Tawhid is	the belief that Allah sends guidance to all people through angels, prophets and holy books.
Risalah is	the belief in life after death.
Akhirah is	the belief in one God.

2. Explain each of the three beliefs of Islam.
3. Why do you think Allah chose to use so many different ways to guide people? What does the fact that Allah had to send so many Prophets tell us?
4. If a person believes in life after death – paradise and hell – how might that affect the way they live their life now? Use some examples to explain your thoughts.
5. 'This life is far more important than an afterlife'. Do you think this is true? Give some reasons why. What might other people say to contrast with your ideas?

The major world faiths

6.2 The founder of Islam – Prophet Muhammad

Learning objectives
- To learn about the key elements of the life of Prophet Muhammad and the early Muslim community
- To learn about the Night of Power
- To explore the qualities of leaders

Big question
What sort of a leader would you follow?

570 CE	Muhammad's father dies, just before Muhammad is born. His home city is Makkah.
576 CE	In accordance with tradition, Muhammad is raised by Bedouin Arabs until the age of two. His mother dies when he is six. He goes to live with his grandfather, tending sheep.
581 CE	Muhammad goes to live with his uncle – a trader – after the death of his grandfather. He learns to be a businessman.
595 CE	Muhammad marries Khadijah, a businesswoman in her own right. They have six children, two of whom are boys who die very young.
600 CE	Muhammad becomes disillusioned with the society he lives in. It is corrupt, ignores the poor and needy and is fuelled by money and pleasure-seeking. He begins to go to the hills alone to meditate and find calm.
610 CE	The Night of Power. While meditating in a cave at Mount Hira, Muhammad is confronted by the angel Jibra'il who orders him to read words from a scroll. Muhammad protests that he cannot read. The angel holds him and squeezes him tight. This happens three times. On the third occasion, Muhammad begins to speak the words from the scroll – he would later say it was as if they were already in his heart. The angel seems to disappear, but when Muhammad runs to the cave's entrance, all he can see is the face of the angel many times in the sky. Muhammad is to be the final Prophet, and his job is to warn and guide humans through messages from Allah. He receives further revelations of the Qur'an throughout his life. He shares these revelations with his family and friends – they recognise him as a Prophet from Allah.
621 CE	In a revelation, Prophet Muhammad is instructed to go public with the message of Islam. Everyone who accepts Prophet Muhammad's message has to change their lives to live in a purer, more disciplined way, but businessmen have to change more than anyone. The businessmen reject his message – not least because it attacks their selfishness, and urges them to share the wealth they greedily cling to.
622 CE	As more people convert to Prophet Muhammad's message, the businessmen hatch a plan to have him murdered. Forewarned, he is able to escape with his followers and flee to Madinah. This is the Hijrah.
627 CE	By this time, the Makkan businessmen have sent armies to fight three battles with Prophet Muhammad and his followers – at Badr (624 CE), Uhud (625 CE) and Ahzab (627 CE). At Ahzab, Prophet Muhammad's army is overwhelmingly victorious – the way is now open for Muhammad to return to Makkah.
630 CE	Prophet Muhammad returns to Makkah as the leader of a big community. He sets up the Ka'aba as the centre of worship of Allah. The city becomes Muslim.
632 CE	Prophet Muhammad delivers his last sermon in Makkah. Knowing he is close to death, he returns to Madinah where he dies in the arms of his wife. His tomb is in Madinah and many Muslims visit it as a pilgrimage. Islam believes there has been no Prophet after Muhammad, that he was the last – the Seal – of the Prophets.

6 Islam

> 'Muhammad is not the father of any of your men, but he is the Messenger of Allah and the Seal of the Prophets; and Allah has full knowledge of all things.' (Qur'an 33:41)

> 'Read: In the Name of your Lord who created. Created man from a clot. Read: And your Lord is the Most Generous. He who taught by the pen. Taught man what he never knew.' (Qur'an 96:1–4)

▲ The cave at Mount Hira, where Muhammad's role as Prophet began

▲ Saudi Arabia, showing Makkah and Madinah

From an early age, Muhammad faced challenges. This must have made him resourceful and resilient. He was successful in business. He was chosen to be the Prophet of Islam because of his good character. He must have been a charismatic person because people came to listen to him, and his words persuaded them to accept the teachings and copy the new religious practices he was carrying out. He must have been brave because he led an army three times against much bigger armies. Muslims see Prophet Muhammad as their role model.

Activities

1. Describe Muhammad's life before he became a Prophet.
2. Explain what happened on the Night of Power, and how this was a life-changing event for Muhammad.
3. Explain what the Hijrah was and why it happened.
4. Imagine you have been asked to write an obituary for the life of Prophet Muhammad. This is a piece of writing published after a person's death, which tells the reader about a person's life and their importance.
5. In your opinion, what was the most important event in Prophet Muhammad's life? Justify your choice.

The major world faiths

6.3 The holy book of Islam – the Qur'an

Learning objectives
- To learn about how the Muslim holy book was formed
- To understand the key messages of the Qur'an
- To reflect on the importance of holy books for believers

Big question
How do you look after important documents?

Muslims believe Allah tries to help humans to behave in the right way so that they can enter paradise after Judgement Day. They believe Allah has sent guidance to humans through revelations, which became 'books'. These were all versions of Allah's book, which Muslims call Umm al-Kitab. He used five Prophets to give this guidance:

- Prophet Ibrahim (Abraham), who received the Suhuf (scrolls)
- Prophet Musa (Moses), who received the Tawrat (Torah)
- Prophet Dawud (David), who received the Zabur (Psalms)
- Prophet Isa (Jesus), who received the Injil (Gospel)
- Prophet Muhammad, who received the Qur'an.

▲ The Qur'an

Muslims believe each of the first four was either changed and made inaccurate by humans, or lost. The versions we have now are still important, and so should be read and respected, but the Qur'an is the only book that was never changed. It is the most important as it remains the word of Allah.

▶ About the Qur'an

Qur'an means 'recitation'. Prophet Muhammad recited the Qur'an, as if from memory – but he could not write it down as he could not read or write. (Look back to page 92 to remind yourself how Prophet Muhammad first received the Qur'an during the Night of Power.) Over the space of 23 years, he received revelations from Angel Jibril, which gave him more of the Qur'an. Sometimes these came as he slept, and caused him to talk aloud in his sleep. The people around him recorded what he said on whatever they could find – paper, wood, leather, stone, leaves. It was only after his death that Caliph Abu Bakr had everything put together into one book. Four copies were made, which he sent to different parts of the Muslim world. Two still exist – in museums in Tashkent and Istanbul.

The Qur'an is made up of 114 chapters, or surahs. Altogether there are 6,236 verses, or ayahs. The Qur'an is written in the Arabic which Prophet Muhammad spoke, and Muslims around the world learn to read it in this language. A Muslim who has completely memorised the whole Qur'an and so can recite all of it is given the name hafiz, which brings respect from others.

All Muslims should read the Qur'an as it is the word of Allah, but there is no set order of reading. A Muslim could decide to read the whole Qur'an over time from cover to cover. They might read sections of it each day. They might open it at random and read. They might read specific sections depending on the day, or events. The sound of the words is believed to be special and to bring a blessing to the reader. Every Friday at the mosque, the imam (religious leader) will give a sermon which is based on a section of the Qur'an. Every day, as they pray, Muslims recite short sections of the Qur'an.

▶ The message of the Qur'an

The Qur'an has five key messages:

1. Allah is good and powerful.
2. There will be a Judgement Day at the end of time.
3. Allah's goodness and power make it necessary for humans to worship Allah.
4. We should be generous to others, because Allah is generous to us.
5. Muhammad is the Prophet of Allah, and tells people how to live in the way Allah requires in the Qur'an.

As the Qur'an is difficult to interpret, Prophet Muhammad's sayings and actions were also recorded in the Sunnah and Hadith. These help Muslims to understand how to do what Allah tells them they must do in the Qur'an. So, for example, the Qur'an demands they pray five times a day, but it is the Sunnah and Hadith that tell them what to do when they pray.

▶ Looking after the Qur'an

Being the word of God, the Qur'an is the most special of words, so it has to be cared for and shown respect. Muslims show great respect to the Qur'an. They always wash before reading the Qur'an, so that they don't put any dirt or grease on it. More importantly, it is a symbol of being physically and spiritually clean before reciting the words of Allah. Many place it on a special stand to read from it. They keep it on a high shelf when not in use – so that no other book is higher. They keep it covered when not in use.

Activities

1. Write out this table so that the two halves match up correctly.

Umm al-Kitab	The Psalms of Dawud
Suhuf	The holy book of Islam
Tawrat	Chapters and verses of the Qur'an
Zabur	A person who can recite the whole of the Qur'an from memory
Injil	Scrolls of Ibrahim
Qur'an	Mother of the book – Allah's book of guidance in heaven
Hafiz	The Gospel of Isa
Surah and ayah	The Torah of Musa

2. Explain why only the Qur'an, out of all the Muslim holy books, is believed by Muslims to be the actual word of God.
3. Explain the message of the Qur'an for Muslims.
4. Imagine you had a bookshop which sold copies of the Qur'an in English and Arabic. To show respect, you have decided that each copy sold will include a card helping the buyer to understand respectful ownership and use of the Qur'an. Design and make that card.
5. 'The guidance given in the Qur'an is what makes it the most important book for Muslims.' Do you agree with this statement? Explain your arguments.

The major world faiths

6.4 The Muslim place of worship – the mosque

Learning objectives
- To know the form of a mosque
- To consider how Muslims have established places for worship in Wales
- To reflect on how society shapes the way people express their beliefs

Big question
How magnificent should religious buildings be?

Mosques come in all different styles, depending on the country in which they are built. The first Muslims to come to Wales had to worship in their own homes. Later, as the communities got bigger and had enough money, they converted existing buildings into mosques. The final stage might be to create new buildings for the specific purpose of being a mosque or Islamic centre An example of this is the Newport Central Mosque. However, many communities find the building they have to be the right one, especially if it was originally built for worship such as the Berea Mosque (formerly a chapel). As of 2022, Wales had about 40 mosques, most of which are buildings converted from another purpose. Many are former Christian churches, such as the Swansea Mosque (St Helen's Road). Some, usually in places where the community is very small, such as in Carmarthen, are converted houses.

Key beliefs
The Mosque is the House of Allah. Mosques are built as a place of worship, but also as the central point of the community. Mosque means 'place of prostration' – a place to bow down to Allah.

▶ Outside the mosque

The most obvious way in which to identify a mosque is by the sign outside it, but many mosques give other clues as well.

There might be a crescent moon and star, the key symbols of Islam. The star has five sides for the five duties Muslims keep (the Five Pillars). The moon was used by travellers in the desert to help find the way; Islam helps humans to 'find their way' and do as Allah requires.

Many mosques have a notice board to inform people of prayer times – Muslims pray five times each day, and Muslim men should attend the mosque to pray as often as they can. Of course, a Muslim can pray whenever they want to, but there is a duty to pray at fixed times. This is salah.

Purpose-built mosques often have towers, from which the call to prayer is given, and domes. These are traditional features of mosques in the places where British Muslims originally came from, such as India, Pakistan and the Middle East.

▲ Mosque in Malaysia

▲ The Dome of the Rock, Jerusalem

6 Islam

◀ Berea Masjid Mosque, formerly Berea Chapel. A Welsh converted mosque

▶ Newport Central Mosque. A purpose-built Welsh mosque

▶ Inside the mosque – key features

Prayer times are dictated by sunrise and sunset, so the times change daily by a few minutes. Most mosques have clocks for worshippers to get their timing right.

Muslims have to complete a ritual wash before praying. This is called wudhu. It symbolises that the person is fit to pray, as outer cleanliness equals inner cleanliness. Mosques have facilities for this, which may be taps in a washroom or a fountain in a yard.

Worshippers enter the hall and are immediately faced with the Qiblah wall. This is the direction in which Muslims face when praying towards Makkah. In the wall is an arch or more decorated section, which is the mihrab. This is usually highly decorated with calligraphy from the Qur'an, and represents the Ka'aba (the black box which is the House of God in Makkah).

At the front is a raised platform for the imam (religious leader) to use. It raises him so that he can be seen and heard by all when giving a sermon at Friday prayer, when all men are expected to attend.

The prayer hall is carpeted, and is not furnished. Muslims pray by bowing, standing, kneeling and prostrating. The carpet usually has a prayer mat design to help with spacing for the prayer process.

Mosques – both outside and in – can be spectacular, or can be simple. They are built or re-designed to give glory to Allah, and space for worship of Allah. They are the centre of a Muslim community.

Activities

1. What is the place of worship for Muslims called?
2. Use the information from these pages to make your own booklet about the mosque. Include the features that help people to recognise it as a mosque and the features inside a mosque; explain any of its symbolism and explain why it is an important building for Muslims.
3. 'People should always pray at a place of worship.' What do you think? Explain your ideas.

The major world faiths

6.5 Belief and prayer – the Pillars of Shahadah and Salah

Learning objectives

- To recognise the start point of Muslim faith – a statement of belief
- To understand how Muslims pray
- To reflect on how a basic belief influences religious practice

Big question

Does one basic belief drive all of a person's behaviour?

Key beliefs

The Five Pillars of Islam are five duties for all Muslims. They are Shahadah (statement of faith), Salah (prayer), Zakah (welfare contributions), Sawm (fasting during Ramadan) and Hajj (pilgrimage). They are called 'Pillars' because the religion rests on them.

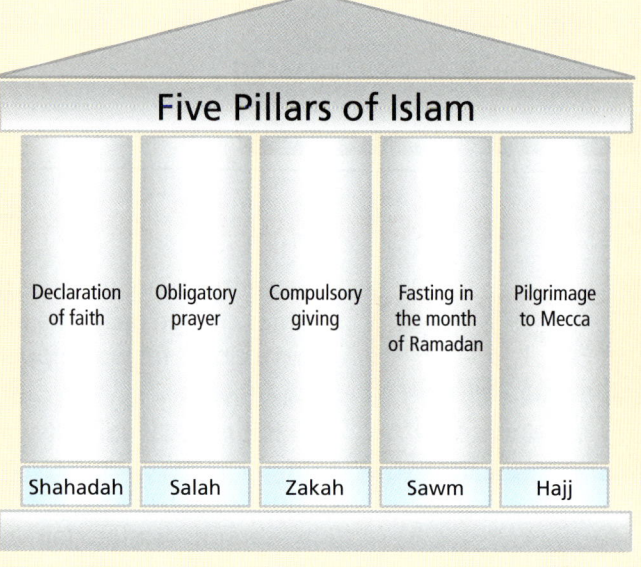

▶ Shahadah – the First Pillar

The Shahadah is the Islamic statement of belief. It sums up what Muslims believe. It says: 'There is no God but Allah. Muhammad is the messenger of Allah.'

This Arabic text is the Shahadah. It is shown here on the outer wall of a mosque in Kuala Lumpur.

Shi'a Muslims believe that Ali was so important to the beginning of the Muslim community after the death of Muhammad that they sometimes add the following to the end of the Shahadah: 'Ali is divinely appointed authority.' This is not necessary to say but is said to confirm their belief in Ali being Muhammad's successor and the first Imam.'

Muslims use repeated geometric patterns instead of images of people or animals. The Shahadah is often written with a geometric pattern as a backdrop.

The words of the Shahadah are the First Pillar. It is because they believe these words, that Muslims carry out the other Pillars.

The Shahadah runs throughout a Muslim's life. They are the first words whispered into the ear of a new-born baby. The Shahadah forms part of the Adhan – the call to prayer, five times a day. The words are repeated as a person dies or said for someone as they die.

▶ Salah – the Second Pillar

Salah is prayer, which takes place five times a day, in the mosque if possible. This can be done at home or in the mosque.

Before prayer, Muslims remove their shoes to enter the mosque, and carry out a washing process (wudhu). Being clean on the outside represents being clean inside the mind, and therefore ready to pray.

At noon on Friday at the mosque, a special prayer (Jummah) takes place which also includes a sermon (**khutbah**) given by the imam. This allows the imam to teach Muslims about the Qur'an or about issues that are affecting the community at the time.

Muslims stand in rows, side by side facing the Ka'aba in Makkah. In their minds, they focus on God, telling him they will now pray.

The most important position is kneeling on the floor with the forehead touching the floor. Sunni Muslims place their head directly on the carpet whereas Shi'a Muslims place their head on something natural e.g. a wooden block or clay block from Karbala (a city holy to Shi'a Muslims). This shows total submission to Allah, and the belief that Allah is greater than anything else.

Prayer involves set movements and words to go with each movement. The movements are in a sequence known as a ra'akah, or unit. Shi'a and Sunni do this slightly differently, for example, their hands and arms are positioned differently whilst standing in prayer.

Salah is important because it teaches Muslims many qualities. It teaches discipline: meeting at the correct prayer times. It teaches humility: realising Allah is the most important figure in life. Muslims realise they depend on Allah and are thankful for what Allah provides. Praying five times a day at set times throughout the day means that a Muslim's thoughts are regularly brought back to Allah as they go through the day. A Muslim should then realise that nothing is more important than Allah.

Activities

1. What is Salah?
2. Describe Muslim prayer.
3. Sunni and Shi'a practise their faith a little differently. Give examples of this from the first Two Pillars.
4. What do you think is the most important part of Salah for Muslims? Why?
5. 'A person should not need constant reminders of Allah in their daily lives.' Give reasons to disagree with this statement.

The major world faiths

6.6 Devotion and thankfulness – the Pillars of Zakah and Sawm

Learning objectives
- To know about the Pillar of Zakah and its demands on Muslims
- To know about the Pillar of Sawm and its demands on Muslims
- To explore the concepts of devotion and thankfulness

Big question
Why do people celebrate when they have completed difficult tasks?

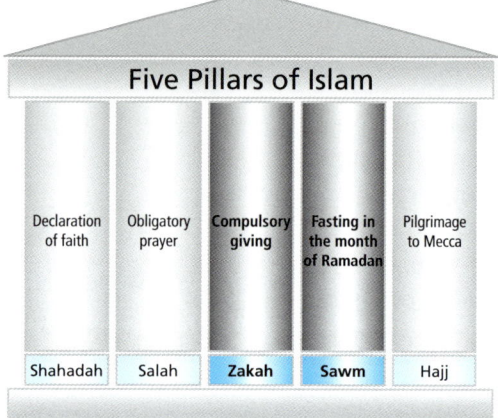

Key beliefs
Zakah – the Third Pillar, welfare contributions

Sawm – the Fourth Pillar, fasting during the month of Ramadan

Eid ul-Fitr – the festival of fast-breaking, which happens after Ramadan

▶ Zakah – the Third Pillar

Zakah is giving to charity from your own wealth. It is a duty for all Muslims. It is given to the mosque during Ramadan, and then distributed to benefit poor Muslims in the community. In some Muslim countries, it is collected as a tax by the government. Zakah is compulsory as a Pillar of Islam. It is given anonymously so people cannot make a show of what they are giving. Only Allah knows the amount given.

In Islam, all wealth is a gift of Allah; humans only have wealth on loan from Allah. They should look after it and will be judged on how they use it. Wealth should be used to help all people, especially those in need. It is like a test from Allah for those who have money to help those who do not.

Zakah is believed to cleanse and purify your wealth. It shares out Allah's blessings and improves lives by providing money to needy people. It brings love into giving, and prevents greed. It makes people pleased to help others, and brings rewards in paradise.

Zakah is 2.5 per cent of earnings after all bills are paid. For Muslims, paying Zakah follows the Qur'anic teaching to think of others and share Allah's wealth around. The wealthier a person is the more they pay. Shi'a Muslims also pay Khums, which is 20 per cent on annual savings. Many Muslims also give Sadaqah (charity).

Activities
1. What is Zakah?
2. Imam Ali said that if all people paid their Zakah no one would be poor. What do you think he meant?

Sawm – the Fourth Pillar

'Sawm is about going without food – but it is also about being a better Muslim and person. It reminds us how often daily life gets in the way of our worship of Allah. For Ramadan, Allah is our focus with more time in the mosque and reading the Qur'an. We also don't watch too much TV, listen to too much music or spend too long playing computer games as none of these gives real benefit to us. We also try to live better by being nicer to each other rather than saying mean things.'

'Ramadan focuses on Allah being the centre of life, which should then carry on for the rest of the year. Perhaps Allah knows how we slip and don't do things right and Ramadan was his design as a reminder. We realise we waste time, and forget what is really important in life. The fasting reminds us what it is like to be poor every day. It also brings discipline to mind and body and reminds us how lucky we are.'

'Ramadan for me is a month I look forward to – but at the same time I don't, as I know how hard Sawm (fasting) is. My community fasts during Ramadan for 29–30 days. Only during the daylight hours though. So, we get up early, have a light meal and then don't eat for the rest of the day till nightfall. Ramadan is a special month; the time the first verses of the Qur'an were revealed.'

'Each day of fasting is ended by Iftar – sharing something sweet like dates, followed by a simple meal. I share the Iftar with my family but in Makkah about a million people share it together! The last Iftar is the night before Eid-ul-Fitr, a massive celebration of completing the fast … now I have to think about the year ahead and being more focused on Allah.'

Activities

1. Design a two-sided postcard. On one side, show why fasting is a really positive experience. On the other side, create an image to represent this month of fasting.
2. 'Doing Sawm makes a person more likely to give Zakah.' Do you agree with this statement? Give reasons for agreeing and disagreeing.

'On the first day of the month after Ramadan, it is Eid ul-Fitr, the festival of fast-breaking. My family attends the mosque. The imam gives a sermon on the discipline we have shown in keeping Sawm and how this fulfils a duty to Allah. I always feel a bit proud of how much devotion I could show because this month was dedicated to Allah. I also feel thankful that I completed it. In some ways I am more thankful that I can stop fasting – millions of people across the world cannot because they are so poor. The day becomes a huge party. Extended families meet up for big feasts, to catch up and to exchange gifts. This is a day to reflect on how we can take the discipline of Sawm into the rest of the year, but it is also a day everyone really enjoys and celebrates.'

The major world faiths

6.7 Dedication and resilience – the Pillar of Hajj

Learning objectives
- To know the process of Hajj
- To understand the importance of Hajj in showing devotion to Allah
- To explore the concepts of dedication and resilience

Big question
Do people show enough resilience?

Key beliefs
Hajj is the Muslim pilgrimage to Makkah. This Fifth Pillar must be done once in a lifetime or as often as can be afforded.

Five Pillars of Islam

Declaration of faith	Obligatory prayer	Compulsory giving	Fasting in the month of Ramadan	Pilgrimage to Mecca
Shahadah	Salah	Zakah	Sawm	Hajj

▶ Hajj – the Fifth Pillar

'Hi I'm Alliyah and I'm going to explain what the Hajj meant to me this year. I don't just want to describe the journey to you – you can easily research that on the internet – I want you share in my experiences: the feelings, thoughts and sights of this special journey for me.'

'On Hajj we wear Ihram. Men wear two white pieces of cloth: one over the shoulder, the other around the waist. As a woman, I chose white too. Seeing everyone all the same, you have nothing to judge them on – money, style, etc. – there is only their character to know.'

'To be in this massive crowd all walking round the Ka'aba, seeing the Ka'aba and feeling the excitement of everyone brought me tears of joy. You are part of a sea of people – millions together – it is such an intense experience. To do here what Prophet Muhammad had done – to walk in his footsteps and show my love for Allah – will stick in my mind always.'

'Some pilgrims are lucky enough to touch the black stone. It is linked to the prophets – to Adam, Noah and Ismail, whoever was the one given it – it came to Earth from heaven and is a gift of Allah. I was close enough to touch it. It was a very powerful moment.'

6 Islam

'Zamzam is the spring that was given to Ibrahim's wife, Hagar. She searched everywhere for water for her son in the desert. Allah rewarded her faith with the spring water. I got a bottle to take home for my family. We believe it has life-giving qualities and can cure illnesses.'

'Next was Safa and Marwa, two hills where Hagar frantically searched for water. I guess many of us would have given up looking for water in the desert, but she didn't and was rewarded. I realised how easily I give up when things are difficult. I need to be more resilient.'

'The Mount of Mercy is the main act of Hajj. We prayed from noon until dusk, asking for forgiveness. Here Adam and Hawwaa (Eve) were reunited after being sent from paradise, showing that Allah forgave them. To pray for so long was hard – thinking about my life … and in the sun! Walking away I felt refreshed in my soul.'

'I spent the night collecting pebbles, praying and reading my Qur'an. In the morning we travelled to Mina, with its three pillars representing Shaytan (the devil). He had tried to tempt Ibrahim not to sacrifice his own son after Allah had told him to as a test of faith. I thought how easily we are all tempted by Shaytan. We have got to be strong. We threw the pebbles at the pillars to show strength.'

'At the end, we had our hair trimmed. The men get it shaved! We paid for a lamb to be slaughtered as a sacrifice to Allah. This is a festival day for Muslims everywhere – Eid ul-Adha. All over the world, Muslims go to their mosque to hear a sermon about dedication and sacrifice. On Hajj we also reflected on the resilience we have shown in completing the Hajj in the time set. Muslims everywhere pay for an animal to be sacrificed, and its meat shared with the poor. Then they all celebrate with their families – food, gifts, happiness. Eid reminds us we must sacrifice our lives to Allah, and do his will, but it also reminds us that Allah gives us everything so we must be grateful.'

Activities

1. What is Hajj?
2. Write the stages of Hajj, and for each explain what Muslims do, and why they do it.
3. Alliyah has described her Hajj journey. Write a list of ten descriptive words you think she might use to describe her journey.
4. Which part of Hajj do you think might have had the greatest effect on Alliyah, and why?

The major world faiths

6.8 Islam in the Welsh community

Learning objectives
- To explore the concept of giving in Islam
- To learn about how Welsh Muslims have given to their wider communities
- To reflect on how beliefs can shape social action

Big question
Is it better to give or to receive?

Key term
Hadith – a collection of the sayings of Prophet Muhammad which help Muslims to do as the Qur'an says

▶ What do the Islamic Hadith say about giving?

'Those who prevent the supporting of orphans and the feeding of the poor are said to be "those who reject the faith"'

'Nothing shall ensure the welfare (and interests) of your religion except generosity.'

'You will not believe until you love for your brother what you love for yourself.'

'Generosity is to help a deserving person without his request.'

'Spend … and I shall spend on you.'

'Protect yourself from hell-fire even by giving a piece of a date as charity.'

These lines from the **Hadith** suggest that giving is essential to being a Muslim and that Allah wants people to be generous in every way possible. By sharing our wealth, Allah's test is passed. The wealth of any person is a gift, and only by sharing wealth does a person show their respect for that gift. If Muslims give and are generous then Allah will reward them well.

There are three ways to give financially:

1. Zakah – the Third Pillar demands 2.5 per cent payment on savings. All wealth is on loan from Allah so a Muslim should use their wealth in a way Allah would want. Allah allows unequal wealth as a test of the rich to provide for the poor.
2. Khums – this is paid by Shi'a Muslims, and is a 20 per cent tax on business profits paid once a year. It is to be spent for the good of Allah.
3. Sadaqah – this is voluntary giving – more like charity. This can be any act of kindness, not just money.

More than just money

What else can be given to show generosity? Not everyone has money to give. Charity is any act of freely giving for the benefit of others. Anyone – even the poorest – can give their time, their expertise or their attention. It is normal for British Muslim communities to be linked to a large range of charitable organisations. Some of these organisations are Muslim, for example, Islamic Relief Worldwide, but many Muslims support organisations set up by other religious and non-religious charities. These organisations work locally, nationally and across the world to help the poor, those who are suffering, the homeless and others. Muslims volunteer their time to collect money and items to help these people. Others go one step further and work in areas that are troubled and where people are struggling.

Helping out in the Covid-19 pandemic

During the Covid-19 pandemic, the Rabbaniah Islamic Cultural Centre in Cardiff extended its foodbank to help support families in crisis. Welsh foodbanks had to step up to provide for the greater demand caused by the pandemic. The demand in Cardiff was greatest; the city's foodbanks received 118 tonnes of food for distribution.

Local volunteers from the Grangetown and Riverside area of Cardiff helped to put together and deliver food parcels, as well as baby milk and nappies. The parcels contained staple foods like pasta, rice, tins, sauces and so on – enough to keep a family going for a week. Even though the Muslim community attending the centre was fasting for Ramadan, it recognised that the wider community was not, and some in that wider community were in great need. Each week about 30 volunteers helped to pack and deliver about 150 food boxes for families who had registered and qualified for support.

Al-Ikhlas Cultural and Education Centre in Cardiff was established in 2013. It provides many services to the local community as well as being a centre for education. It hosts a Youth Forum weekly where young people can improve their job prospects by getting guidance on CV writing, mock interview practice and job-seeking support. The centre also runs a foodbank.

During the pandemic lockdown, food poverty became an increasing problem across the UK. Al-Ikhlas spotted a chance to contribute to being part of the solution, and continued an initiative which they had set up in a previous Ramadan. Iftar is the meal which is eaten in the evening of each day of the Ramadan fast. Up to 300 Iftar meals were made fresh and delivered every evening of Ramadan. Al-Ikhlas sought donations from the local community, and worked with a local supermarket to provide the ingredients. Many people, including the Labour MP Jenny Rathbone, helped to make the meals and then distribute them around Cardiff.

Activities

1 Explain how a Muslim might be encouraged by their beliefs and the teachings of the religion to help others.
2 Explain three ways in which Muslims give financially.
3 Explain how Al-Ikhlas Cultural and Education Centre is helping its local community.
4 Do you think religious believers should focus their resources on their own community or more widely? Explain the reasons for your answer.

7 Hinduism

7.1 Key beliefs about God in Hinduism

Learning objectives
- To learn about the Hindu concept of God
- To understand the way that Hinduism sees God in all
- To reflect on why people want to believe in a power beyond this world

Big question
Can we ever know what God is like?

Talk it out
There is no scientific evidence to prove God exists, but billions believe God exists.

Why do you think people want to believe in God?

The Trimurti
To help them start to understand God, many Hindus break down Brahman into the Trimurti. Trimurti means 'three forms', which are:

- Brahma – the creator: God creates everything
- Vishnu – the preserver: God supports everything in creation
- Shiva – the destroyer: God brings everything to an end

For Hindus, as for people from all religions, questions like 'What is God?' can only be partly answered. Hinduism is a pluralistic religion; it accepts there are many different ways of understanding God. Some Hindus focus on the idea of one God; this is Brahman – the Ultimate Reality. Hindus believe that Brahman is everywhere and part of everything; that God can never be seen and understood fully; that God has no limits and is beyond our existence; and that God is too powerful for us to see or understand fully. Religious traditions which believe in one God tend to break their ideas of God down in different ways. Christians understand God through the Trinity, while Muslims understand Allah through Allah's 99 names. Many Hindus have a similar way of trying to say what God is like – through images that represent qualities of the divine.

The deities
Many Hindus focus on aspects of the personality of Brahman, made into individual characters (deities). For examples, Saraswati is the deity of all learning. Each deity represents one or more of the qualities of God. Each quality can be represented as an image or statue (called a murti). These murtis are believed to host the presence of the deity, so are worshipped.

Activities

1. What is the name of God in Hinduism?
2. How is Brahman described?
3. Study the image of the Trimurti and read the annotations carefully.
   a. Make a list of all the qualities of Brahman that the Trimurti describes.
   b. Pick five of these qualities: how could these qualities be shown in a modern way? Draw pictures or write descriptions for your answer.
4. What are deities in Hinduism?
5. Is it right to say that Hindus believe in one God? Explain your reasons.

▶ Why do Hindus use murtis to describe God?

Hinduism is the oldest religion, existing before humans had written language, so instead of using words to describe God they used visual images called murtis. The murtis helped people to understand what God is like. Brahman's nature was explained through the use of murtis. Stories were told and then written about these murtis, showing different qualities – a bit like giving God a personality that people could build a relationship with.

The murtis only *represent* God. Hindus believe that each form is a way to help Hindus understand and relate to God's different qualities. The murtis reflect those different qualities, while hosting the presence of God.

The murtis in the picture below are full of symbolism, helping worshippers better understand their religion and God.

Vishnu preserves and protects everything. Vishnu came to Earth with special powers as avatars (see page 118) to help people.

Vishnu is blue like the sky, showing he is everywhere. He has four arms (showing power) and a long 'U-shape' runs down his forehead with a dot in the middle. Vishnu carries four objects – the conch shell represents the sound of creation; the discus represents the Sun; the lotus flower symbolises beauty, peace and freedom; and the mace (a stick with a spiked head) is his magical weapon. Vishnu is responsible for all these areas of life.

Brahma, the creator of the universe, is shown with four heads, representing the four primary scriptures – the Vedas (Hindu holy books).

Brahma's four arms show power and the forces of creation. He carries a ladle with water (the universe comes from this), beads (a reminder to pray) and a book representing the Vedas (Hindu holy books).

Vishnu stands on a lotus flower. Sometimes he is seen lying on the coils of a serpent with Lakshmi, his wife, massaging his feet, or riding on Garuda, the King of Birds, who is half man, half eagle.

Shiva's third eye shows his wisdom. The cobra necklace shows his power over even the most dangerous creatures. Snakes shed their skin to make way for new smooth skin so this represents his power of destruction and recreation. This cobra is Vasuki, a serpent king.

Shiva's three-pronged spear – a trident (trishool) – represents the Trimurti. The three lines across his forehead represent the three qualities which Hindus believe the universe is made up of.

Shiva is also known as Yogiraj, seen meditating in the mountains as Lord of Meditation. He is also known as Nataraj, seen dancing in a circle of flames as Lord of the Dance. The dance refers to the cycle of creation, preservation and destruction.

The major world faiths

7.2 Key beliefs in Hinduism – karma and reincarnation

Learning objectives
- To learn about the key Hindu beliefs of karma and reincarnation
- To explore the Hindu understanding of the cycle of life
- To reflect on whether religion makes a person more morally good

Big question
Is death the end, or the start?

Talk it out
Do you think it helps people to believe there is something after this life?

Does that belief have a big impact on living this life?

The word **samsara** means 'to flow'

▲ The cycle of samsara: 'Death is certain to the one that is born and birth is certain to the one who dies.' (Bhagavad Gita)

One of the key beliefs of Hinduism is the idea of samsara, the cycle of birth, death and rebirth (reincarnation). Hindus believe we have an atman (spirit) which is born again and again into many lifetimes on its spiritual journey. The journey only stops when the individual discovers their true nature or identity as part of Brahman. This point is called moksha – liberation or freedom from rebirth, and reunion with Brahman.

A Hindu story of karma and rebirth

A simple story from Hinduism about rebirth tells of a priest who is about to sacrifice a goat. This is his main job – sacrificing goats to the gods. The goat begins to laugh, so the priest asks why it is laughing (given it is about to die). The goat replies that for 500 lifetimes, it has been born as a goat to burn off bad karma from a previous lifetime. The priest then again makes to sacrifice the goat, only for it to begin to cry. Puzzled, the priest asks why the goat is now so upset about dying when it will next be a human. The goat tells him that it is not crying for itself. It is crying for the priest 'because 500 lifetimes ago, I too was a priest who sacrificed goats!'

Activities
1. Give the meanings of these words: karma, reincarnation, atman, samsara.
2. How might a person be influenced in their life if they believe in karma and rebirth?
3. Look at the top circle in the diagram of moksha on page 109. Explain some examples of how a person might do this.
4. With a partner, come up with three classroom rules that would generate good karma. As a class consider all the suggestions and vote on the five rules for good karma in a classroom.
5. 'The Hindu idea about life after death is the best explanation for what happens when we die'. What do you think about this statement?

▶ Karma

Hindus believe in karma – that all actions in life have consequences. People in life have choices and these choices create good or bad karma. The soul moves on carrying the karma with it from one body to the next. You might think this means that Hindus don't care about people who are suffering, thinking they must have done something to deserve it in a previous life. However, Hinduism teaches that it is not only an individual's actions that influence the cycle of rebirth. Other forces beyond the individual's control, including the actions of other people, affect it. So, Hindus should not ignore suffering. Only humans create good karma. Animals do not create karma because they do not make moral choices. They act on instinct and so their actions can be neither good nor bad. People who have acted in a wicked manner might be reborn as animals as many times as it takes to burn off their bad karma, although this is believed to be unusual.

▶ Reincarnation

Hindus believe in atman, which is similar to the idea of a spirit that lives within each person. It is this atman (spirit) that is reborn in another body when we die. The process of the atman being born into a new body is called reincarnation. The atman karma shapes its future lives. Hindus are therefore responsible for their own rebirth. In each lifetime, the atman grows until it reaches perfection. Those who build lots of bad karma take more lifetimes to reach perfection.

The whole aim of these rebirths is to achieve the goal of being reunited with Brahman – the ultimate reality. The atman breaks free from the constant cycle of karma and rebirth when it realises its true nature. Hindus call this moksha.

▶ Moksha

Moksha is freedom from rebirth, and reunion with Brahman. It is the aim of life for Hindus. Hindu ideas about karma and reincarnation mean that a person should try to live a good life. They focus on worship of God, think about helping others rather than themselves, treat all life as important and are tolerant of others. The atman slowly comes to understand its true nature – that it is part of or one with Brahman, and sees everything else as not being reality (illusion). At this point, the atman becomes enlightened, and achieves moksha.

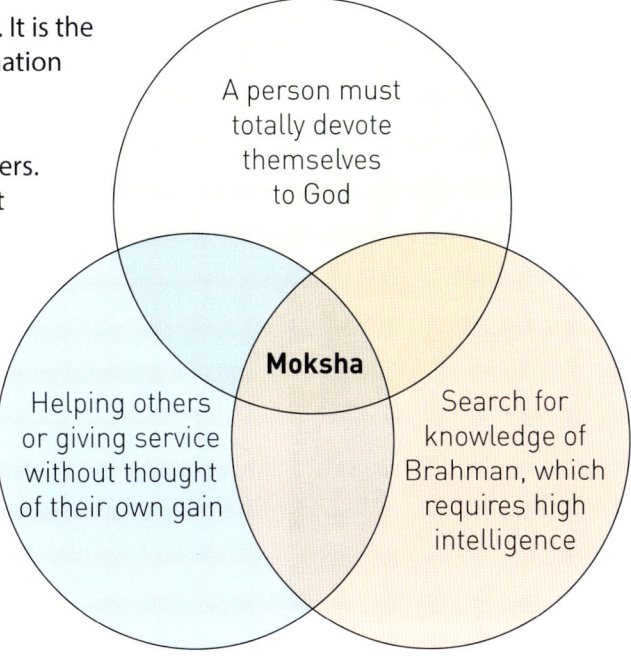

The major world faiths

7.3 The Hindu place of worship – the mandir

Learning objectives
- To know the features of a Hindu place of worship
- To learn about Welsh mandirs
- To reflect on why religious people seek to build their own places of worship

Big question
Should religions build their own places of worship or reuse ones which have become redundant?

Hindu temples are called mandirs and usually cover quite a large area, all of which is considered sacred. They are recognisable because there is usually a gopuram (gate) at the entrance. Purpose-built temples often have ornate entrances carved with images of the deities, but as many Welsh temples are converted buildings, this is not possible, so the gopuram tends to be a decorative feature around the main entrance.

Many UK temples have a large hall, at the end of which is the main shrine. The space in front of and around it is open without furniture. Temples have an external wall to mark the extent of the sacred space.

▲ Shree Swaminarayan Temple, Cardiff

The main sacred space (garbha griha) is usually central in the furthest wall from the door. It is the largest sacred space in the temple containing the statue of the deity to whom the temple is dedicated. Here the priests focus their work. The deity is often draped with garlands of flowers. Offerings such as flowers, fruit and incense are put there. Priests will recite Hindu scriptures and lead worship from this inner sanctum.

Sacred spaces are found all around the outside of the main sacred space on the side walls. Usually smaller and less imposing than the main sacred space, these are dedicated to other deities who are associated with the main deity. Worshippers often make offerings, light ghee lamps (lamps which burn clarified butter as their oil) or incense and say prayers at these sacred spaces.

Many Hindu communities in the UK have had to use redundant buildings – sometimes former places of worship for other religions. For example, Shree Swaminarayan Temple in Cardiff was originally a Jewish synagogue. These buildings have been decorated and refurbished to make them fit for the purpose of Hindu worship. Buying a building is a considerable cost – and many communities never get big enough congregations or enough money to justify the expense.

▲ The gopuram over a purpose-built Hindu temple is often very imposing.

▲ The sacred space at the India Centre, Cardiff

7 Hinduism

An arti tray is a tray with a lamp on it that is often lit by five wicks. Worshippers pass their hands over the lit flame and then touch their foreheads as a kind of blessing. There are often lit oil lamps around the temple.

At each shrine there is a bell for the worshippers to ring to announce their presence to the deity when their worship begins. The sound is believed to help a worshipper focus, to welcome the deity and dispel evil.

Sights and sounds of the Hindu temple

Offerings can be seen all around the temple. They may be garlands of flowers or trays of beautiful flowers and fruits which can be bought outside temples from local shops and sellers. Coconuts are often offered to the deities, after being smashed open on the ground.

Most temples have several priests associated with them, usually of different ages and with different roles. These are people who dedicate their lives to the temple and worship. At Welsh temples, they live in the community, study the sacred texts and lead worship. Hinduism has many rituals for worship, and these have to be learnt so that no mistakes in words or actions are made.

Hindu symbols are found on many shrines – the most common being the swastika, a symbol of good fortune; or aum, the symbol of Hinduism. Aum is thought of as the sound of the universe being created. It is used as a mantra that is repeated during worship.

Activities

1. What is the special name for a Hindu temple?
2. Use these words to describe a Hindu temple: gopuram, garbha griha, sacred spaces, offerings, priest.
3. What evidence is there to show that one of the sacred spaces is the most important?
4. Imagine you are a tour guide for a temple. Produce a simple guide to the building that you could hand out as you take your visitors around. Make it clear and colourful.
5. 'The statues and decoration in temples make it easier to focus on God.' What do you think? Give reasons for agreeing and disagreeing with this statement.

The major world faiths

7.4 Acts of worship in Hindu temples

Learning objectives
- To understand the central role of worship for Hindus
- To understand how worship at the temple might take place
- To reflect on the value of having different forms of worship

Big question
Should a religious person worship every day and always in the same way?

'Let me meditate on the glorious light of the creator. May this light guide our minds and inspire us with understanding.'
(*Gayatri Mantra*)

Key terms
Puja – act of worship in Hinduism

Arti tray – tray used during worship; contains lamp and representation of five elements; worshippers can take blessing from this

Hindu temples are open all day, every day. Many temples employ Brahmin priests who are available all the time to worshippers. It was traditional for priests to come from the Brahmin group within society, but this is changing so that some Hindu communities now accept any appropriate person to train to be a priest. All temples have priests, Brahmin or otherwise.

▶ Puja

Puja means ceremonial worship of a deity via a murti (image or statue, pronounced 'moorti'), which follows a set form. In different parts of India, where Hinduism began, many varied forms of puja take place, which are often influenced by the culture of the area. In the early morning at the temple, the murti on the main sacred space will be washed and dressed by the priests – often with flower garlands. Water, food and flower offering are made, while prayers or mantras are chanted. As well as the main puja, there are other small rituals which can be seen as worship. The priest's role is to perform these rituals.

▲ Worshippers around an arti tray seeking the deities' blessing

▶ The arti ceremony

An arti ceremony is the greeting of the deity – various offerings are made by moving them in a clockwise, circular motion in front of the deity. A bell is rung while people meditate on the deity. The priest brings a tray with an arti lamp on it and the worshipper draws their hands over the lit flame and over their foreheads. They take back some of the flowers offered and sprinkle water on themselves. After this, kirtan (stories) and bhajan (hymns) are sung.

As the lamp is waved in front of the deity, the worshipper believes it becomes filled with the love and energy of the deity. When they pass their hands over the flames, they take these blessings on themselves. On the **arti tray** along with the lamp are items to represent the five elements – space, fire, water, air and earth – showing that the whole of creation is offered to the deity.

▶ Darshan and havan

Darshan is an act of personal worship to a particular deity. The worshipper stands before the deity, bows their head, holding their hands together. Some prostrate themselves (lie on the floor) to show respect. This can be done at the main or side sacred spaces. They make offerings, drink holy water (charanamrita) and are given some of the sacred food. This food is called prashad. At other times, you might see a havan – a fire sacrifice where rice and grains are thrown into the fire while prayers are offered. Coconuts are also smashed to represent the destruction of one's ego in the hope of becoming a more spiritual person.

▶ Prayer and meditation

Prayers and the reciting of mantras are part of most religious activities. Hindus are encouraged to meditate on the scriptures in order to purify their minds and work towards a better rebirth. If people pray, they are less likely to behave badly. Worshippers can also listen to sermons which improve their understanding of the scriptures.

> 'Whatever the ardent devotee may offer, be it leaf, fruit or water, that I willingly accept for it was given with love.' (*Bhagavad Gita*)

> 'Learn to meditate ... Thus you will master the senses, the emotions, the intellect ... and free yourself from anger and desire.' (*Bhagavad Gita*)

▲ Priests dressing a temple deity

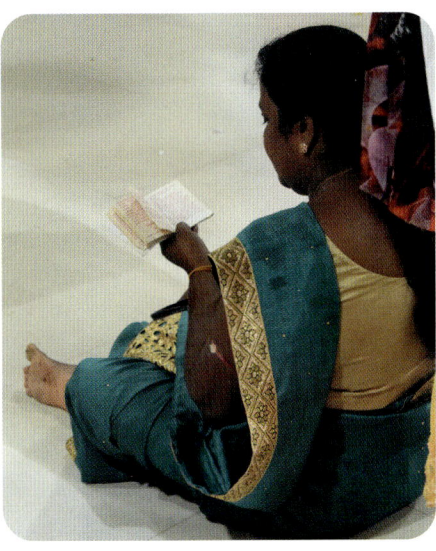

▲ A Hindu woman reading scriptures in the temple

Activities

1. a What is puja?
   b What happens during puja?
2. What is the arti ceremony and why is it important?
3. Draw pictures to show each type of worship in the temple and write an explanation to accompany each picture.
4. What do you think the three quotations from the holy books mean? Write your own versions using words that make sense to you.
5. 'Having many ways to worship makes it more difficult to get it right.' What do you think? Give reasons for agreeing and disagreeing with this statement.

The major world faiths

7.5 The home as a place of worship for Hindus

Learning objectives
- To learn that the home is an important place of worship for Hindus
- To understand how acts of worship might be done in the home
- To reflect on the relative values of the home and temple as places of worship

Big question
'Home is where the heart is.' Is that true?

It is a duty for Hindus to worship every day. This might be done at home or temple, or at another place sacred to Hindus, for example, in a natural setting. For the first Welsh Hindus, home was the only place of worship available – early communities were too small to build or acquire premises for worship, and worshipping in natural settings could draw negative attention. While it is true that Hindus now have a number of Welsh temples, not all Welsh Hindus are close to those temples or can attend daily. This is true for any Hindus who are not living in a Hindu country. However, they still have to worship daily, so a home temple is the perfect solution. A home temple can be small or large – some Hindu homes devote a whole room to it. Hindu homes are usually managed by the woman of the house, and the home temple is also her responsibility. For Hindus, every day starts with an act of worship – a puja.

▶ What happens at worship in the home?

A small murti (statue or picture) of the deity the family worships is central to the temple, and is surrounded by other images, and any offerings that have been made. An arti tray is also there to be used in puja.

The woman places a spot of coloured paste on the forehead of the murti between the eyes, then on her own forehead and on the foreheads of any members of the family who are present. She then prays, focusing on God in a quiet, peaceful way. The spot, called a tilak, represents successful worship and meditation.

Every puja starts with Ganesha puja – a prayer performed for good luck. Ganesha is the destroyer of obstacles and evils, and represents wisdom.

Offerings are made – ranging from grains of rice to flowers and lighted incense sticks. Even the smallest offering is welcomed by God, as it is the intention that matters. Being poor is not a barrier to worship.

The room is cleaned and the mother or grandmother of the house usually leads the worship. She first washes and puts on clean clothes to be respectfully ready to pray.

Many Hindus offer a tray of fruit – as they do at the temples – reminding them that everything comes from Brahman and they should be thankful for all that they have.

Reading scriptures sets the family up for the day reminding them to live the day in the best way possible – being respectful and kind to others as well as themselves.

The woman pours water over the murti to clean it and dresses it with garlands and clothes.

The arti lamp is lit and waved in front of the murti. The woman passes her hands over the flame, and then passes them over her eyes and head to receive the blessings of God.

7 Hinduism

'It is important for me to begin the day thinking of God and there is no better example to set for my family, especially my children. Thinking of God will hopefully set their minds on the right track so that they can face the challenges of the day with a good mindset. This will then keep their actions good – all working towards good karma and a better rebirth next time. I am proud to lead the puja and pass on our religion to my family. We chose Ganesha as our deity because he is the son of Shiva and we believe he will bring good fortune. Having the sacred space at home feels like God is always with us in all we do each day.'

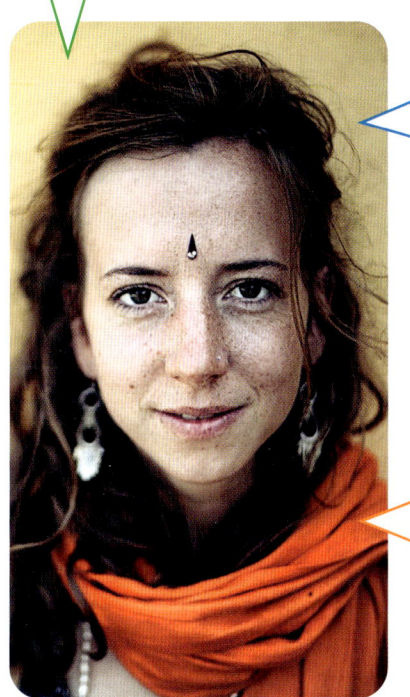

'Puja involves all the senses. We see the image of the deity to whom we give our worship. We chant the name of the deity as part of our prayers, so we say and hear those sacred words. Lighting incense creates sweet smells, reminding us of the sweetness of Hindu teachings, and how by understanding them our life is better. We offer food to the deity, which we will eat later as blessed food. Part of puja is meditation, and this refreshes the mind and soul. By worshipping in the morning, we are fully awakened for the day.'

'There is a temple in my community, but having a temple at home shows the importance of our religion to my family. As a Hindu, I know we can worship anywhere. You see, true worship is from the heart and in the heart, giving full devotion to Brahman – our heart is always with us wherever we are. The home temple makes worship easier in the morning when I have so many things to do to get my family ready for the day. It also means I can worship at any time when I am at home, for example if someone has become ill. I do go to the temple – that is a sacred space, the priests are there, my community is there. I am lucky to have the temple. My sister lives in Bangor, where there is no temple. She has to rely on her home shrine, as do many other Hindus in Wales.'

Activities

1. Draw a sacred space in the home, including the main features and label them with explanations.
2. Explain how the family worship at home.
3. Explain why Hindus worship at the start of the day, before work or school.
4. 'Temples are the best place for worship.' Do you agree with this statement? Explain your opinion.
5. 'Having a sacred space at home ensures a person worships every day.' What do you think? Give reasons to agree and disagree with the statement, and make sure you include a justified conclusion.

The major world faiths

7.6 Holy places for Hindus

Learning objectives

- To learn about two places that are holy to Hindus
- To understand why Hindus make pilgrimages
- To reflect on whether pilgrimage is a responsible practice in the modern world

Big question

If you could go anywhere, where would you go, and why?

The Hindu word for pilgrimage (a special journey to a sacred place) is yatra. Pilgrimage is important for Hindus for several reasons: the scriptures say it brings good karma, it strengthens their faith as during pilgrimage everything is focused on their religion, and they visit places of importance to the religion and its history. Also a Hindu might go on pilgrimage to complete a promise to a family member, so it shows respect to them. There are many different places that Hindus can visit on pilgrimage. We will consider two: Vrindavan and Varanasi.

▲ Sri Krishna Balaram Mandir in Vrindavan, one of the major ISKCON temples

▶ Vrindavan

Vrindavan is sacred to Vaishnavites (followers of Vishnu). They believe that Krishna (an avatar of Vishnu) spent much of his childhood here, having been adopted by cowherds after his uncle wanted to kill him. He looked after the cows and played in the forests with the other cowherders. The forests are believed to be sacred at Vrindavan.

There are over 5,000 temples in Vrindavan, dating back many centuries. New ones are planned, including the one in this picture currently being built by **ISKCON** Hindus.

Friends of Vrindavan (FoV)

Friends of Vrindavan (a conservation project) was set up in 1996 to reverse the damage done to Vrindavan by the vast number of pilgrims who visit. The FoV works to protect the environment by:

- planting trees and renewing parts of the sacred forest
- clearing lakes and waterways of the litter and plants which were blocking them
- sending out street cleaning teams to work in the worst-affected parts of the city
- managing recycling projects that employ orphans, widows and other vulnerable people.

Caring for this sacred place, its environment and its people are important aims of FoV and come from their Vaishnavite principles of love and devotion.

7 Hinduism

▶ Varanasi

The city of Varanasi is built at the side of the Ganges. It is the oldest continuously inhabited city in the world, having been inhabited since at least 2000 BCE. The city has thousands of temples, and is dedicated to Shiva. Many Shaivite Hindus go to Varanasi to visit temples, carry out worship and learn from the holy men and women. Historically, almost all renowned and important Hindu holy men and women have visited or lived at Varanasi, making the city very holy.

The Ganges River – Mother Ganga – is believed to be a living goddess, and bathing in her waters brings great blessings, even freedom from rebirth (moksha). Hindus believe it helps a person's rebirth if their ashes are scattered in the Ganges, so many people are cremated at ghats (steps leading to the water) beside the Ganges at Varanasi. Families of Hindus from around the world bring the ashes of their relatives to Varanasi to scatter them in the Ganges.

The Green Pilgrimage Network

Varanasi – along with Vrindavan – is part of the Green Pilgrimage Network (an organisation which includes all religions). Millions of believers every year want to show their devotion by making a pilgrimage, but this causes problems for the environment. These two factors have to be balanced. Hinduism sees the Earth as 'mother', and believes she should be respected and cared for. Also, everything we need is given to us by the Earth, so when we damage it, we eventually harm ourselves. The aim, therefore, is to make Vrindavan and Varanasi models for caring for the environment – by the use of environmentally friendly products and materials, recycling and tidying, protecting nature and cleaning polluted areas.

▲ Volunteers of the Ganga Action Parivar planting trees

Activities

1. Give three reasons why Hindus go on pilgrimage.
2. For Vrindavan, answer these questions:
   a. Which group of Hindus are most likely to visit?
   b. Why do they go?
   c. What might they do there?
3. For Varanasi, answer these questions:
   a. Which group of Hindus are most likely to visit?
   b. Why do they go?
   c. What might they do there?
4. a. How does pilgrimage affect the environment?
   b. Why is this such a problem for Hindus in terms of their faith?
   c. How is the Green Pilgrimage Network trying to help?
5. Create an 'Environmental pilgrim guidance' leaflet which tells people how to behave in an environmentally friendly way when they travel to one of these places.
6. 'Making a pilgrimage is the best way to show your devotion to God.' Do you agree with this statement? Give some reasons to agree, and some to disagree. Write a conclusion to justify your point of view.

7.7 Hindu celebration of Diwali

Learning objectives
- To explore the origins of a Hindu festival
- To understand how Hindus celebrate this festival today
- To consider why religions share their festivals with others

Big question
Do festivals need great stories?

Key beliefs
Most Hindus believe that Vishnu (one of the three gods of the Trimurti) has been incarnated (born in human form) on Earth at least ten times, each time when humans had greatest need. A Hindu holy scripture – the Bhagavad Gita – explains: 'For the protection of the good, and for the destruction of the wicked, for the establishment of Dharma, I am born from age to age'. The form that the god takes on Earth is called an avatar, and has special powers. Rama and Krishna are the most famous and widely worshipped of Vishnu's avatars.

▶ The story of Diwali

The Ramayana is one of the Hindu holy scriptures. It is the story of Rama and Sita.

Rama was the seventh avatar of Vishnu. He incarnated with his consort, Sita, to end the rule of a ten-headed demon king called Ravana, who was terrorising the world. Rama was born as a prince to a king who married three times. The mother of another of the king's sons wanted her son to be the next king. She conspired against Rama, and he was banished with Sita from the kingdom.

They lived in the forest with Rama's brother, Lakshmana. Rama always told Sita to be watchful when he went away hunting. One day, Sita was tricked then kidnapped by a many-headed demon king, Ravanna, and taken away to the island of Lanka. The monkey king, Hanuman and others helped Rama search for her, and eventually tracked her down. Rama's forces built a great bridge between the main land and Lanka, then crossed over.

Rama demanded Sita be freed, but Ravanna refused to give her up, and so there was a great battle between the forces of Rama and those of Ravanna. Hanuman had to find medicines to heal the many wounded on Rama's side. Eventually, Ravanna was defeated – Rama gave him the chance to surrender, but he refused. Rama was a great bowman, and killed Ravanna by shooting him with an arrow.

The couple were reunited, and returned home to reclaim the throne. On their journey, villagers lit their way with small lamps.

How Diwali is celebrated

Diwali is the festival of lights. It takes place on the last day of the Hindu lunar year. People are encouraged to resolve any issues that may have built up during the year, forgiving others and moving on from any troubles. Families put lines of small lamps or candles, called diya lamps, along windows and outside walls to remember how the villagers lit the way for Rama and Sita. These diya lamps are kept lit all through the festival; they represent the light of knowledge, which Hindus work hard to achieve so that they can attain moksha (liberation) and reunion with Brahman.

In the UK, Diwali is not a bank holiday, so Hindus have to get time off work if they want to celebrate for the whole period of the festival. Many workplaces do, however, give their employees a day off work. The festival lasts five days. This includes preparation time during which homes, temples and offices are thoroughly cleaned. Hindus visit the temple daily for worship. On the third day it is traditional to give offerings to Lakshmi (the goddess of wealth), and light up the houses. People wear their finest clothes, eat special foods and visit friends and relatives, often to share meals and stories. Rangoli patterns – intricate colourful patterns – are drawn on the floor outside houses. In families, the story of Rama and Sita is retold. Many films have been made of the story, which are screened at cinemas and on TV.

Temples are decorated for the festival. Every year, Cardiff's Shree Swaminarayan Temple has a huge firework display at the end of Diwali – a traditional way to celebrate for Hindus everywhere in the world. Cardiff hosts a Diwali Mela (fair) with stalls, crafts, food and performances of the story of Rama and Sita, as well as other entertainment, such as Bollywood and Bhangra music and dance. Hindu communities from all over South Wales attend, as well as many from further afield. Non-Hindus are also welcome; this is a way to build community understanding and community relations. The Hindu Cultural Association has held a ten-day Diwali celebration annually for more than 14 years, producing resources for the National Museum for Wales.

During the Covid-19 pandemic, celebrations for most festivals were different, and toned down to become more family-centred. Shree Swaminarayan Temple in Cardiff distributed craft boxes so that children could decorate their homes for the festival. The Welsh Government, partnered by the Indian Embassy, hosted a week of online Diwali events, which everyone could access – Hindu or not. Diwali represents the triumph of good over evil, and the ending of a period of great suffering for humans. As a festival of hope, it had the perfect message for a pandemic.

Activities

1 Explain what an avatar is in Hinduism.
2 Retell the story of Rama and Sita in fewer than 100 words.
3 Describe how Hindus celebrate Diwali.
4 'The most important part of Diwali is its message of hope.' Do you think everyone might agree with that? Explain your reasons. Give your own justified opinion.

The major world faiths

7.8 Hinduism in the Welsh community

Learning objectives
- To explore the role of Hindu believers in their wider community
- To learn about the social action carried out by Hindus in Wales
- To reflect on the impact of Hindu beliefs on the actions of Hindus

Big question
What counts as kindness?

Key beliefs
Hindus believe there are four pathways or yogas, to achieve moksha (liberation from rebirth, and reunion with the Divine). Anyone can follow any path, or follow several. By following these paths, they are committing to working on their spiritual development. These pathways are: karma yoga (action), bhakti yoga (devotion), jnana yoga (knowledge) and raja (meditation and self-discipline).

▶ Shaping action through key Hindu virtues and beliefs

'Selfless service' is an idea deep-rooted in Hinduism. Hinduism describes four paths to attaining moksha, one of which is karma yoga – the path of action. Karma yoga demands good actions which shape the attitude of Hindus to the suffering of others and the world around them.

> When I help others, people see that I, a Hindu person, am part of the big community. People come to appreciate the good of my religion.

> I believe that Brahman is part of every living being, including animals and plants. My religion is to worship Brahman to eventually achieve freedom from rebirth, and reunion with Brahman. So I have to respect life – it is Brahman. I show this through my actions – how I treat others, how I help others. It also means looking after the world for everyone now, but also those of the future.

> I believe my atman (spirit) is destined to be reunited with Brahman, but I must work to make that happen. All my actions either help me to reach that goal or prevent me from reaching it – so I have to be sure to do good, not harm.

> The Hindu holy books tell us many qualities we should try to develop in ourselves – virtues, or positive qualities. These include compassion, honesty, service to others, non-violence, tolerance and more. You can only develop qualities by practising them. Beliefs, virtues, anything – they help no one if they are just ideas in your head.

> As Brahman is in all, I believe in ahimsa (non-violence). This means not hurting others, but it isn't about being passive in life. Ahimsa is about doing something for the good – help not harm – making change happen, good change.

Selfless service – Skanda Vale

Skanda Vale is a multi-faith monastic community in Carmarthen, which has its roots in Hinduism. There are three Hindu temples there. The community was founded by Guru Sri Subramanium in 1973, and is run by the Community of the Many Names of God, who recognise the relevance of all religions in the search for spiritual truth. Over 90,000 pilgrims visit each year, and a community of monks and nuns live there permanently. Their spiritual path is one of devotion to the divine and service to all. These are two of the four paths to moksha – bhakti yoga (path of devotion to God) and karma yoga (action).

Skanda Vale receives more food donations than the community needs. All the food is offered to the deities and blessed. Each year, at least 80 tonnes of that food is given to different charity groups, including 20 tonnes to mainly Welsh charities, such as Fare Share, Cardiff Foodbank, the Refugee Food Kitchen, MIND and domestic abuse services. The community has far more than it needs, so it shares with those who are in the greatest need. This is an act of compassion and service, and shows respect for life.

Skanda Vale has an animal sanctuary in its grounds, where cows, donkeys, ponies, birds and two temple elephants are cared for. Caring for these animals teaches people the value of all life, a belief central to Hinduism.

In 1987, Guru Sri Subramanium had a serious heart attack which put him in hospital. While recovering there, he was saddened to realise the depth of loneliness and fear of patients who were dying. While giving good medical care, the hospital staff simply did not have extra time to spend with the patients. This led Guru Sri Subramanium to set up the Skanda Vale Hospice in Llandysul. It is staffed mainly by volunteers, who make a difference to society by providing safe and compassionate care for the dying. The hospice care is free, and funded entirely by donations. When people are near to death, they need love and care – and the hospice provides it.

The India Centre, Cardiff

This centre provides a place for worship for Hindus. It also tries to build understanding in the community of Hindu and Indian culture by holding courses and events to which non-Hindus are welcome. Events based around food, clothing, and Hindu festivals and stories build relationships within the wider community, and from understanding and relationships comes peace and harmony.

▲ The India Centre in Cardiff

'At the India Centre, we hold cultural events, and events in partnership with local communities. It is about a cultural exchange, and intergenerational exchange and raising awareness of our faith. It is important for the whole community and our religion.' Versha Sood

Activities

1. What are the Hindu virtues?
2. When a person works to develop the Hindu virtues, how do you think:
   a. the person can be changed?
   b. society can benefit?
3. Explain how Skanda Vale expresses its beliefs through examples of social care.
4. 'Everyone should contribute to improving society.' Do you agree? Explain the reasons for your answer.

8 Sikhism

8.1 Key beliefs in Sikhism

Learning objectives
- To learn Sikh beliefs about God
- To learn Sikh beliefs about rebirth and liberation
- To reflect on whether a person can always 'do the right thing'

Big question
What does it mean to 'do the right thing'?

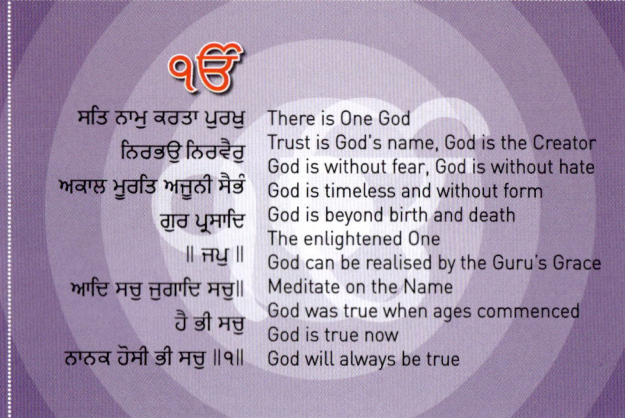

There is One God
Trust is God's name, God is the Creator
God is without fear, God is without hate
God is timeless and without form
God is beyond birth and death
The enlightened One
God can be realised by the Guru's Grace
Meditate on the Name
God was true when ages commenced
God is true now
God will always be true

Sikhs believe in one supreme God. Guru Nanak, the founder of Sikhism, wrote the Mool Mantar, a poem which describes God (see above). The poem says that God is timeless, without beginning or end; that God is the creator of all and cannot hate or discriminate, because God sees all equally. It says that God has no gender, is everywhere and in everything, and is available to anyone for a personal relationship – whatever their religion – because there is only one God. The first line of the poem is 'Ik Onkar'. It is a symbol which represents God and means 'there is one God'. Sikhs believe that there is one reality or essence, which is in everything and which keeps everything going, and that this is God.

▶ A Sikh's goal in life

Sikhs believe everyone has within them a 'divine spark' – God living within each and every human being. This is our soul. For Sikhs, the aim of life is for that divine spark to be reunited with God. Sikhs believe that anyone can be reunited with God; they just have to follow the right path, and be a good person. Reuniting with God is called mukti or 'liberation'. It is called this because at this time, a person's soul would be freed from being reborn into life as an animal or a human.

Sikhism says that to be human is to have been reborn in the highest form of life. Of all the creation, only humans have the ability to choose between right and wrong, and to understand morals. All of our actions, thoughts and words will have an impact on what our next life is like, making it better or worse. This idea of being born many times is called reincarnation. When a soul achieves mukti, it stops being reincarnated. It becomes one with God again – this is the ultimate goal for a practising Sikh.

▶ The symbol of Ik Onkar, meaning 'there is one God', is a common feature of Sikh gurdwaras; it reminds them of the whole Mool Mantar

▶ Achieving liberation (mukti)

Sikhs believe the way to achieve liberation is for a person always to be thinking of God, and making sure their behaviour and thoughts are fit for God. In this way, the soul becomes more and more pure. This is called being God-centred, or gurmukh. If a person always thinks of God, then they will always treat others well, try to help others, be content with their lives and try to make a difference. If they are always thinking of how to serve God, and remembering that everyone is their equal, and is a part of God, it comes naturally to them to 'do the right thing' for much of their daily life.

Sikhs work at being gurmukh in many ways, for example:

- reading passages from the Guru Granth Sahib to know about God
- studying their religious beliefs with others in the sangat (Sikh community)
- doing acts of selfless service (sewa) through donations of money and time, and concentrating on their own spiritual development
- living according to Sikh principles.

The opposite of this is to be self-centred, or manmukh. This means always taking care of our own needs first, and becoming increasingly materialistic. This is a selfish way to live. Sikhs believe that living in this way makes it more difficult to be reunited with God, because such a person only sees their own needs and desires, which can be hurtful to others.

Activities

1. What does 'Ik Onkar' mean?
2. Describe Sikh beliefs about God.
3. Write out this table so that the two halves match up correctly.

Mool Mantar	Being self-centered, thinking only of your own needs and desires
Soul	A poem that describes God
Gurmukh	The divine spark within each of us
Manmukh	The cycle of birth, death and rebirth
Reincarnation	Liberation from being reborn, to be reunited with God
Mukti	Being God-centred, thinking always of God and God's creation

4. Give some reasons why a person might try to be gurmukh.
5. Give some reasons why it is easy for a person to be manmukh.
6. Design a poster of words and images that show the key Sikh beliefs.
7. Do you think that believing in reincarnation makes a person behave better or worse? Explain your answer.

The major world faiths

8.2 Founders of the faith – the ten gurus

Learning objectives
- To know the importance of the ten gurus in Sikhism
- To know the key events of the life of Guru Nanak
- To consider the importance and impact of role models

Big question
Who counts as a role model for you?

Sikhs follow the teachings of the ten gurus. The gurus started the religion, then led the community as it grew. Sikhs believe these gurus (teachers) were very special people, who had already achieved mukti (liberation). They believe that God sent them back to human life to help and guide others.

The ten gurus led the Sikh community at these times:

- Guru Nanak, 1469–1539
- Guru Angad Dev, 1539–52
- Guru Amar Das, 1552–74
- Guru Ram Das, 1574–81
- Guru Arjan Dev, 1581–1606
- Guru Hargobind, 1606–44
- Guru Har Rai, 1644–61
- Guru Har Krishan, 1661–4
- Guru Tegh Bahadur, 1665–75
- Guru Gobind Singh (Rai), 1675–1708

Activities
1. Who were the ten gurus?
2. Why were the gurus important?
3. Write about the founder of Sikhism.
4. Choose one of the gurus to research and create an information sheet on that guru.
5. Write a short article about the Guru Granth Sahib to help someone else in your class to learn about it.
6. Guru Gobind Singh established the Guru Granth Sahib as the final guru. Why do you think this was important for the religion?

▲ The ten gurus of Sikhism

▶ The founder of Sikhism

Guru Nanak founded the faith after he had had a religious experience. He was born into a Hindu family. His teachers said he was an extraordinary student, full of knowledge. He married and worked as an accountant. His closest friend was a Muslim.

Every morning, he would bathe in the river. One day in 1499, he simply disappeared while bathing. No one could find him. He reappeared in the same place, three days later, in a state of bliss. His first words were, 'There is no Hindu, there is no Muslim.' He proclaimed that there is only one God and that he had been in the presence of God for the days he was missing. He said that God had given him knowledge about God, reality and human life, and that he had achieved mukti. He gave up his job and wealth, and devoted his life to teaching God's words.

From that point on, Guru Nanak spread the message of Sikhism. He travelled extensively around Asia, meeting people of all faiths. Many became his followers, so he set up small communities as he travelled for them to come together for worship and meditation. Eventually, he set up the first Sikh community at Kartarpur. This became a Sikh town, and people came from far way to hear him teach and to follow his teachings and values. Guru Nanak saw that these people came without places to stay or food, and so he ordered that all the people who came should be fed. He also ordered that everyone should eat the same (vegetarian) food and should eat together, without any hierarchy. This demonstrated that everyone – regardless of gender, wealth, status, age, background or ability – was equal in the eyes of God. Equality is a core belief and practice in Sikhism – central to all the teachings of the faith.

▲ The Guru Granth Sahib – the living Guru

The practice of shared eating became the langar, a practice that is now an essential part of Sikhism. Guru Nanak wrote many hymns in praise of God, which form a large part of the Guru Granth Sahib, the Sikh holy book.

▶ The other gurus

Each guru made contributions to the religion and its practice. Guru Angad Dev developed the language in which the Guru Granth Sahib would later be written. Guru Amar Das sent out missionaries to spread the Sikh faith. Guru Ram Das established the holy city of Amritsar. Guru Arjan Dev (the first Sikh martyr) produced the Adi Granth, the first Sikh holy book. Guru Hargobind developed the Sikh concept of holy war and formed the Sikh army. Guru Har Rai continued the development of Sikh warriors and distributed free medicines. Guru Har Krishan, a child Guru, emphasised helping the needy, regardless of gender, status, religion or race. Guru Tegh Bahadur fought for the rights of Hindu and Sikhs to worship in Muslim-governed states. Guru Gobind Singh created the Khalsa and compiled the Guru Granth Sahib.

The gurus established the religion, and how to live by it. They taught and lived its values: the oneness of God and the equality of all. They were the inspirational role models that Sikhs still look to today.

▶ The living guru

Guru Gobind Singh decided that after him there would be no more human gurus. The teachings of the gurus were to be codified into one book – the Guru Granth Sahib – which would be the living guru because its teachings would never die, and it would always lead the religion. Guru Granth Sahib means 'master book by the teacher', which shows that the words were spoken by gurus. 'Guru' means 'teacher' so demands respect.

The Guru Granth Sahib is made up of hymns by some of the gurus, and other holy people from Hinduism and Islam. It is written in the gurmukhi script which Guru Angad Dev created, and split into 5,894 shabads (hymns). Every copy is identical so that no single copy can be considered better than any of the others. It has 1,430 pages. The first shabad is the Mool Mantar. The Guru Granth Sahib is believed to be God's words channelled through the gurus.

When the human gurus lived, Sikhs went to them for worship and to hear their teachings. Today every gurdwara has a Guru Granth Sahib, so every Sikh can attend to hear God's message.

The major world faiths

8.3 The Sikh place of worship – the gurdwara

◀ Gurdwara Nanak Darbar, Cardiff

Learning objectives
- To know about the features of a Sikh gurdwara
- To explore how gurdwaras reflect key Sikh beliefs
- To reflect on whether it is better to have a special place for worship

Big question
Why do believers want a special place for worship?

The Sikh place of worship is the gurdwara, which means 'door to the guru'. The first Welsh Sikhs worshipped in their own homes until the community was large enough to justify a specific building. Wales now has four gurdwaras – one in Swansea and three in Cardiff. Three of these are buildings that were converted to be gurdwaras. The gurdwara in the picture above is one of these.

The gurdwara is very important to the Sikh community. It is the place where they worship, but also where the community of Sikhs (sangat) can come together to support each other's faith. Many celebrations are also held there, such as weddings.

The building is recognised by its saffron-coloured flag, a yellow-orange flag that winds all the way up the flag pole to fly freely at the top. On it is the symbol for Sikhism – the Khanda – which shows that the building has been dedicated to worship.

▶ Other parts of the gurdwara

Sikhs take off their shoes and cover their head before entering the prayer hall, so there is always somewhere for storing shoes.

Sikhs believe the Guru Granth Sahib should be treated as a living guru. There is therefore a small room with a special space in which the Guru Granth Sahib rests when it is not a time for worship.

Guru Nanak said all worshippers should be given food when they attend the gurdwara, so gurdwaras have kitchens, called langar. Enough food is cooked so that everyone can have a full meal, and the community can eat together. The food is vegetarian so that anyone attending, Sikh or non-Sikh, can eat together. The langar is about service to others, and equality.

8 Sikhism

The Guru Granth Sahib is the holy book (Granth) of Sikhism. It is made up of hymns and poems written by the gurus, and Sikhs believe it is the word of God. It is read in every act of worship. In the gurdwara, it has its own room when it is not being used.

Sikhism teaches that the Gurus should all be respected, as they have all contributed to and are role models of Sikhism. Hence it is normal to see pictures of all the Gurus, especially showing what they did. These are found throughout the gurdwara, not just in the diwan hall.

When worshipping, everyone faces the Guru Granth Sahib. It lies on a throne, called a palki. Over it is a canopy, called a takht. Both of these are highly decorated to show the importance of the Guru Granth Sahib. The palki and takht are at the centre-front of the prayer hall. Sikhs sit on the floor when they worship so they have to look up to the Guru Granth Sahib – again showing respect, but also showing the equality of the worshippers.

The Mool Mantar is a poem written by Guru Nanak about God. It begins 'Ik Onkar' (there is one God). It describes God's qualities. Every gurdwara has this written on the wall at the front to remind people who they are worshipping.

The Guru Granth Sahib is read by a granthi. This is a member of the Sangat who is respected by all, and who is able to read fluently and correctly. It is an honour to have this role. In the picture this is a man, but women are also allowed to do this role.

When Sikhs go to worship, they bring gifts, or offerings, for the Guru Granth Sahib. This is usually flowers, money or food. Worshippers take their offerings to the front and lay them near the palki before they begin worship. The food goes to the langar, and the money to the upkeep of the gurdwara.

Activities

1. How could you recognise a gurdwara from the outside?
2. Draw a plan of the inside of a gurdwara. On it, label and explain what each of these are: palki, takht, Guru Granth Sahib, Mool Mantar.
3. What evidence can you give to show that Sikhs respect the Guru Granth Sahib?
4. What evidence can you give to show that equality is important in Sikhism?
5. 'It is better to have a special place for worship.' What do you think of this idea? Explain your opinion.

The major world faiths

8.4 Worship at the gurdwara and the Guru Granth Sahib

Learning objectives
- To learn how Sikhs worship
- To recognise the central importance of the Guru Granth Sahib in Sikh worship
- To reflect on the importance of showing devotion

Big question
What difference does music make?

Talk it out
Look at the picture of the girl. What do you think is happening?

She is in the gurdwara. What might she be doing?

Sikh worship is based around prayer, using the hymns of the Guru Granth Sahib, and others. Few Sikhs have a copy of the Guru Granth Sahib, but many have a gutka. This is a small book with a selection of hymns in it. Reading the gutka is a form of prayer because it focuses a person's mind on God. A Sikh can read this anywhere, but in the gurdwara there are many symbols of the religion which help them to understand Sikh beliefs. The girl in the picture above is reading her gutka.

Before worship starts, the Guru Granth Sahib is carried from its resting room to the palki. Someone will hold it up high above head-height as it is carried past the worshippers. A person walks ahead of it, sprinkling water onto the floor. The Guru Granth Sahib is considered a 'living guru'. Just as respect is given to important people, so respect is given to this holy book. An important person in Indian culture would have the floor cleaned before them, and their head shaded – so the same signs of respect are shown to the 'living guru'.

▲ The Guru Granth Sahib being carried high above the heads of worshippers to its place for worship

▲ A Sikh granthi reading the Guru Granth Sahib

Once on the palki, the Guru Granth Sahib is opened at random and that shabad (hymn) is read out. This becomes the main reading for the day, and will be re-read many times.

The service (diwan) can last many hours, and people come and go during that time. When people arrive, they go to the palki to give offerings to the Guru Granth Sahib. When giving their offerings, usually flowers, food or money, they bow their heads to the floor.

Throughout the service, the Guru Granth Sahib is read by a person called a granthi. This is a special honour, and can only be done by someone with the skill and capability to pronounce the words correctly. This person must also be respected in the community and deemed as a good person. To help people understand what is said, a group of musicians called ragis will be singing shabads (hymns from the Guru Granth Sahib). Music is important because it helps people to feel closer to God, to understand the words of God and to enjoy the service. It is important that people understand the words, so that they know how to live a good life for God.

Each person who attends worship receives some karah parshad to eat. This is a mixture of flour, semolina, butter and sugar which has been blessed. It is considered a special food from God. The fact that everyone is given some demonstrates equality.

After worship, a person might go to the langar to eat some food with others. The making and serving of food is a form of sewa (service to others), which is an act of worship in itself.

▲ Karah parshad being prepared for sharing in the service at a gurdwara in Cardiff

▶ Focusing on the name of God

Sikhs have a duty to keep God in mind. For many this is done by repeating the name of God (Nam Japna), or by meditating on God (Nam Simran). Meditation can help people to understand religious truths, as well as being good for their health. Keeping God in mind should make a person keep to a morally good code, and so be a 'better' person to others, doing God's will and work.

Activities

1 Use the text to give the Sikh term for each of the following:
   a Sikh place of worship
   b Sikh act of worship (service)
   c Person who reads the Guru Granth Sahib aloud
   d Sikh musicians in the gurdwara
   e Sikh prayer book
   f Repeating the name of God
   g Meditating on God

2 Imagine you had been taken to a gurdwara by a Sikh friend. Write a letter about what you saw on the visit. Make sure you include all aspects, from bringing the holy book from its resting place through to eating in the langar. You might like to use some of the information from Topics 8.2 and 8.3 as well (pages 124–7).

3 'Music is the most important part of an act of worship for many Sikhs.' Give two reasons for agreeing and two reasons for disagreeing with this statement.

The major world faiths

8.5 Becoming a Khalsa Sikh – the Amrit Sanskar

Learning objectives
- To know what happens in the Amrit Sanskar ceremony
- To understand the historic importance of the Amrit Sanskar
- To reflect on why people make formal and greater commitments to an ideal

Big question
Why do we have ceremonies of commitment?

This important Sikh ceremony goes back to Guru Nanak, who initiated new entrants to the faith. Guru Gobind Singh (Tenth Guru) combined that ceremony with the creation of the Khalsa. It is called Khande-di-pahul.

Talk it out
What do we mean when we talk about commitment? Can you give any examples? How does someone show their commitment? Do you think taking part in a ceremony of commitment makes a person more committed?

▶ The origins of the Amrit Sanskar

Guru Gobind Singh was originally called Guru Gobind Rai. He led the Sikhs at a time when they were persecuted by Hindu and Muslim rulers. He often spoke about Sikhs being prepared to fight for justice and against persecution and harassment. In 1699, at the Vaisakhi festival, he spoke to crowds of Sikhs about faith, courage and bravery. He asked if any of them would be prepared to die for what they believed in. Eventually, one came forward, was taken into a tent, and the crowd heard the sound of a beheading. Guru Gobind Rai asked the same questions four more times. Each time, a person stepped forward; each time, the crowd believed them to be stepping forward to their death. At the end, Guru Gobind Rai brought all five out from the tent, still alive, dressed in saffron (yellow-orange) robes, with turbans and swords. He praised their faith and courage, saying they represented a new kind of Sikh – the Panj Pyare (Five Beloved Ones). The Panj Pyare would dress and act differently to show their new status, showing a new level of commitment. These five and others who joined them became known as the Khalsa. Guru Gobind Rai took amrit from the Panj Pyare, and was renamed as Guru Gobind Singh, his name as the tenth guru. The original event is celebrated every year at the Sikh festival of Vaisakhi by Sikhs across the world.

The ceremony today

The Amrit Sanskar ceremony usually happens in a gurdwara, which will be closed to public worship for the ceremony. Anybody can worship, but not everyone is prepared to be a member of the Khalsa. Only Sikhs who are already members of the Khalsa can attend the ceremony. Everyone attending wears the 5Ks, and five beloved ones fully dressed in saffron robes like the original five were, administer the ceremony. A sixth member reads from the Sikh holy book, the Guru Granth Sahib and prayers are also said. One of the five 'beloved ones' reads out the duties that the new member must follow. The new member kneels on their right knee, as this shows that they are ready to fight for their faith. Each person drinks five handfuls of amrit (water with sugar stirred into it using a kirpan which is blessed). Five handfuls of amrit are also sprinkled on their eyes, and on their hair. Then there are more prayers. Finally, everyone eats the blessed food, karah prashad.

Being a Khalsa Sikh

Khalsa Sikhs wear the 5Ks. These are:

1. Kesh – uncut hair. Sikhs do not cut their hair – they wear a turban to protect it and show respect for God. Men also have a beard. They do not change what God has made.
2. Kara – a circular, steel bangle/bracelet. Steel represents strength, and a circle represents God, who has no beginning or end, and is eternal.
3. Kangha – a comb in their hair. This represents cleanliness and purity of body and mind.
4. Kirpan – a knife. This shows determination to fight for justice.
5. Kachera – breeches (shorts). These are a reminder that historically Sikhs had to be ready to fight in battle (shorts gave freedom to move quickly, unlike the normal Indian clothing of the time). In modern times, they also symbolise modesty.

Khalsa Sikhs commit to pray every day, to pay daswandh (a tenth of their earnings) to the gurdwara, and to follow the Sikh code of conduct and the gurus' teachings. They commit not to eat halal (ritually slaughtered) food, not to behave in a sexually immoral way, and not to use tobacco, alcohol or drugs.

Khalsa Sikhs are role models for their community. They make a commitment to focus on their own spiritual development, but also to help others with their spiritual development. They show this through supporting others in the community, and by being active in the work of the gurdwara at festivals and throughout the year.

Activities

1. Explain briefly what the Amrit Sanskar is.
2. Draw a storyboard of the origins of the Amrit Sanskar.
3. Imagine you had seen the Amrit Sanskar ceremony today. Describe what happened.
4. Many Sikhs do not become Khalsa Sikhs. Give some reasons why you think this might be.
5. Explain how Khalsa Sikhs show their commitment after the ceremony, in their daily lives.
6. Do you think it is important to have a ceremony of commitment when you join something? Give reasons for and against, before giving your own opinion.

The major world faiths

8.6 Amritsar – the spiritual centre of Sikhism

Learning objectives
- To learn why Amritsar is an important place for Sikhs
- To explore what Sikhs do when they go to Amritsar
- To reflect on the importance of physical places to religious and non-religious people

Big question
What makes a place special?

Talk it out
Have you ever been somewhere and decided it was very special? Is there a place you have an ambition to go to? What makes it special?

For Sikhs, **pilgrimage** is not a duty; it is done by choice. Although there are special places for Sikhs, it is their choice whether to go or not. Guru Nanak said that 'God's name is the real place of pilgrimage'. He told Sikhs to make their pilgrimage by thinking about the word of God, and getting a greater understanding of what God is. For him, pilgrimage was something in our minds, a journey to the 'divine spark' within.

However, from the very start of Sikhism, people came to Guru Nanak from near and far to hear his teachings. Therefore, it could be said that travelling to the guru was always part of the religion. Nowadays, every gurdwara has a copy of the Guru Granth Sahib – the living guru – so you could say that Sikhs still travel to the guru regularly, they just don't have to travel so far. Many Sikhs, however, do still make a pilgrimage to one place that is very special to all Sikhs. That place is Amritsar, in the Indian part of the Punjab region.

Key term
Pilgrimage – a journey to a place that is important to the religion. Many religions have places of pilgrimage. The journeys to them are often not easy, which means that greater devotion is needed in order to make the journey.

▲ The Golden Temple (Sri Darbar Sahib) of Amritsar facing the Akal Takht

▲ Sikhs bathing in water at the Golden Temple

8 Sikhism

▶ How Amritsar came to be

'Amritsar' means 'pool of nectar'. Guru Ram Das (the fourth guru) first began to build it after he had been given the land by the Emperor Akbar. On the land, there was a small pool, which was made bigger. Guru Ram Das' son, Guru Arjan Dev (the fifth guru), continued this work and also built the Golden Temple (known as Sri Darbad Sahib and completed in 1604) in the middle of it. He put the Adi Granth (the first holy book of Sikhism, which had only just been completed) inside it, and prostrated himself. A walkway was built so that worshippers could get to the Golden Temple. Over time, many other buildings were constructed around the edge of the pool, including rest houses and a langar hall. The most important of these buildings is the Akal Takht, the foundations of which were laid in 1606 by Guru Hargobind (the sixth guru). Important decisions that affect the worldwide Sikh community are made here.

▶ About the Golden Temple

From the outside, the Golden Temple glitters in the sun. Its upper half is covered in sheets of gilded copper, and much of the artwork is also gold. It has four doors – one per side – to show that everyone is welcome, regardless of where they are from. On entering, a person has to step down into the Temple, and then look up to the Guru Granth Sahib. This shows humility and respect. The inside of the temple is black and white marble, and many of the fittings, such as the lights, are gold.

Early each morning, the Guru Granth Sahib is brought from the Akal Takht, carried on the head of the lead granthi. The cushions (below the Guru Granth Sahib) and romallas (squares of silk that cover the Guru Granth Sahib) in the Golden Temple will have been changed, and scented water sprinkled around the holy book. Once it is placed on the palki, the Guru Granth Sahib is opened at random and the passage is read. The Ardas Prayer is recited, and the ragis begin their hymns.

At the end of the day, at 9.45 pm, the Guru Granth Sahib is returned to the Akal Takht.

▶ What might Sikhs do at Amritsar?

- Many Sikhs bathe in the waters around the Golden Temple, believing this brings a blessing from God. This water is believed to have healing qualities.
- They enter the Golden Temple, prostrate themselves before the Guru Granth Sahib, make offerings, listen to the readings and share karah parshad.
- They eat at the langar, sharing food with the thousands who eat there every day.
- At the main entrance, they can visit a museum dedicated to Sikh history, which houses items owned by the gurus. They can walk around the complex to visit the shrines and memorials of important Sikhs.
- Some Sikhs volunteer their time, for example in the langar, or medical centre – acts of sewa (selfless service to others).

Activities

1. What is Amritsar? Why is it important to Sikhs?
2. How did the Golden Temple come to be built?
3. What kind of things do Sikhs do when they go to Amritsar? Which do you think is the most important and why?
4. Imagine you have visited the Golden Temple. Write a postcard home about what you saw. Design a Sikh stamp for the postcard.
5. 'All Sikhs should visit Amritsar at some point in their lifetime.' Do you agree? Give reasons and explain them to show different points of view.

The major world faiths

8.7 Living as a Sikh

Learning objectives
- To know the three Sikh principles for living
- To explore how these principles affect daily life
- To reflect on how a religion provides a code for living

Big question
Should religion be all day, every day?

Sikh daily life is shaped around three principles which were taught by the gurus. These are Nam Japna (meditation on the name of God), Kirat Karni (living an honest lifestyle), and Vand Chakna (sharing). This means that Sikhs should live every day in the way the gurus taught, the way God wants – and this covers everything in their daily life. Let's explore each further.

▶ Nam Japna

A Sikh's religious duty includes doing the following every day:

- Getting up before dawn and bathing, then meditating on the name of God until sunrise
- Praying three times a day – in the morning, in the evening and before bed – reciting specific prayers (nit nem) each time
- Reading scriptures – either the Guru Granth Sahib or a gutka (prayer book); at least five verses is a recommended amount
- Attending worship at the gurdwara if possible.

By doing these things, Sikhs remain constantly aware of God throughout the day. They are less likely to do anything morally wrong or against their religion if they have God in mind all the time.

▶ Kirat Karni

Living an honest lifestyle influences the sort of job a Sikh has. Many Sikhs work in the caring professions, where they can help others. The only rules around work, however, are that a Sikh should not be in a job that involves going against their religion or exploiting others. They should earn money through honest and lawful means; they should not steal it or win money by gambling, both of which are against the moral code for Sikhs.

Kirat Karni is also about the way in which people conduct themselves – how they behave towards others. Sikhs are encouraged to be disciplined, and not selfish. There are five vices which Sikhs try to avoid: lust, anger, greed, jealousy and self-centredness. All of these characteristics make a person less kind to others, and less God-centred. At the same time, there are five characteristics that Sikhs should try to develop in themselves: truthfulness, compassion, contentment, humility and love. All of these make a person nicer to others and less selfish, and so more God-centred. It is easy to see which kind of a person most people (Sikh or not) prefer – the one with the positive characteristics.

The Rahit Maryada is the Sikh code of conduct and is a guide to how Sikhs – wherever they are in the world – should live. As well as describing the right way to worship, and the wording for important ceremonies, it also tells Sikhs what they may not do. Sikhs should not drink alcohol or take any drugs (other than medicines).

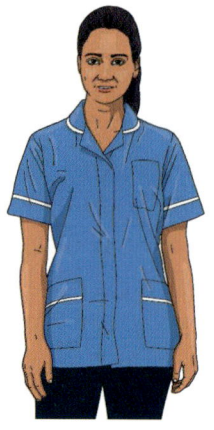

▶ The three principles of Nam Japna, Kirat Karni and Vand Chakna

Nor should they smoke. They should not eat halal (Islamic ritually slaughtered) meat, though in fact most are vegetarian anyway out of respect for God's created world and life. They should – especially if they are Khalsa Sikhs – wear the 5Ks as a symbol of their disciplined life and devotion to God. They are encouraged only to spend time with good people, and to avoid those who are a bad influence.

▶ Vand Chakna

Having earned money, it is important to share with others. All Sikhs give daswandh – 10 per cent of their earnings – to the gurdwara. This is a financial contribution to their religion and religious community.

Sikhs also do **sewa** (selfless service to others) in some way every day. Sewa is about sharing your time, finances, energy and intelligence in ways that benefit others.

> **Key term**
>
> Sewa – selfless service to others; a duty for Sikhs

> In the gurdwara, the langar (community kitchen) is a really good way to show all three principles taught by the gurus. If I work in the langar, I serve others and share my time and energy with them (Vand Chakna).
> The work is honest and is helpful to others (Kirat Karni).
> It is done for God, so God is in mind (Nam Japna).

Activities

1. List the three principles of living for Sikhs.
2. Why do you think some religious people try to follow their religion in all aspects of their lives?
3. Referring to the three principles:
   a. How do Sikhs worship God on a daily basis?
   b. How does Sikhism influence the jobs people have?
   c. How does Sikhism affect the way a person behaves or treats others?
4. Worship is very important to Sikhs. They believe if you always think about God, you will behave better. Do you agree? Explain your answer, showing you have thought about more than one point of view.
5. Thinking about Kirat Karni, which of the virtues would you find most difficult to keep? Why? Which virtue would you find easiest to work on? Why?
6. Is it possible to follow the Sikh way all day, every day? Explain your answer, using examples to support your argument. Write a counter argument.

8.8 Sikhism in the Welsh community

Learning objectives

- To learn how equality motivates Sikhs in their local community
- To learn about sewa (selfless service to others)
- To reflect on how Sikhs are helping to support their local communities by putting beliefs into action

Big question

Is it better to help when asked, or just to help whenever there is chance to do so?

'Sikhism is a religion of service. It is a religion for the community, for humanity and for the universe.' (*Gurmit Singh Randhawa*)

▶ The beliefs that motivate Sikhs

Sikhism teaches that God created everyone. This means that all are equal – regardless of religion, race, gender or ability. Sikhs also believe that God created a place for everyone and that the world is for everyone. They believe that humans should learn to live as brothers and sisters, with regard and care for each and every other person – whether they know them or not.

The Mool Mantar (see page 122) teaches that God is the creator of all – humans, all life, the world and universe. It all exists only because God wills it to exist and God is within all. Believing this, a person cannot want to hurt anything.

Sikhism teaches that the more a person reads the Guru Granth Sahib, the more they are helped to live a good life, because the hymns are 'nourishment for the soul'. The Guru Granth Sahib teaches a person how to live by three principles (pages 134–5):

- Nam Japna – always thinking about God
- Kirat Karni – living a truthful life, by developing good habits and working hard to avoid those attitudes and behaviours which hurt yourself and others
- Vand Chakna – sharing with others.

▶ Sewa – selfless service to others

Guru Nanak said that sewa is good for mental health, good for spiritual health and good for society. As it is about helping others or showing devotion to God, he also said it was a kind of love. By doing sewa, a Sikh becomes more God-centred (**gurmukh**) and less self-centred (**manmukh**), which helps their soul become purer and closer to achieving mukti (liberation from rebirth).

There are three kinds of sewa. Almost anything done to help others without seeking a reward can count as sewa.

Key terms

Gurmukh – being God-centred, focused on God at all times

Manmukh – being self-centred, selfish; thinking only of oneself

	Tan	Dhan	Mann
Meaning	Body – helping out in a physical way	Money – helping others financially	Mind – attitude; helping in a sincere way
Example	Doing an errand for someone or serving food in the langar	Paying daswandh (10 per cent of earnings) to the gurdwara or giving to charity	Being a musician in the gurdwara or teaching children about Sikhism

▶ All part of the religion

Helping others and working to improve the world is part of what it means to be a Sikh. Every gurdwara has a langar (community kitchen). Very large gurdwaras provide free vegetarian meals every day to anyone. The langar at Amritsar feeds 100,000 people every day, and double that on festival days. The gurdwaras in Wales serve free food one day a week to anyone who attends. For Sikhs attending the service, the community meal is part of worship.

Helping outside the gurdwara

Welsh Sikhs also take the langar to those in need. At St Mary's Street in Cardiff, a langar distributes 250 meals every Saturday in a two-hour period to those in need. Since 2014, at Newport Street, Cardiff, at 3 pm every Saturday, a group of Sikhs, including university students, have been giving out cartons of cooked food to the homeless.

▲ Sikh volunteers distributing meals in Newport Street, Cardiff

Many gurdwaras receive more offerings of food than they can use, and the excess is redistributed via charities and foodbanks. The gurdwaras in Wales have accommodation on site, or available for travellers. These are mainly taken by Sikh visitors, who know about the duty to help others – but would be open to all.

Reading or watching the news, we are constantly made aware that someone somewhere needs help. In recent years, the UK, for example, has suffered as a result of flooding and the Covid-19 pandemic.

During the Covid pandemic, Welsh Sikhs donated over 100,000 dinners to hospitals, those on lower incomes and the housebound. Sikhs in Cardiff made significant donations of money and food to provide a langar for those in need. The money raised also paid for food parcels filled with basic items, which were distributed to residents of Cardiff and beyond who were in need. In all these situations, the people receiving the help also got a chance to chat with someone, and enjoy some companionship. Loneliness was a huge problem during the pandemic, and giving someone some of your time costs nothing – Sikhs offered theirs as part of sewa.

Khalsa Aid

Khalsa Aid is a Sikh aid organisation, set up to carry out sewa through organised means wherever it is needed in the world. For example, Khalsa Aid Sikhs went to help out in Indonesia when the country was hit by a tsunami. It also works to help in disasters in the UK, for example, it called on Sikhs volunteers when there was serious flooding in the UK, including in Wales. Sikhs from all over the country travelled to flooded areas. They filled sandbags, helped evacuate people, staffed supply bases, distributed food – whatever could be done to help where homes and communities were flooded.

To be a Sikh, is to love God, live morally well, love all and serve all – without discrimination and without exceptions. Helping is part of the Sikh religion, rather than something that is done only when there is an emergency. The help Sikhs give during a disaster or emergency is an extension of what they are doing all the time, as part of their religion.

Activities

1. Explain Sikh beliefs about the equality of all people.
2. What are the three principles? How do these influence Sikhs to help others?
3. Explain what sewa is.
4. How is Sikhism contributing to its local communities in Wales?
5. Is the duty of sewa the biggest motivation for Sikhs to help others? Explain the reasons for your answer.

9 Buddhism

9.1 The life of the Buddha – before enlightenment

Learning objectives
- To know about the early life of the Buddha
- To understand how his early life would influence his later life
- To reflect on the idea of 'life-changing' events

Big question
Do you know any stories of events that changed people's lives?

▶ A special one

'Buddha' means 'awakened one' – it is a title not a name. Siddhartha Gautama is the human name for the Buddha. He was born in about 563 BCE in Lumbini, which is modern-day Nepal, to King Suddhodana and Queen Maya.

Even before his birth, there were signs that Siddhartha was to be a special human. His mother dreamt that a white elephant with six tusks had entered her right side. This was interpreted to mean that her child would be special.

Queen Maya was on her way to her parents' home for the birth of her child – as was the custom at that time. While passing the gardens of Lumbini, she felt the urge to walk among the trees. While she was there, she realised she was about to give birth. The trees bent down for her to hold. Without any pain, she gave birth to Siddhartha, who walked and talked immediately. Lotus flowers blossomed with each of his first seven steps, and he said 'I am the chief of the world, Eldest in the world. This is my last birth.'

After Siddhartha had been born, his father invited people from near and far to pay their respects to this new prince. A greatly respected holy man, Asita, visited, to give him a blessing. As Asita held the baby, he proclaimed that Siddhartha would either become a great king, or a great religious leader. He also said that if Siddhartha saw four sights – old age, illness, death and a holy man – being deeply affected, he would choose the religious path. The King immediately resolved to shield Siddhartha from all of these, as he wanted his son to be a king.

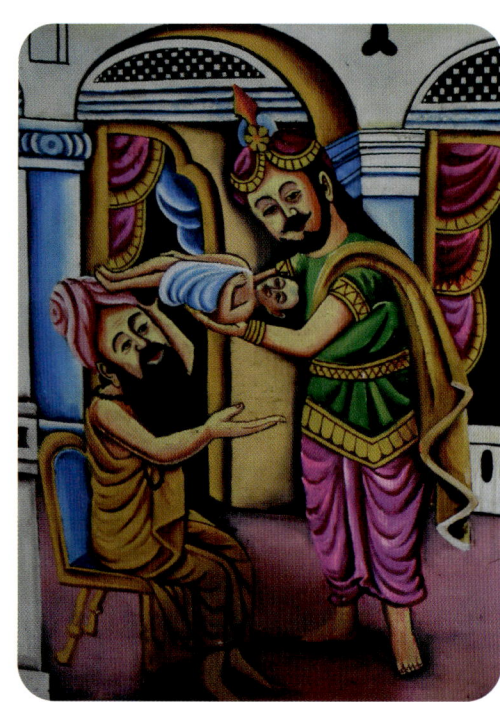

The King had several palaces, and he moved his family around them with the seasons. Siddhartha had a life of immense luxury, never wanting for anything. He was highly educated by teachers who came to the palace. He had many friends and was a skilled sportsman. He married Yusodhara, and they had a son. All this took place within the palaces and their grounds so that there was no chance of him seeing the four sights.

The Four Sights

Siddhartha was happy with this life, but not content – he felt there was something more. He asked his father to allow him to leave the palace and see the world outside it. Eventually, his father agreed but he was to be accompanied by his servant, Channa. On the King's orders, along a specific route the streets were cleared of any evidence of the four sights.

The precautions failed. Siddhartha saw each sight in turn: an old person, an ill person, a dead person at their funeral, and a holy man. He had never seen any of these before, and was shocked and puzzled. He asked his servant if the first three would happen to him. Channa answered that he would certainly become old and die, as this is what happens to everyone, whoever they are and however much money they may have. He also explained that ill-health can strike anyone and it makes them feel terrible. Siddhartha noticed that although the holy man must have known these things about people as he lived in the real world, not sheltered in a palace, still he seemed quite content and undisturbed. Channa explained that the holy man had found a way to live, a path through the suffering that Siddhartha had just learned about.

Siddhartha was deeply moved by his experience – he vowed to find a solution to the suffering of the world. At the age of 29, in the night, he left the palace, his wealth and family behind. He began his spiritual quest (search).

▶ The spiritual quest

For a few years after leaving the palace, Siddhartha learned different forms of meditation from a series of masters. He learned how to calm his mind, to focus and to reflect deeply. In spite of this, he found no solution.

Then he met six ascetics (people who deny themselves all luxuries and are very self-disciplined) who told him that he needed to decide what was his biggest craving, and deny it to himself. Siddhartha chose food, and therefore starved himself, eating only a few grains of rice a day, not washing and spending most of his time meditating. He became very weak, and lost so much weight that it is said his backbone could be seen through his stomach. He was close to death, but no closer to the solution to the problem of suffering.

Activities

1. Imagine you are King Suddhodana. Write diary entries for each of these days: Queen Maya's dream, Siddhartha's birth, Asita's prophecy, and the day Siddhartha left the palace. In your diary entries, explain what has happened, how that makes you feel and what you are going to do.
2. Explain what happened on the day of the Four Sights. Why do you think it had such an impact on Siddhartha?
3. 'Siddhartha Gautama was determined to solve the problem of suffering.' How true do you think this statement is? Give reasons for your answer.
4. 'The Four Sights was a life-changing event for the Siddhartha Gautama.' Do you agree? Give reasons for your answer.

9.2 The life of the Buddha – the enlightenment and beyond

Learning objectives
- To learn about the Buddha's enlightenment
- To understand how the main teachings of Buddhism came from the Buddha's enlightenment experience
- To reflect on how insight leads to leadership

Big question
Have you ever had a 'lightbulb moment'?

Key term
Asceticism – a religious way of life in which a person deprives themselves of all luxuries, and lives on the bare minimum

▶ Rejecting asceticism

Siddhartha had realised that depriving himself of even the simplest things was not going to give him the solution to the problem of suffering. This realisation came when he heard a man in a boat talking to his son about stringing a musical instrument. The man was telling his son that if he tightened the string too much, then the sound would be wrong, but that if he tightened it too little, again the sound would be wrong. There was a precise amount – a middle way. Siddhartha realised that his life of luxury and his life as an ascetic were like those two 'wrong' ways.

At the same time, a young woman offered Siddhartha some yoghurt – it is still common to offer food to holy men. He took it and ate it, thus breaking the rules of his asceticism. Stepping into the river to bathe he considered whether to give up his search. He dropped the yoghurt bowl into the river and decided that if it travelled against the flow, he would resume his meditation and not stop until he solved the problem of suffering. The bowl moved against the flow.

Seeing what he had done, his ascetic friends left him, calling him weak-willed. Washed and refreshed, Siddhartha settled under a bodhi tree to meditate. The place where he settled was Bodh Gaya.

▲ Representation of the Buddha at the point of his enlightenment

▶ The enlightenment

Siddhartha vowed to meditate until he achieved enlightenment – to know the truth about the nature of all things. That night is split into four sections:

1. At first, the demon Mara tried to persuade, tempt and frighten Siddhartha into giving up his search for enlightenment, by sending his daughters and armies. He demanded to know what right Siddhartha had to fully realise the truth about suffering. Siddhartha recalled all his past lives, and saw how each one had contributed to making him ready for enlightenment. He then called on the Earth as a witness to this right. Mara left him.
2. Entering a deep state of meditation, Siddhartha's first realisation was that everything is impermanent (is subject to change) but connected to other things – there is a chain of existence. This is known as the Three Universal Truths.
3. Next, he realised that people suffer because of craving, or desire. To end suffering, craving must be ended. This was to become his first major teaching: the Four Noble Truths. It includes the Three Universal Truths.
4. Finally, he extinguished (put an end to) the Three Poisons of ignorance, anger and desire within himself – these are negative emotions that lead humans to selfishness. By doing this, he attained enlightenment. He was completely awakened – the Buddha.

▶ Teaching others

Immediately after the enlightenment, the Buddha considered staying alone until his natural death. He had solved the problem of suffering; his journey was over. However, the god Brahma visited him and urged him to go and teach others. Brahma agreed that many people were nowhere near ready for enlightenment, but said there were many who were just waiting for the right teaching, and they would become enlightened themselves. The lotus flower is a Buddhist symbol of this – its roots grow in mud at the bottom of a pond, a stem grows through the water to the surface where its flower emerges into the air, finally to open under the sun. Brahma was telling the Buddha to be the sun helping the flowers (people ready to be enlightened) to open.

The Buddha went to find his former friends, the ascetics, who were in the deer park at Sarnath. They realised immediately that he was enlightened, and sat to listen to his teachings. They fully understood what he said and became enlightened.

The Buddha spent the rest of his life teaching others. His teachings were based on the truths he had realised while becoming enlightened. He used his own insight to explain truths to others, and was recognised as a great speaker. As people felt the truth of what he said, so more came to him, and organised their lives around his teachings. They saw him as their leader. He realised that most followers needed a programme to follow in their everyday lives, without having to be there listening to him. They had to work on their own enlightenment. This was to become known as the Noble Eightfold Path and is the programme of self-discipline that Buddhists still follow today.

The Buddha died at the age of 80 at Kushinagar, just after giving his final sermon.

▲ The Buddha's first students were his former friends, the ascetics

▲ Painting of the Buddha at death

Activities

1. Draw a map of Northern India. On it mark these places: Lumbini, Bodh Gaya, Sarnath, Kushinagar. Write explanations for why each of these places is important to Buddhists today.
2. Describe what made the Buddha give up his life of asceticism. Do you think any one incident was more important than the others?
3. Describe the four phases of the Buddha's enlightenment.
4. What did the Buddha do after becoming enlightened?
5. 'It was the insight achieved during his enlightenment that helped Siddhartha Gautama to become a great leader.' Do you agree? Explain your reasons.

9.3 Key teachings of the Buddha

Learning objectives
- To know the basic teachings of Buddhism
- To understand the logic behind the Buddha's teachings
- To reflect on whether religion is 'common sense' or 'supernatural sense'

Big question
Are you more persuaded by something that makes sense to you, or by something you are told?

The Buddha realised religious truths which led to his enlightenment. These truths form the basis of all Buddhist teachings. He realised these Truths during his enlightenment.

▶ The Three Universal Truths (the Three Marks of Existence)

The Three Universal Truths are three characteristics that are true of all things. To understand suffering, a person needs to understand these three things, because not understanding them leads to suffering.

1. The truth of suffering, dissatisfaction (dukkha). The Buddha said that everything leads to suffering, even good things. Some suffering is obvious. If you fall and hurt yourself, if you are ill, if you do something and are punished: in all cases, you suffer. Some suffering is not so obvious until it is pointed out. Think about your best holiday, how fantastic it was – it still feels great, still makes you smile. Now think about the fact that the holiday is over, and you are in school. Do you still feel great? Or are you a little sad? Even good things make us suffer, because they do not last.

2. The truth of impermanence (anicca), the idea that nothing lasts. The reason those good things make you suffer is often because they are in the past, and we want them to be now. The Buddha said that everything is impermanent, and nothing lasts forever. Think about the world around us. Can you think of anything that cannot change or be changed, that cannot be spoilt or die?

3. The truth of no permanent self (anatta). When the Buddha saw the Four Sights, he realised that his body was impermanent. When he became enlightened, he realised that humans and all sentient beings are made up of five factors (body, feelings, thoughts, consciousness and perception). These are always changing, so Buddhists do not believe in a permanent soul. Let's test this idea. Are you exactly the same person you were when you woke up this morning? If you have eaten, washed, walked and learned then the answer is no, because the food is now absorbed, the washing removed some dead skin cells, the walking improved your muscles, and the learning added to the knowledge in your brain.

I wish I was still on holiday.

That delicious food has gone off.

A year older – how different you look.

▲ Which Universal Truth is shown through each of these statements?

All of this sounds like common sense and quite obvious when it is pointed out. It is no surprise therefore that people wanted to hear more.

▶ The Four Noble Truths

Buddhists believe that the Buddha's teaching is a cure for a person's illnesses and troubles. The Buddha used a well-known Indian medical formula to help explain the Four Noble Truths to his friends:

1. What is the illness?
2. What has caused the illness?
3. Does a cure exist?
4. What remedy does the patient need in order to be cured?

1. The First Noble Truth – the illness (suffering)

   The illness is the suffering and unhappiness that everyone feels at some time in their life. If you think about it, there is always suffering of some sort, whether it is mental, emotional or physical. This is dukkha (suffering). It is also one of the Universal Truths.

2. The Second Noble Truth – the cause of the illness (the cause of suffering)

   The cause of unhappiness is craving. We are never content with what we have, so become unhappy and want more. We always think something else will make us feel right. Even when we have a good experience, we don't want it to end, or we want to have that experience again, which makes us suffer (just think of the best experience you have ever had). This is tanha (craving).

3. The Third Noble Truth – the cure (the cessation of suffering)

   It is possible to be happy and free from craving. This state of perfect freedom and happiness is the same as enlightenment. If we don't crave things, then we don't suffer. By knowing the true nature of things, we don't crave them. This is nirodha (cessation).

4. The Fourth Noble Truth – the remedy (the path leading to freedom from suffering)

   The way to overcome the craving that causes our unhappiness is to follow the Noble Eightfold Path. This path is sometimes called the Middle Way; it is a middle way between extremes. The Buddha had once lived a life of luxury as a prince; then he tried a life of extreme hardship – the ascetic life. The Noble Eightfold Path is a middle way, a programme for self-discipline to achieve enlightenment. The Noble Eightfold Path has eight elements which cover ethics, meditation and wisdom. This is magga (the path to Nirodha).

This is another logical line of reasoning. It makes sense when you read it – which always makes something easier to understand.

Activities

1. What are the Three Universal Truths? Use examples to explain each one.
2. Explain the Four Noble Truths.
3. Do you think that the Three Universal Truths and the Four Noble Truths are straightforward teachings? Give reasons for your answer.

The major world faiths

9.4 Key beliefs in Buddhism

Learning objectives
- To know some key beliefs of Buddhism
- To understand how key beliefs and teachings have an impact on what people do
- To reflect on whether a person needs to be religious to follow a religious programme for living

Big question
Are symbols valuable?

One of the main symbols of Buddhism is the dharmachakra, an eight-spoked wheel. The spokes remind Buddhists of the Noble Eightfold Path, their programme for living as a Buddhist on their journey to enlightenment. The wheel reminds them of the teaching of samsara – the cycle of birth, death and rebirth.

▶ The Noble Eightfold Path

The fourth Noble Truth, the Buddha's remedy to our unhappiness, is to follow the Noble Eightfold Path.

All Buddhists try to work on these eight 'rights' in their daily life. Buddhism has never taught that people should ask God for favours. The Buddha always taught his followers that their spiritual path was their own work to do, and that by following this programme they could come closer to achieving enlightenment. Buddhists follow the whole path – not just one or two bits of it. The Noble Eightfold Path includes aspects that train the mind and the body, and therefore bring good physical and mental health. This means we can say they could be good for everybody, not just Buddhists.

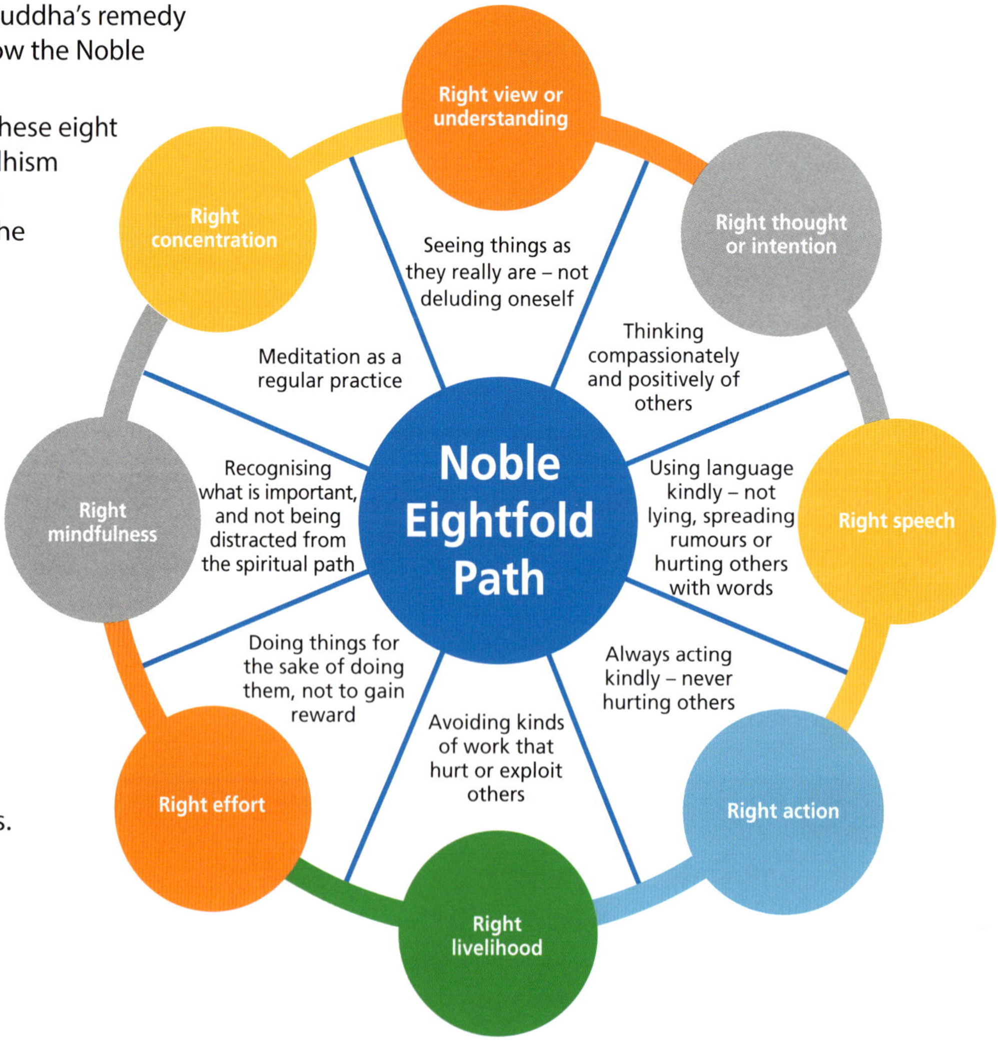

Noble Eightfold Path:
- **Right view or understanding** – Seeing things as they really are – not deluding oneself
- **Right thought or intention** – Thinking compassionately and positively of others
- **Right speech** – Using language kindly – not lying, spreading rumours or hurting others with words
- **Right action** – Always acting kindly – never hurting others
- **Right livelihood** – Avoiding kinds of work that hurt or exploit others
- **Right effort** – Doing things for the sake of doing them, not to gain reward
- **Right mindfulness** – Recognising what is important, and not being distracted from the spiritual path
- **Right concentration** – Meditation as a regular practice

144

9 Buddhism

> For me, the Noble Eightfold Path just makes sense. A big chunk of it is about being a decent person – help not harm. Then there is work on my own self – making me more aware and focused. It is a calming way of life. Gareth

▶ Believing in karma, rebirth and Nirvana

Buddhists believe that every action has a consequence, which we may or may not see, and which might be big or small. This is the law of karma. Karma is generated by words, thoughts and actions, and affects both this life and future lives.

Karma is part of the cycle of samsara, the cycle of birth, death and rebirth. Buddhists believe that when one life ends, our impermanent self keeps being reborn into physical lifetimes in different forms. This keeps happening until a person achieves enlightenment. Once enlightened, they understand the true nature of all things, and extinguish the Three Poisons (anger, desire (wanting) and ignorance) which are keeping a person bound to the wheel of samsara.

Nirvana is:

- enlightenment; awakening to the truth; being freed from suffering, desire and anger
- no longer being affected by the wheel of samsara
- understanding that there is no permanent self, everything is changing, so there is nothing to cling to or crave
- the end of ignorance, greed and anger within yourself
- the aim of life for Buddhists.

Activities

1. Draw a dharmachakra. Label each spoke as one of the eight parts of the Noble Eightfold Path, and write a short explanation of each.
2. In your life, do you already try to keep any of the eight parts (now that you know what they are)? Will there be any others you might keep in the future? Use examples to explain yourself.
3. What is karma, and how does it link to the wheel of samsara?
4. Why is Nirvana the aim of life for Buddhists?
5. 'The Noble Eightfold Path is just a common-sense way to live.' Do you agree? Give reasons for agreeing with and disagreeing with this statement, before writing a justified conclusion.

9.5 Monasticism in Buddhism

Learning objectives
- To learn the role of **monasticism** in Buddhism
- To explore Buddhist monasticism in Wales
- To reflect on the value of monasticism in the modern world

Big question
Do people in the modern world need a space for time out?

Any religion that uses monasticism does so in order to provide a dedicated living space for individuals to devote their whole life to a spiritual path. Monastic communities have religious spaces, such as temples; living spaces, such as cells for the **monks** or **nuns**; communal spaces; and usually work spaces, such as workshops, to provide products to raise funds for the monastery's upkeep. Some monastic communities are self-sufficient (can provide for their own needs), while others rely on the laity.

Buddhism has a strong tradition of monasticism. The Buddha's first community of followers followed a monastic way of life, after the example of the Buddha who had left his family and given up his wealth to focus on his enlightenment. They devoted all their energy to their spiritual path. During the Buddha's life, monks began to wear simple robes, have a simple diet, and follow a strict and lengthy set of rules – a tradition which is still kept today. Wherever you go in the Buddhist world, you will see Buddhist monks and nuns.

▲ Choje Lama Rabsang, a Tibetan Buddhist monk, the resident teacher of Palpung Changchub Dargyeling in Brynmawr.

▶ Welsh Centres of Buddhism

The Welsh landscape and environment has encouraged the setting up of Buddhist monasteries. Nature allows a person the perfect space away from busy towns and cities for meditation and focus, and Wales has plenty of that. Many of the Welsh Buddhist Centres have very small monastic communities – perhaps only the teachers are resident. They all offer meditation classes for visitors, and many offer retreats (a short-term Buddhist monastic experience). They represent many different forms of Buddhism.

Tiratanaloka Buddhist Retreat Centre for Women (Brecon)

This is a community of eight Buddhist nuns. They offer training for the ordination of others into the order, as well as a space for Buddhist retreats for Buddhists of the Triratna order, which is a Western form of Buddhism. They maintain contact with all of the women who have attended their retreats and programmes, to support them in their spiritual path. The community is based in Brecon.

The Samatha Trust (Llangullo)

This national centre for the whole UK teaches a form of Theravada meditation. Its monks and teachers teach in person and online. The Centre also has facilities for residence and retreat.

Lam Rim Buddhist Centre (Raglan)

This is a meditation and retreat centre that follows the Tibetan (Mahayana) form of Buddhism. A small community lives there, but many more visit for short and long periods each year on group retreat. It also has solo retreat facilities; its visitors often include renowned Buddhist masters. Buddhist conferences and workshops are hosted there – both for Buddhists and those interested in the faith or in meditation.

9 Buddhism

I wear the maroon robes of Tibetan Buddhism. I teach other monks for their Yeshe degree (a degree in Buddhist philosophy) at my monastery. The Tibetan name for a monk is trapa – scholar – to show we are all learning. For all the monks, the day starts with morning prayer which last for two or three hours. I spend time every day in meditation, I read scriptures and I take classes with my students. I might also spend some time with ordinary Buddhists chanting scriptures for them. Our food is simple vegetarian fare.

I wear the saffron robes of the Theravadin tradition. My monastery is actually the temple which the laity attend. I start the day with the other monks in morning prayer, and later do some work around the temple to keep it tidy, perhaps cutting grass, moving old offerings and so on. I also devote time to my spiritual studies: meditation, reading scriptures, listening to lectures on the Dharma from my teachers. Our food comes from the community – we walk an alms round for them to freely give us food each day, and they also provide food as offerings to the temple.

I live at a very small monastery which is a community for women. Each day is structured around the spiritual path, beginning with prayers, then study of scripture, which is often led by the leader of our community. We are self-sufficient, so grow all our own food. This is just one of the physical tasks around the monastery, all of which the nuns take part in. We also organise women's retreats (several days or weeks spent on meditation and reflection).

I wear the robes of a Zen monk. My tradition strongly believes in the importance of service to others, so I spend part of every day on that. It helps teach me humility. My day is very structured, giving specific time to specific things. I try to do everything focusing only on that thing. When I eat, I eat; when I walk, I walk. This is a skill that helps me focus entirely on prayer when praying, for example. Each day I study scriptures and meditate for long periods.

Key terms

Monasticism – the practice of devoting one's life to a spiritual path, including living as part of a community of people doing the same

Monk – a man who has devoted his life to the spiritual path by taking religious vows, and lives in a community of others with the same ideal

Nun – a woman who has devoted her life to the spiritual path by taking religious vows, and lives in a community of others with the same ideal

Laity – those people who follow a religion but are not ordained (have not taken religious vows)

Alms round – monks going into their local community to be given food by Buddhists as a gift

Activities

1. What is monasticism?
2. Why is monasticism important in Buddhism?
3. There are many kinds of Buddhism. Using the information on this page, what similarities of life for the different forms of Buddhist monk and nun can you point out?
4. 'Monasticism is not important in our world today.' Do you agree? Explain your reasons.

The major world faiths

9.6 The Buddhist place of worship – temples

Learning objectives
- To learn about the key features of a Buddhist temple
- To explore a Welsh Buddhist temple
- To consider why religious buildings are open to all

Big question

Should religious buildings be open to everyone?

Buddhists worship at temples. Temples are places of meditation, teaching and for showing reverence to the Buddha through making offerings. Where temples have another function, they might have another name. For example, Thai Buddhist temples usually have monks living in the grounds, and these are viharas. Tibetan temples are part of monasteries where monks study Buddhist philosophy so are known as gompas.

Buddhist temples are open every day; people come and go when they want to. Western Triratna Buddhists do hold a special day when lay Buddhists can hear sermons about Buddhist teachings. There is no duty of worship in Buddhism, rather Buddhists should focus on their own spiritual development, seeking guidance from the monks at the temple when it is needed. It is still true, however, that many lay Buddhists do go to temple to pay respects to the Buddha and venerate him.

Temples reflect the culture of their country. There are temples from five different countries in the collage on this page. Try to pick out some similarities and differences. The features of temples in a particular country make them easy to spot. Temples in Wales are often buildings that used to have a different function; many are old houses, for example. This is true of most Western Buddhist temples, where communities have not enough wealth (or space) to build new ones. There are, however, some purpose-built temples in the UK.

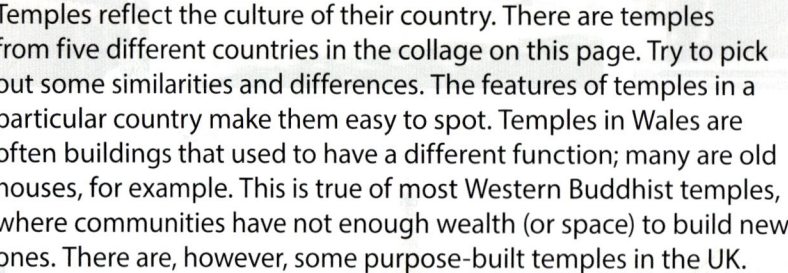

148

The most important part of any temple is the shrine room. This is usually central to the whole complex in a purpose-built temple, but will be a main room in a converted temple.

▶ Shrine room at Palpung Changchub Dargyeling Buddhist temple, Brynmawr

▲ Offerings of incense, food and flowers are made, often together as a single offering

There are usually many statues of the Buddha in a shrine room, one of which will be central and imposing. Often there are three large statues, especially in the Mahayana tradition, in front of which many other statues are placed. Buddhists do not worship the Buddha, they venerate him (show him great respect). The Buddha found the solution to suffering, and gave them practices and guidance to attain enlightenment, so they are thankful to him and show this in their worship.

The statues are posed as if meditating – whether the statue is seated, standing or lying down. Meditation is the key practice for Buddhists, and the Buddha achieved enlightenment through meditation.

When Buddhists visit a shrine, they usually make offerings to show respect. These are symbolic, for example:

- flowers – to show everything is impermanent
- incense – the scent of which goes everywhere, as do the teachings of the Buddha
- candles – the light of which represents Buddhism showing the way
- food – for the monks whose blessings they seek.

In Buddhist countries, temples are open all day and to anyone – Buddhist or not, so long as they are respectful. In the UK, many temples are open only on certain days or with appointments. All temples though give a welcome to all.

Palpung Changchub Dargyeling (Brynmawr)

The Tibetan Buddhist Centre in Brynmawr opened in 2009 in a former Welsh Baptist church. The centre has a large shrine room which hosts acts of veneration, meditation and classes. The Centre also has a community venue in Brynmawr where non-religious well-being activities are open to the whole community. A resident teacher – Choje Lama Rabsang (who you can see on page 146) – came to the UK from Tibet to teach Buddhist philosophy to Western Buddhists in 2001. Several nuns and monks reside at the centre, Buddhists come from all over Wales and the UK to take part in retreats, and a large Buddhist community attends.

Activities

1. What are the different roles of Buddhist temples?
2. Why are Buddhist temples different in different countries?
3. Draw a Buddhist shrine room. Include the Buddha and offerings. Label each to say what it is, and what it symbolises.
4. Do you think it helps society for religious buildings to be open to anyone? Explain your ideas.

9.7 Buddhist celebration of Wesak

Learning objectives
- To learn about Wesak
- To explore how Buddhists celebrate Wesak
- To reflect on the concept of remembrance

Big question
Do we celebrate a person's life or their death?

Wesak is the most famous of all Buddhist festivals. It is celebrated by Buddhists all across the world every May and recalls the birth, enlightenment and death of the Buddha.

▲ The Buddha's birth, enlightenment and death

▶ The origins of Wesak

The Buddha is said to have been born on the full moon day of the month of Vesakha, at Lumbini. He is said to have become enlightened on the same night years later at Bodh Gaya, and then to have died, years later, on the same night at Kushinagar.

It is normal for believers to celebrate key dates in the life of a founder of a religion. Many historically important people's lives are celebrated in certain countries, for example, Martin Luther King Day is 17 January. You celebrate the birthday of members of your family each year. We celebrate these as important events. We also reflect on a person's passing on the anniversary of their death. For Buddhists, the three most important events of the Buddha's life can be celebrated in one festival: Wesak, which is celebrated especially by the laiety.

Buddhists want to celebrate Wesak because:

- The Buddha founded the religion, so is an important person.
- He became enlightened which is the goal for all Buddhists.
- He gave teachings which will guide a person to attain enlightenment, which helps everyone.
- His life and teachings provide the best example to follow to attain enlightenment.

> Wesak is a time of joy, even though we remember the Buddha's passing. We are thankful for his teachings, and that he showed the way to enlightenment. Wyn

> Our temple holds special Wesak services at the weekend nearest to the date. In Wales, Wesak isn't a holiday, so this way all can join the celebrations. Neula

▶ How do Buddhists celebrate Wesak?

Wesak is not a bank holiday in the UK, so Buddhists have to take time off work in order to celebrate. Temples often open for celebrational services on the weekend nearest to Wesak.

There are some practices that are common to Buddhists everywhere in the world:

- Lay Buddhists make a lot of offerings on this day, because they can gain greater karmic merit. They might give alms to the monks and nuns, offer food to the poor, donate money to temples and charities or help those in need. The alms can be financial or practical.
- Buddhists attend the temple to venerate the Buddha, and make offerings. On this day, they are more thankful for his life and what he did which helps them today – his teachings, his example, his advice on living. Special services are held at most temples which include sermons on the Buddha's life and his teachings, and especially how Buddhists can follow these today. Many chant mantras (short religious phrases repeated over and over to concentrate the mind) and say prayers; some seek personal advice and teaching from monks.
- Some Buddhists focus on their religious practice. All Buddhists keep the Five Precepts (see page 153), while monks keep ten – so lay Buddhists might choose to live by the Ten Precepts for the festival. The precepts are guidelines for living in the right way. In Buddhist countries, such as Thailand, it is common for young men to live at the temple for 30 days before Wesak as novice monks.
- Light is important in the festival. Many Buddhists light candles, float candles and decorate their homes with light. The light reminds them that the Buddha's teachings lit the way to enlightenment.
- Water is also important, with statues being splashed or cleaned with fragrant water. The fragrance reminds that the Buddha's teachings are sweet.

> I keep the Five Precepts every day, but at Wesak I go a bit further and keep the Ten Precepts. I also do a bit of volunteer work, as thanks to the Buddha. Aled

Activities

1. What does Wesak celebrate?
2. Why is it important to celebrate Wesak?
3. Explain the different ways in which Buddhists celebrate Wesak, and explain the symbolic nature of each.
4. Do you think it is important to remember the contributions people make to society? Explain the reasons for your answer.
5. Does everyone deserve to be remembered and celebrated? Explain the reasons for your answer.

▲ Candles in lotus flower cases, floating on water at Wesak

The major world faiths

9.8 Buddhism in the Welsh community

Learning objectives
- To learn the religious motivation behind Buddhists helping others
- To understand how the Buddha's teachings are put into practice for the benefit of the wider society
- To reflect on whether it is beliefs or principles that underpin social action

Big question
Do people do things for society because they want something for themselves?

Talk it out
If you could make a change to your local community, what would it be? Why?

Is that change something that directly benefits you? Or is it something that benefits others? Or that benefits everyone?

What does that tell you about your motives?

While becoming enlightened, the Buddha remembered all of his past lifetimes. In those memories, he saw that he had helped others in many of them. In one lifetime, reborn as Prince Sattva, he saw a tigress at the foot of the cliff he was walking along. The tigress was starving to death. She had cubs, and was going to eat them to stay alive. So, he threw himself off the cliff and died near her – giving her food, and sparing her cubs.

When the Buddha first became enlightened, he was not going to teach anyone. He intended to continue his spiritual practice alone until his death. The god Brahma persuaded him he had much to give in supporting others to enlightenment. Brahma persuaded the Buddha that there were many people ready to be enlightened – they just needed a little help, and the Buddha was ideally placed to provide that. The Buddha's teachings are summed up in this quote from the **Dhammapada**: 'Not to do any evil; to cultivate good; to purify one's heart – this is the teaching of all the Buddhas.' Buddhists believe that some enlightened beings have chosen to continue to be reincarnated so that they can help those in need. Other unenlightened beings have taken a vow to help all beings become enlightened. All these beings are called **bodhisattvas**. Many are venerated for their compassion, such as Guanyin.

The Dalai Lama, spiritual head of Tibetan Buddhism, summed up the Buddha's teachings in two points: first, you must help others; second, if you cannot help someone, you must not harm them. These are the principles behind the Five Precepts.

Key terms
Bodhisattva – a person whose actions are motivated with deep, impartial, loving kindness to all beings; who has put off their own full enlightenment to be able to help all sentient beings (any being that has feelings or can feel pain) become enlightened

Dhammapada – Buddhist holy scriptures which are collections of the sayings of the Buddha; verses of truth which are the best known of all Buddhist scriptures in the Western world

Activities
1. How does the story of Prince Sattva guide Buddhists in their attitude to helping other sentient beings?
2. What are the Five Precepts? Give examples of keeping and breaking the precepts.
3. Which of the precepts would make school a better place if everyone followed them? Explain your ideas.
4. 'Life is better for everyone when everyone believes it is right to help others.' Do you agree? Explain your ideas.

9 Buddhism

▶ What are the Five Precepts?

All Buddhists keep a set of precepts (guidelines for living). For monks and nuns there are at least ten, but for all others there are five. Keeping the precepts in a positive way generates good karma for their rebirths; breaking the precepts has a negative effect on future rebirths, taking them further from enlightenment.

1. The First Precept is not to harm other sentient beings. This means anything that can feel pain – so not just humans. Harm is mental and emotional as well as physical. Helping others is the positive way to keep this precept.
2. The Second Precept is not to take anything that is not freely given. This means no stealing, but also not persuading someone to give you something when you know they don't want to really. Also, money and material items are not the only things that can be stolen. This can also refer to time, ideas, etc. Being generous with what you have is the positive way to keep this precept.
3. The Third Precept is to abstain from sexual misconduct. This means behaving properly in sexual relationships, both emotionally and physically. Remaining faithful is the obvious positive way to keep the precept.
4. The Fourth Precept is not to use false speech. This does not just mean lying, but also refers to gossiping and any hurtful use of language. Using words kindly is the positive way to keep this precept.
5. The Fifth Precept is not to use intoxicants that cloud the mind. This clearly means drugs and alcohol, but it can mean anything that distracts you completely. The positive way to keep this precept is to live a moderate life.

Buddhism is a religion that is about helping others. It is not possible to be a Buddhist and not help others. By helping others, you also help yourself because in this life you get a sense of well-being from helping others, and if everyone helped others, then life for everyone would be nicer. In karmic terms, keeping the precepts generates good karma, which makes rebirths better. Better rebirths make the path to enlightenment easier.

> I became a Buddhist about five years ago. My town doesn't have a temple, so once a week I go to one which is about an hour away from home, to meditate with others. My religion isn't just something I do on that day, though – it is all day, every day. I try to be really alert to my actions and how they affect others. It is easy not to think about what you do, and hurt someone else without intending to, but by being aware and mindful, I can affect people in a positive way. The pandemic was really hard for so many people. My job let me work from home, so I had more time on my hands. I decided to use that for the good of others. I volunteered to deliver food parcels and prescriptions locally. Whenever I delivered anything, I made sure to spend some time with the receiver, chatting with them. Many people get very lonely, so even if I only gave them fifteen minutes of my time, I was able to lift their spirits.

> I have been a Buddhist for a long time now – and am part of a small community. We have been fund-raising for a while and have started the process of buying some land. Our intention is to rewild this land. We will be planting groups of trees – a fruit orchard as well as trees for a small wood. There will be some pathways created in and around this land, with spaces to sit to eat, reflect and chat. I feel very calm in natural environments, and am helped by that calm in my meditation and in my mood. We hope to work with our local community on this project, and then share it with them. The world belongs to everyone, and can help everyone. It is something to care for and to share.

10 Values and ethics
Identity and belonging

10.1 Identity and belonging

Learning objectives
- To explore the question 'Who am I?'
- To consider the many groups a person belongs to, and how these groups complement or clash
- To reflect on whether humans need to be part of bigger groups

Big question
Are you always the same whoever you are with?

Key terms
Belonging – the sense of being part of something (a place or group)
Identity – the qualities, beliefs, personality, looks and/or expressions that make a person who they are

Read about this young man. What is he saying that is part of his identity? What examples of belonging is he sharing?

> I usually hang around with three friends. We went through primary and secondary school together. We all go to Dr Mz, the youth drop-in.

> I am 15 years old; I was born in Carmarthen.

> I'm one of four kids – the only boy in the family.

> When I was a kid, I thought I wanted to be a footballer. Now I know I am better at other sports, but I'm not going to make it as a professional without too much hard work and self-discipline.

> My mum works in Lampeter at the university there. Dad does house conversions and other building stuff.

> I like working things out, and am quite determined and resilient really. Some of my mates give up at the first hurdle, but I don't.

> We learn Welsh at my school. I am proud to be Welsh. The Welsh language is part of my identity, and of anyone Welsh, so I think it is important we keep using it and keep it alive.

> I go to Air Cadets and might join the RAF when I finish school, but I might go to university instead (or first). My parents say I can get a degree then join up at a higher level.

> Some people say I am quite serious, and get on with tasks and show good discipline. My mates say I am a 'funny guy', plenty of jokes. It all depends what I need to be really.

> I'm not religious. My mum goes to church, and my dad does on special occasions. I was brought up going to church, but they let me decide for myself when I got old enough. I think all that matters is being a decent person.

154

10 Identity and belonging

▶ About identity

Your **identity** is what makes you you. It is a combination of all kinds of things: your looks, your ideas, your hobbies, your likes and dislikes, your skills – all sorts of things. And this can change; for example, as you get older you change your looks, new ideas or information or influences can change and shape your ideas, new opportunities can inspire new hobbies, your food preferences will change, you will learn new skills, and so on. Buddhism teaches that there is nothing permanent about us, and when you think of how much we each change, you can see that this is true.

> **Talk it out**
> What is your identity made up of? What changes have there been to it since you were small? Why did they happen?

▶ About belonging

Sociologists say that humans are social beings: we enjoy, even need, companionship. This means we feel a need to belong. The most obvious sense of **belonging** we have is those who surround us as we are growing up, those we spend most time with for the crucial developing years of our lives. As we get older, we get opportunities to belong to other groups: a street community, friendship groups, schools. Throughout life we belong to and then leave many groups, even if we might feel a sense of nostalgia for them, or return to reunions with others from the group – like school reunions. Throughout life we get chances to belong to new groups – for example, work colleagues.

> **Talk it out**
> What groups do you belong to? What are the benefits of belonging to each group? What do you have to do to keep belonging? Are there any drawbacks to belonging to any particular group?

When we belong to a group, we get lots of benefits: companionship, friendship, a shared idea or goal, support on physical and emotional levels, and more. However, we also owe something to any group we belong to; we have to back the group, support others in it, help it meet its goals, and more. We get things from being in a group, but we also have to give to the group so that it remains strong.

Activities

1. Draw a silhouette of yourself. Add labels around it to show aspects of your identity, and examples of belonging.
2. Explain why it is important to belong to groups. Use examples to demonstrate your points.
3. Use examples to explain why sometimes there are drawbacks to belonging to groups.
4. What do you think is the biggest influence on a person's identity? Using examples, explain your ideas.

Values and ethics

10.2 Shaping or being shaped?

Learning objectives
- To think about your own worldview
- To consider how your worldview has been shaped by the groups you belong to
- To reflect on the positive and negative influence of groups

Big question
What influences your ideas and decisions?

▶ What is a worldview?

A worldview is a particular philosophy of life or idea about the world; for example, many religious worldviews are based on the idea of a battle – good versus evil. Most religious people believe in a God, so their worldview focuses on that; whereas those who are atheists usually focus their worldview around human beings. A humanist worldview is based on reasoning, evidence and the idea of treating everybody equally. A person's worldview shapes the principles they go on to live by.

> Hi I'm Effi. I am agnostic – I don't think we can prove if there is or isn't something divine. I can think of reasons to believe there is a God, and reasons why there isn't. However, I also believe that people are all the same, they have the same worth, just with different opportunities, which makes life easier or more difficult. I think we have to live in a way that isn't going to hurt anyone else, and if possible, people should do things to make life a bit better for someone else. Science has a lot to give to help us do that, but we have to use science wisely. Don't forget that humans can twist science to do bad things. So that is my worldview: be nice and do good because we all live in the same world.

What about you? What is your worldview? Do you think you will have the same worldview throughout your life?

▶ How do people get a worldview?

The biggest influence on a person's life, and so on their worldview, at least until their teens, is usually their parents or carers. You spend your most formative years with them – learning to walk and to talk, learning manners and morals, and so on. If your parents or carers hold a certain worldview, it is likely you will hold that worldview as a child.

Once you go to school you are likely to meet other people with other worldviews. In lessons, you are exposed to more different ideas. These can influence you to modify or change your views. For example, you might debate issues such as the death penalty or environmental ethics. This helps you to form your own attitude to the issue, and so becomes part of your worldview.

Society also has a growing influence, especially the media with its news stories, media influencers and personalities. As you see and hear these, you may find your worldview being influenced.

Travel exposes you to new situations, different cultures and histories, and different ideas and ideologies. This can be a big influence, especially if you stay in one place for an extended time. It helps to shape you as a person, and the worldview you are building for yourself.

Many people belong to a religion, and this gives them a worldview to believe in. They don't have to work out their own unique worldview. For example, Christians believe there is a God who is the supreme creator of everything. They believe they are stewards of this world, so have to look after it. They believe God will judge them after death, so their behaviour in this life has to be good. Believing in and worshipping God, and doing good deeds are the two duties for Christians.

10 Identity and belonging

> My influences were my parents. They got divorced when I was six, and I live with my dad now. Their lifestyles are really different, so I get different ideas from each. With one I do loads of outdoor stuff – walks, gardening, rock-climbing. I know I have to keep my body healthy, not just my mind. With the other, I do more cultural stuff – theatre and film, reading and we discuss all sorts. So I value the arts, you could say. School influences me because of what I am studying, especially subjects like RS and sociology – you get to hear lots of different views that you can weigh up for yourself. I help out at the local churchyard on Saturdays, keeping it tidy. I chat with lots of the people who go, and a lot of them are old so they have interesting things to say – they always make me think. I think that I was shaped by my parents, but then all the other groups I am in are changing that all the time, little by little. I feel I have an opinion of my own now, not just what my parents thought.

▶ Are influences always good?

Most people who are trying to influence others certainly believe what they say is right, so from their point of view, their influence is good. However, some people manipulate others. Their worldview is a selfish one, based around what is in it for them. Some worldviews are self-evidently good ones, such as 'help all, harm none'. It is up to each person to have enough information to be able to decide if they want to follow a certain worldview or not. For example, you can read what a religion teaches, decide it makes sense to you, and use it to shape how you behave towards others and the world. Alternatively, you might read it and think it makes no sense to you or you don't agree with it, so disregard it.

There are lots of examples of 'bad' influences, where a worldview persuades someone that it is fine to do something most people think of as wrong. Many people in prison thought they had a right to hurt others in some way, for example. There are also plenty of groups existing online or in society who spread messages of hatred towards certain others in society.

What about you? How has your worldview been influenced by the different groups you are part of?

> I think the groups we belong to are basically good because they are supporting us. However, I think sometimes they can go a bit far. I play for a girls' football team, and they tried to stop me playing for school. My friend's brother got in with a group who made him steal some stuff to stay in the group. (He was stupid enough to do that, and to get caught! The group didn't back him then.) Also, the ideas a group has can be very destructive. In history, we are studying Nazi Germany, which is the perfect example of a worldview that is destructive. I think you have to use your intelligence and common sense to sift through what groups say, and not just buy it all. But I do realise that that can be very difficult at times if you want to stay part of the group.

Activities

1. What is a worldview? Give an example.
2. How do people get their worldviews?
3. How much influence do the different groups we belong to have in shaping our worldview?
4. Do you think belonging to a group is more important than what the group stands for? Explain your ideas.

What about you? Do you think influences are always good? Give example of some good and bad influences.

157

Values and ethics

10.3 What is morality, and how do we get it?

Learning objectives
- To learn about the argument from morality for the existence of God
- To learn different views about morality and its origins
- To reflect on the links between morality and actions

Big question
Where do we get our ideas of right and wrong?

▶ Where do we get our sense of morality from?

Religions tell us that our **morality** – sense of right and wrong – comes from God. They tell us that God is supreme, absolutely fair and just, and can never be wrong, and that God provides laws through revelation and the holy books, which should guide our sense of right and wrong. This doesn't mean that all religious people follow the rules of their religion slavishly. Many interpret these for themselves, as they acknowledge God's gift of intelligence, and that we live in an ever-changing world.

Non-religious people believe that morality comes from humans themselves. **Humanists**, for example, believe that humans should use their intellect, reasoning and experience to work out what is right or wrong. They also say that morality should be shaped by empathy (sharing the feelings of others) and respect for others. They argue that the proof of something being right or wrong is the good or bad outcome it leads to. Something leading to a lot of suffering can't be good, for example. They also argue that good outcomes are more likely if we empathise with and show respect for others. Many people take a **utilitarian** stance. This means they always try to do what is the best for the most people. This does mean that individuals can lose out in a decision – because the majority gain from it.

Your morality comes from different sources, including all those groups you belong to. For example, if your friendship group thinks it is acceptable to drink alcohol underage, you are likely to so the same. Your parents or carers gave you your first sense of morality, but then each new group adds to and shapes it. It might even be that you operate on different moral systems depending on who you are with, or what group you are in. If you are in Army Cadets, for example, you may follow rules more strictly when at a session with them than you do elsewhere (because the Armed Forces operate on rules). As you get older, your sense of morality will change as new contacts, new experiences, new knowledge all influence it.

Key terms
Religion – a belief system that relies on the existence of a supernatural or divine being

Morality – a sense of right and wrong; principles that distinguish between good and bad behaviour

Humanist – a non-religious person without a belief in a god, who advises humans to look to reason, empathy and human nature for solutions.

Utilitarianism – the principle that an action is right if it brings happiness, and the aim is to bring the greatest happiness to the greatest number

Pragmatism – thinking or acting in a reasonable and logical way to get a satisfactory outcome without relying on rules or beliefs

Is our morality shared?
Imagine that your class has been stranded on a desert island, and will be there for an unknown period of time. You have to come up with some rules that everyone will agree to. These rules have to be able to keep everyone safe, and prevent people from losing trust in each other.

What would be the five most important rules for everyone to follow? Write your five, then compare with someone else's. If there are differences, discuss and agree on five.

If you were to extend that task to bigger groups, then to the whole class, you would probably find that you all agreed on the top four or five rules.

What does it tell you about morality when we all have the same basic ideas?

10 Identity and belonging

▶ The argument from morality for the existence of God

Some philosophers, such as Immanuel Kant and C.S. Lewis, have pointed to the fact humans seem to have a shared sense of morality. This, they say, proves there is a God.

Simply put, this is how their argument goes:

- everyone has an instinctive idea of what is right and wrong. No one needs to be told what they should or should not do in any given situation – they already instinctively know (though that does not mean that they will do the right thing, and we can all think of examples where someone did not do the right thing!).
- Laws from different countries are strikingly similar on crucial points (such as it being wrong to kill, to steal, and so on), as well as on what they think is the worst thing to do (take a life). Even remote tribes that have had only very limited contact with the outside world, use the same basic set of rules. So, even without every group in the world meeting to discuss a set of rules, it is true that every group in the world still comes up with the same basic set of rules.
- This being the case, morality must come from somewhere outside humans (as it didn't rely on them contacting each other), and that can only be God. So, morality proves God exists.

You might argue that morality is just something that happens naturally, or it is just part of who we are part of human nature. C.S. Lewis disagreed. He questioned how a random event, the Big Bang, could generate morality, which is so uniform across the world. He believed there had to be a great intellect behind it, building it into the design of humans – as far as he was concerned, that is God.

▶ Does morality matter?

You could say that it doesn't matter what people think is right or wrong, just as long as there are certain principles in place. Or just as long as actions only have positive consequences. In other words, morality is something in our heads, and what matters is what we do. This is **pragmatism**.

> I don't believe in God, however, I can see that morality is common generally across the world. I think that morality is just part of evolution. As the human species has adapted and evolved, we have become a highly social species. Humans need others, need companionship. The only way to survive when you are with others is to have a shared sense of what is right and wrong – so everyone operates according to shared rules and values. This means people look after themselves and each other – and the species continues to survive. Morality has come from a natural process, not God. Ibra

Activities

1. What is meant by morality?
2. Where do people get their idea of morality from? Is it fixed?
3. Outline the argument from morality for the existence of God. How strong an argument do you think this is for explaining human morality? Explain your ideas.
4. Read Ibra's idea in the speech bubble above of how humans acquired morality. Ibra is a humanist. Explain his idea of evolutionary morality. Do you agree with him? Explain your answer.
5. In your opinion, how closely are morality and actions linked? Explain your ideas.
6. 'Act as if whatever you do makes a difference.' Do you think it would improve society if everyone believed and acted on this? Explain your ideas.

Values and ethics

10.4 Beliefs – values – behaviour

Learning objectives
- To recognise the link between **beliefs** and **values** and **behaviour**
- To explore some **dilemma**-based thinking, and consider the consequences of decision-making
- To reflect on whether the law or what society expects has more influence on our actions

Key terms
Beliefs – ideas we hold as true without proof, which shape our identity and actions
Values – ideas of what is important
Behaviour – how people conduct themselves
Dilemma – a difficult choice which has to be made, often with only bad options
Advocate – someone who publicly supports or recommends a person or cause

Big question
Why do we keep laws and rules?

Most of us live our lives by a set of values. Values are our principles – what we think is important. These might have originally come from a set of beliefs. Those beliefs and values then affect how we behave; in fact, at times, they control our behaviour. See some examples in the table below.

Beliefs	Values	Behaviour
Milo believes in God. He believes that God created all life.	This belief makes him value life, so he thinks it should be protected and cared for.	So Milo works as a paramedic, and literally saves lives every day.
Gwen believes that humans have a responsibility to look after the world because we live here and it is an amazing thing.	This belief makes her value the environment and animals.	So Gwen does volunteer work in a local nature reserve, and donates to several animal charities.
Aisha believes in freedom of speech as a fundamental right.	This belief makes her value the society she lives in and the laws that protect that right.	So Aisha is an **advocate** for freedom of speech, and also a campaigner for those in other countries where there is no freedom of speech.

Values are personal to each of us. As a general rule, most people agree on the same big values – for example, everyone believes human life is important. Religious people believe that human life is important because their religion tells them it is made specially by God, or is part of a cycle of rebirth. Non-religious people might start from themselves – 'My life is special, so all life is special' – or recognise that humans are uniquely different from all other species because of their ability to think and reason, which makes them special.

Once you dig deeper, though, the fine detail of our values might be different.

Activity

Work with a partner, and discuss whether each of the following lives is special. For each one, explain why it is or is not.

a A young person who has had an accident that has left them in a coma from which they will never awaken.
b The foetus of a woman who needs surgery that will terminate (end) the pregnancy.
c A person who has abducted, assaulted and murdered five children.
d A homeless war veteran, who has been awarded many medals, but who has drug issues.
e A talented athlete with a good chance of winning Olympic medals.

You probably didn't quite agree on all of those, or had different reasons for your views. This shows you that as we explore situations, we might change our values and attitudes.

One last thing: would it make a difference to your answers if you personally knew any of these people?

Absolute and relative morality

Morality is not always straightforward or clear cut. People do not always agree on the same things, and their morality can change depending on circumstances. When they decide something is always right to do, in every circumstance, they are using absolute morality – morality that is unchanging and fixed. It might be that some of the rules a person keeps carry more weight than others, so they can break one rule to keep a 'higher' one. For example, in Judaism there is a key rule of pikuach nefesh – the need to save a life outweighs the need to obey other laws. So for Jewish people even though they should not work on the Sabbath, if they needed to get medical help for someone on that day, they could do. Most people, most of the time use relative morality – judging what to do based on the information they have and the details of a situation. The step is then acting on what they think should be done.

Behaviour

Do you think a person always acts on their beliefs and values? Might there be times when they ignore them?

Depending on how serious or important the dilemma is, many people find their values challenged. They might compromise. Acting on your values can be very difficult – if you believe you are at risk then you might not act. Sometimes values can clash. You might believe life is special and must be protected. This becomes more complicated if there is a choice between two lives; for example, if you had to hurt someone else in order to defend yourself against an attack. Generally, however, a person can stick to their values in how they act.

Something else that affects our behaviour is law and social norms (what society accepts). If you break the law, you could get punished, and no one wants to be punished. Society tells us what is acceptable and what is not, and this might sometimes mean that you avoid doing something or choose to do something.

Can you think of any examples of laws or social norms that influence our actions?

Even if we disagree with the law or social norms, the consequences and pressures make us keep them.

Talk it out

Which do you think is a stronger influence: the law or social norms?

Does it depend on the situation?

Activities

Man jailed for theft of food and goods

1. Look at the headline. What do you think of it? Is it fair?
2. Do any of these make a difference to your answer?
   a. The man was a friend or yours.
   b. It was your shop he stole from.
   c. He has done this many times before.
   d. He did this because he had no money and needed to feed his family.

Activities

1. What do we mean by 'values'? What are yours?
2. How do beliefs lead to values and then to behaviour?
3. Explain, using examples, what is meant by absolute and relative morality.
4. Give two examples of how the law affects our behaviour. Give two examples of how social norms affect our behaviour.
5. 'Sometimes we have to ignore our values and act against them.' Do you agree with this statement? Explain your reasons.

Values and ethics

10.5 Religious influences on morality

Learning objectives
- To explore some general moral attitudes from religious sources
- To understand where religious morality comes from, and how important it is to believers
- To reflect on whether religious believers should break the law

Big question
Which is more important: your principles or the law?

The Golden Rule is a principle nearly everyone can agree with – whatever their religious or non-religious beliefs. It is written in many different ways, but they all mean the same.

Do as you would be done by.
Do not do to others what you would not want done to yourself.
Want only for yourself what you want for others.
Treat others as you wish to be treated.

You do not need to have religious beliefs to agree with this principle, or to live by it. However, every religion does have a version of it in their scriptures. It is a simple but good way to think, and it is easy to act on.

Religious beliefs come from **revelation** and **sacred scripture**. Many religions believe that God has spoken directly to one or more people, and given them the rules for living which please God, and mean they will have a better next life (whatever that is). The rules are usually based around key principles or values, such as:

- All life is special – humans are the highest species.
- The world is special, and needs to be cared for.
- There is an afterlife, that everybody will move on to, which is influenced by our behaviour here on Earth.
- Worship and service to others are twin duties.
- The most important virtues are compassion (care for others), truthfulness and humility (modesty).

Key terms
Revelation – God revealed to humans; religious truths revealed by God
Sacred scripture – holy books such as the Christian Bible, and other texts believed to hold religious truths, such as the Hadith in Islam

Talk it out
Thinking about your own behaviour, do you generally live by the Golden Rule?

If everyone in school followed the Golden Rule, would school be any different? How?

Do you think society generally needs to do more to follow the Golden Rule?

▶ Religious believers and keeping the law

Religious believers have their own religious laws, but they must still keep the laws of the country in which they live. This does not usually lead to any problems, because many laws are common sense, and many match religious laws. For example, it is common sense that it should be wrong to murder someone – you do not have to believe life is sacred or created by God to agree. No one wants to live in a society where people are not safe from the threat of murder – that is just common sense. It is also against every religion's law to kill someone.

Religions tell their followers to obey the laws of the society in which they live, unless the law tells them to break one of God's laws. Usually society's laws are easy to keep alongside religious laws.

Sometimes religious people do break the law. Of course, not every religious person is a law-abiding citizen, and some do terrible things for which they are punished as anyone would be. Some religious people do things in the name of their religion which break the law and cause a lot of harm. However, some religious people break the law deliberately, but for a reason they see as morally right.

10 Identity and belonging

> **Activities**
>
> Look at these examples:
>
>
> *In my own country, I had been persecuted because of my religious beliefs, so I paid smugglers a lot of money to get me into another country where I rebuilt my life. I didn't trust the authorities not to send me back, so I got false papers and lived there illegally.*
>
>
> *I believe in absolute non-violence because I believe that all life is sacred. Even so, I plotted to kill the leader of my country, and almost succeeded. By his orders, his government was rounding up and killing all people of certain minority groups; many tens of thousands had already been killed. I believed that I had to stop him, to stop his greater evil.*
>
>
> *The Government gave permission for scientists to grow genetically modified crops in fields near my town. What the scientists have done changes what God has created. It is an insult to God. I helped a group of others to burn the fields – committing the crime of arson.*
>
>
> *My religion teaches me that it is wrong to steal, but I stole food for my family. We have only enough money each week to live on, and one week it was too little. There is no foodbank near me, so I had no way to feed my children. I stole the food for them.*
>
> In each case:
> - How is the person breaking the law?
> - Why does the person think it is necessary?
> - Is the law and their religion in conflict?
> - Do you think the person was right to do what they did?

Religions advise their followers to fight for justice, and speak up against unjust laws. In each of the four cases above, the person is breaking a law that they feel goes against God's laws, or for a morally good reason. However, there would be people in their religions who did not agree with their actions. This shows that people have a conscience (an internal sense of right and wrong) which is their own, and this is another influence when they make decisions and act. Religious people see this as the 'voice of God' or being inspired by God; non-religious people may see it as 'good sense' or inspired by the idea of the needs of society.

> **Activities**
>
> 1. Explain what the Golden Rule is, and give some examples of it in action.
> 2. The law is meant to protect citizens. Why might some people break it?
> 3. Explain religious attitudes to the law.
> 4. Do you think religious people should obey their religion's laws, or the laws of the society they live in? Explain your reasons.

11 Rights and responsibilities

11.1 Human rights – the UDHR and the UNCRC

Learning objectives
- To understand the idea and range of human rights
- To explore rights given to children by the UNCRC
- To reflect on the importance of human rights as a non-religious worldview

Big question

What is the most important right a person has?

The Universal Declaration of Human Rights

In the past many countries have written statements of the rights of their people. In 1945, after the end of the Second World War, 51 countries, including the most powerful, came together to form the United Nations (UN). The organisation gave itself a mandate (an instruction or directive) for peace and harmony in the world, jointly working for the good of all, and the support of the weak by the strong. In 1948, the Universal Declaration of Human Rights (UDHR) was written, and then adopted by most countries in the UN (though it is not binding in part or in full).

The UDHR is made up of 30 articles (parts), which are split into two groups:

- those related to civil and political rights
- those related to economic, social and cultural rights.

The first article reads: 'All humans are born free and equal in dignity and rights. They are endowed with reason and conscience and should act towards one another in a spirit of brotherhood.' Everything else then flows from that first idea.

You can find a simplified version of the 30 articles at www.youthforhumanrights.org/what-are-human-rights/universal-declaration-of-human-rights/articles-1-15.html

Let's take a look at some of these rights.

Talk it out

Which are the most important rights?

Should everyone always have all these rights?

How should a government ensure these rights for their citizens?

Everyone is:
- equal
- born free
- innocent until proven guilty.

Everyone should:
- be treated the same way
- respect everyone else.

Everyone has the right to:
- legal protection
- a public trial
- asylum/refuge/protection
- belong to a country
- marry and have a family
- own things and keep them
- free speech and free thought
- meet peacefully with others
- vote
- work
- rest and play
- an education
- basic rights – water, food, shelter, healthcare
- be an artist and enjoy the arts.

No one should be:
- tortured
- unfairly imprisoned.

No one may take away the rights of others.

There must be laws to protect these rights.

11 Rights and responsibilities

Activities

Look at these headlines. Which human rights are being broken?
a More than a million girls under 14 forced into prostitution each year
b Man beaten up for repeatedly making extremely racist remarks
c Tsunami victims denied help by their own government
d New laws rushed in to stop protestors

Activities

1 What is the UDHR?
2 Find out more about the UDHR and create an infornation leaflet for younger students.
3 In your opinion, which right is the most important in the world today? Explain your ideas.

▶ The United Nations Convention on the Rights of the Child

The United Nations Convention on the Rights of the Child (UNCRC) was written in 1991, and is made up of 54 articles that describe the rights of a child. The last nine of these are about how adults and governments can protect these rights.

> I am going to summarise the rights for you. First, it says who a child is – anyone under 18 – and that we should be registered, as we have the right to an identity. It says we have the right not to be discriminated against in any way; that our best interests always come first; and that our parents are responsible for us growing up. There are loads of things about protection – from harm, from the media, from unfair treatment, and so on. Then there are ones that say what we are entitled to: education, basic rights (food, water, shelter, healthcare), justice, special support and so on. It also says we are not allowed to be in armies, or be exploited in any way. You can read it for yourself – UNICEF has a great poster on their website. But really, it starts from the UDHR, and then adds kid-specific stuff because most young people don't have the power they need to protect themselves. So, this tells governments what they need to be doing. It is a shame that a country which signs up doesn't have to keep to it. This is something young people should be fighting for.

▶ Is the idea of human rights more than an idea?

The UDHR and UNCRC set out clearly the rights people should have. Most democratic governments try to build the rights into their laws, but even so they do not always manage to protect them. Some countries seem to protect few of the rights for adults or children.

Together the UDHR and UNCRC set out a worldview to follow. They include the right to religious freedom and expression, but they are not religious rights, rather these are rights for everyone to keep and protect. They provide a 'perfect idea' which everyone can work towards, whether their government does or not, and which aims for the best for all.

Activities

1 Why do you think there are 54 rights for children, but only 30 for humans?
2 What sorts of rights does the UNCRC give to young people? Do some research to find out more detail about these.
3 Why do you think people do not always get their human rights? Use examples to explain your answer.

Values and ethics

11.2 Rights and responsibilities

Learning objectives
- To understand the difference between rights and responsibilities
- To understand why responsibilities are important
- To reflect on whether rights are even more important than responsibilities

Big question
What responsibilities do you have to yourself and to others?

▶ What are rights?

Rights are the things we are entitled to. The UDHR lists 30 rights that all humans are entitled to. In any situation, a person has their own individual rights, not just 'human' rights.

The Amsterdam Declaration, which describes the key principles of humanism, states that humanism supports democracy and human rights. Humanists see human rights as being a recognition of shared human needs and values, something to be protected by all.

Some people feel that their rights are more important than everyone else's. They might not say that, but their selfish behaviour suggests that that is what they believe.

Everyone has rights, but these can be lost as a punishment – for example, the right to freedom is lost for those sent to prison. Not every country or situation gives or protects its citizens' rights. For example, Amnesty International (the world's leading human rights organisation) argues that every country that uses the death penalty as a punishment is breaking the right of humans to fair treatment . This is because Amnesty believes the death penalty to be inhumane (a punishment that is cruel and without compassion). The countries using the death penalty include ones which are signatories to the UDHR.

▶ What are responsibilities?

Responsibilities are the things we have a duty to do. Rights and responsibilities complement each other: to have rights, you have to be aware of your responsibilities. On a simple level, you have the right to an education, but you also have the responsibility to study and learn so that your education effectively prepares you for your future, for example by getting good qualifications. Millions of young people in the world do not get the chance of an education – so some would say you have a responsibility to them to make the most of your better chances.

Responsibilities are really important because they are how we behave towards ourselves, others and the world. If we do not take responsibilities seriously, why should we have any rights? For example, I might believe I have the right to free speech – as does everyone. This means if I think I can say anything I want, then so can everyone else – including abuse, lies and worse. So, my right to free speech means I also have a responsibility to use language fairly, kindly and truthfully. This means I think before I speak so as to not make problems or make things worse. It is by taking responsibilities seriously that we protect people's rights.

11 Rights and responsibilities

▶ Whose rights and whose responsibilities?

Read each of the statements below and for each one identify the rights and the responsibilities that are involved.

> I live in this country as a refugee after coming from the one I was born in. There is a civil war there, which destroyed my home and most of my town. Many of my friends and relatives have died. I was lucky enough to be able to pay someone to get me and my family out of there to come here. The Government are assessing my claim to stay, but at least we have food, shelter and medical care, and my child can attend school.

> My dad took my computer games off me for a month. He had told me to clean my room, and look after my little brother while he was out. I left my brother with his mate – they are both 11 – and went to the shop. There I met my mates, and then didn't get home until after 11 pm. So I was in trouble for not cleaning my room, and for not looking after my brother, and for disobeying dad. He said I was not being responsible enough.

> I believe humans have the right to do as they wish in the world. We live here, and have the intelligence to change things as we wish and make our lives better. We can use the planet – its resources and animals – for our needs because of our status. So I agree with hunting, mining and exploration to find new things for us to use.

> I do what I can not to be a burden on the world. I buy only what I need; I am careful to recycle and reuse; I grow some of the food I need; I do not eat meat; I cycle or take the bus or walk to get to where I need to go; I do not use planes. My carbon footprint is lower than zero. Although I live simply, I feel very content with my life.

▶ Are rights more important than responsibilities?

The idea of rights helps us to realise the responsibilities we have. For example, we all have the right to be treated fairly and in the same way; our Government is responsible for protecting us against discrimination and passes laws to do this.

Taking our responsibilities seriously is what makes everything fair, or at least fairer than it might be. If we just say what our rights are, but do not work hard to make sure those rights are protected (if we ignore our responsibilities), then the rights would just be words, nothing else. For example, if I believe that we have a right to keep the things we have, but then ignore someone who I see stealing something, then there is no point to the belief.

Sometimes, our responsibilities mean that others lose their rights. This may be to keep someone safe or to ensure that society works fairly. For example, I might lose my right to leave school at the end of the school day and have to do a detention, because the teacher is responsible for punishing those who disrupt learning.

Activities

1. What are rights? Give an example.
2. What are responsibilities? Give an example.
3. Using examples, show how rights and responsibilities are both important.
4. Do you think there are times where a person should lose (some of) their rights? Explain your ideas.

Values and ethics

11.3 Religion and human rights

Learning objectives
- To learn about the difference between religious belief and human rights
- To explore reasons why human rights can be broader than religious belief
- To reflect on whether religions should adapt to human rights

Big question
Is anything more important than human rights?

In the Western world, human rights developed around the idea of individual freedom; in the developing world, human rights were often ways in which poorer people gained freedom. Many sociologists would say that everywhere in the world human rights have helped to bring freedom to people who are poor or underprivileged, whereas the rich have always had their human rights. Human rights are very important in an unequal world, because they help to protect people.

Human rights are not absolute, though. A government has the right to limit people's rights, for example, if it is wartime, during a pandemic, or if someone is found guilty of a crime. Rights rely on people respecting each other – so that at an everyday level, our rights are supported by the people we know and the rest of the community.

A person's right to follow a religion and to express their beliefs is protected by the UDHR. However, do religions respect all the other rights in the UDHR for their believers?

Religions share the principles of the UDHR. They believe all humans are equal, and should be shown respect. Respect is fundamental to the UDHR, because it is behind every one of the rights in the UDHR.	Human rights give the right to some things which religions might not agree with – things that are against their beliefs. For example, there is a right to marry and have children. Some religious believers would say that is only true for opposite-sex couples; the UDHR is interpreted to include same-sex couples.
Religions all tell their followers they should obey the laws of the country they live in. Where governments put human rights into law, religious believers are supporting human rights. In some countries, where there are human rights issues, religious believers still support human rights.	Human rights are rights because we are human, and the rights are fair. If every country enforced human rights, equality and justice would be the norm. Religions give rights because they believe God has given life and made it special, or because being reincarnated as a human is special. This is seen by some believers as having greater importance.
Most religions believe God gave humans their intelligence and the ability to reason. As God is just, so humans try to copy God. The UDHR was written by humans, so the principles must be in tune with religious belief and law.	Some religious people might say that some human rights are being interpreted too freely. They say that humans can be selfish, and do lose sight of God's laws, which makes them give rights where they should not.

11 Rights and responsibilities

▶ Being a religious citizen

Most people in the UK are British citizens (legally recognised members of the country). Some people have special papers allowing them to stay in the country, either temporarily or permanently. Some people have applied for citizenship because they claim refugee status or asylum. This means there are dangers for them if they go back to their own country – either because of the situation in the country, such as civil war, or for them personally, for example because their political views have made them a target of the rulers.

Being a citizen brings many rights within the country. It also brings responsibilities to be aware of and rules to respect.

Anyone who is a citizen can also be a religious believer. Religious believers follow the rules of the country because their religion tells them to. Generally speaking, British law is based on religious law. Both are based on respect, so the religions would agree with the laws as they are based around respect. However, what happens if the laws and the religion clash, which they sometimes do? Read the examples below.

> My father died suddenly. The doctors want to do a post-mortem. In my religion, we should not desecrate (damage) a body and should bury it whole. The post-mortem goes against both of those beliefs. Should we agree to the post-mortem, or fight it?

▲ Grace

> My great-grandfather was a Quaker and when the Second World War started, he was called up to fight. Quakers are pacifists – they don't believe in violence. The draft papers said he had to join the army – in wartime, of course, a soldier has to fight. What do you think he did?

▲ David

> I am a Sikh. My headmaster says my turban breaks school uniform rules. A turban is part of my identity as a Sikh, and it is my religious duty to wear it. I have not been to school since I have been banned from wearing my turban. I use the internet and books to help me study and keep up with my subjects. What should I do?

▲ Desi

Activities

1. Why are human rights important?
2. Why might religion and the law clash?
3. Explain why some people say that religious beliefs and teachings protect human rights, and why others say they don't.
4. 'Human rights are more important than religious rights.' Do you agree? Explain the reasons for your answer.

Grace's family did not give permission, but the law can take that right away. Her father's body was subjected to a post-mortem exam before being released to the family for burial.

David's great-grandfather claimed his right to be a conscientious objector (someone who refuses to join the armed forces for moral or religious reasons). He was given a job in the UK for the war effort at home, but was subjected to persecution and abuse, and was called a traitor.

Desi's case went to court and the House of Lords. It was ruled that, for Sikhs, wearing a turban is a religious duty, and schools have to respect that religious right. He went back to school and wore his turban as per his religious duty.

169

Values and ethics

11.4 Social justice

Learning objectives
- To understand the concept of social justice
- To explore why social justice is important in Wales today
- To reflect on the importance of social reformers in Welsh history

Big question
Is Wales a fair society?

Justice is fairness. Social justice is a term used to describe initiatives and programmes to make society fairer, especially for the most vulnerable and poorest in our society; it brings greater fairness to society. If you think about the society you live in, there are lots of examples of inequality. Social justice covers all the initiatives (new ways of doing things) and laws that try to make society fairer.

There are four aspects to social justice in the UK today:

- human rights – everybody has the same rights, and those rights are protected
- access – everyone gets the same opportunities
- participation – everyone has a voice in society, and their voice is listened to
- equity – everyone is given the help they need to be on the same level.

Social justice, then, is about making sure everyone's human rights are respected and protected. It is also about taking away barriers that prevent a person from enjoying those rights. At times, this means giving them something others do not get (the benefits system is a good example of this). Social reformers are people who make change happen in society to bring greater social justice. Some make changes happen in their local area; others ensure laws change so everyone is affected; still others set up initiatives that go worldwide. Here are three Welsh examples of social reformers.

▶ Some Welsh social reformers

Robert Owen (1771–1858)

Born in Newtown, Powys, Robert Owen spent most of his working life outside Wales (in Manchester, London, Scotland and the USA). However, his ideas and the way he ran his businesses was revolutionary for its day, and paved the way for much social reform.

▲ Robert Owen's grave in Newtown, Powys

Owen's factories ran on the principle that the workers were as important as the equipment, if not more so, which was the opposite of the norms of the day. This meant he gave his workers many rights. For example, at the time, it was normal to employ children from workhouses from the age of five to work fifteen-hour shifts. He employed only from the age of ten, reduced the length of their shifts, banned corporal (physical) punishment and set up an infant school. As a result of better working conditions, his workers were happier and more productive. His ideas also led to change in the laws of the UK.

Owen's shops followed principles which later became the basis of the co-operative movement, which is now a worldwide movement. First, he bought in bulk so that the price was lower. Then, he sold at a price that gave a low profit – so that people got cheaper goods, making his shop popular. People could afford more, making life easier.

Owen's ideas spread through society, and became a movement for social change everywhere. When he died, he was a member of the Spiritualist Church. He is buried in Newtown, Powys.

11 Rights and responsibilities

Betty Campbell (1934–2017)

Betty Campbell was born in Tiger Bay, Cardiff; her father was killed serving in the Second World War. She won a scholarship to St Margaret's Girls' High School at 11. In spite of excelling in her studies, she was often told she would never succeed, which made her more determined and was a source of motivation for her.

In 1960, Cardiff Teacher Training College admitted women for the first time to train to be teachers; Betty was one of them. After beginning her teaching career in Llanrumney, she returned to Mount Stuart Primary School in Butetown, Cardiff, where she taught for 28 years, becoming head teacher. In the 1970s, she began teaching about black history, slavery and apartheid. She believed it important that young people understood their culture, neighbours and community, and the impact historic injustices had had on the status and development of communities. She taught children to be proud of their heritage. Her school became known across the UK for its excellence on multicultural education. She also taught workshops in Cardiff, showing the contribution that different communities had made, for example when fighting in the World Wars. From her work, Black History Month was born. She also became a member of the Committee for Racial Equality.

Betty became a member of Cardiff Council, speaking and fighting for her community. In 2021, Cardiff Council erected a statue in Betty's memory. She is an inspiration – working class, black, female, she showed that we can overcome barriers and prejudices to make real our dreams, that we are in control of our future. As a passionate advocate for black culture, she championed multiculturalism in Wales.

Aneurin Bevan (1897–1960)

Aneurin ('Nye') Bevan was born in Tredegar in 1897. Following in his father and grandfather's footsteps, he became a miner after leaving school at thirteen. Six years later, Nye had become a union activist, fighting for the miners rights, particularly to change unsafe mining practices. In 1926, Britain was hit by general strikes – Nye was at the forefront of these protests, becoming widely known, and stepping into politics as a local counsellor in Monmouthshire. In 1929, he was elected MP for Ebbw Vale, though often found himself at loggerheads with his own party leadership as well as the opposition.

After the Second World War, Bevan became part of the Government. He oversaw the building of over a million new homes as part of the rebuilding of Britain. His most important contribution came in the form of the National Health Service. He believed that 'no society can legitimately call itself civilised if a sick person is denied medical aid because of lack of means'. Healthcare in the UK at the time was very mixed and localised; his vision was for a free service, which was publicly funded and Government-led. This he set up, and it continues to be part of British identity today, remaining the 'envy of the world'.

Bevan was a lifelong atheist and humanist who believed passionately in making things better for ordinary people. He believed in the dignity of all, and that human rights were everyone's rights, not just those with money. Through his union work, which improved rights and working conditions for miners, and his NHS, he put those beliefs into reality.

Activities

1. What is social justice?
2. Describe the work of these three Welsh social reformers.
3. Explain how the work of each of these three social reformers might have had an effect in Wales.
4. In your opinion, which of the three made the biggest contribution to social justice? Explain your ideas.

Values and ethics

11.5 Attitudes to poverty

Learning objectives
- To understand that poverty exists everywhere, and is a form of social injustice
- To explore some attitudes to efforts to overcome poverty
- To reflect on whether social justice is just about poverty

Big question
What does social justice make a society look like?

Human society might never be equal. However, society can be much fairer for all than it is. Many laws have been passed in the UK to try to make society more fair. The Government set up the benefits system to help those who could not find employment so that they could still afford the basic rights. The NHS is a healthcare system for all, which enables any person to get appropriate free medical treatment for any and every ailment. Equality laws protect us against unfair discrimination.

Historically, those with wealth have been able to enjoy the full range of human rights, whereas those who are poor or vulnerable have been most affected by **social injustice** and a lack of rights. For example, poor people being forced to do jobs which paid very little or were dangerous.

Key terms

Absolute poverty line – a figure set by the World Bank; currently $1.90 (about £1.40) a day as minimum needed to live on (set in 2011, but still used); about 9.5 per cent of the world population or over 700 million people have less money than this to live on every day

Poverty – lack of the basic essentials for living, relative to the society we live in

Social injustice – a situation where society is uneven, with some members affected by lack of wealth, opportunities and privileges

Absolute and relative

Although there is an **absolute level of poverty** that applies around the world (currently set at living on the equivalent of $1.90 or £1.40 a day or less), poverty is also relative. That means that people in the UK with a lot more than £1.40 a day to live on are still poor because they cannot afford the activities and possessions that most people in the country can afford. For example, a family in the UK might have a home and even be in work, but earn very little; whereas a family in a developing country might have a rough shelter, no water or electricity, and work in the fields for many hours each day. Both cases count as **poverty**.

There are lots of causes of poverty. In the UK, poverty often comes from having no job, or a very low paid one. But the UK does have a welfare system which helps people to find work, and provides some support for them while they are looking. In a developing country, the country itself is poor, and its facilities are not good everywhere, which means most people are also poor. If a person has to walk miles for water, only sometimes has electricity, has no help from the government when they have no money, then they will have a difficult life. Some of the things we, in the UK, take for granted are luxuries elsewhere – we were lucky to be born in such a country.

Activities

Each of these examples counts as poverty. Can you work out why?
1. A family of four who live in a one-room shack without running water or electricity. They have a field on which to grow crops, which give them most of what they need to eat.
2. A homeless person in the UK who sells *The Big Issue*.
3. A family in the UK who depend on Universal Credit.
4. A family in a small village whose income is only £300 per year, while the national average is £3,500.

11 Rights and responsibilities

In an unequal world, how can we make things better for more people? How can we share our good fortune? What could individuals in the UK do to make life better for some of those in developing countries?

▶ Religion and poverty

Many religious people live in poverty, and many religious people give money and time to help those in poverty. CAFOD (the Catholic Agency for Overseas Development), Khalsa Aid, Muslim Relief and Sewa International are all religion-based aid agencies working across the world in places of poverty and in disaster relief. Although they are religious organisations, they do not just focus their help on people of their own religion – they help anyone in need in the area a project is based. In disaster relief, the criteria is only that people need help, and they can provide it.

Religious people believe in the sanctity of human life – that every life is special and should be protected. They believe in the importance of service to others, as a way to show their devotion to God. For example, Sikhism is a religion that is based on service to God and humanity with the aim of bringing about justice. Religious people also believe in good moral actions, like helping those in need. For example, Jesus gave the Parable of the Good Samaritan (Luke 10:25–37) in which a man helps another simply because he needs help – even though their two nations were enemies of each other. The moral codes of all religions can be summarised by the Golden Rule (see page 162) – treat others as you wish to be treated.

So, you could say that religious people should help others because it is a way to help people who share the same beliefs … or that they should help anyone in need regardless of belief because of their own beliefs and teachings about compassion and the sanctity of all life. In any case, religious people are doing exactly that, and trying to bring greater social justice across the world.

Find out for yourself

Research a religiously motivated project which helps to bring greater social justice. Write up your research as a report. As a class, compare these reports to decide which ones are having most impact.

> 'Education is the most powerful weapon which you can use to change the world' – that is what Nelson Mandela said. I work for an aid agency which funds schools and education for women and their children in poorer parts of the world.
>
> — Rahila

> I always try to buy Fairtrade items. This way I know that the farmers who grew those things get a decent amount of money for their efforts and they aren't exploited. Supermarkets stock lots of these now, so it isn't difficult.
>
> — Amarnadh

> I sponsor a child in Bangladesh. The charity is also paying for the school's upkeep and for teachers. It also pays for local women to get training in accountancy and handicrafts so they can set up businesses and sell goods, bringing in money for their families.
>
> — Chiminanda

> I went out to a very remote part of an African country as a volunteer. I trained nurses to improve the level of healthcare in the area – more nurses with better training. My organisation also funded equipment and medicines as part of the project, so infant mortality has been reduced.
>
> — Theodore

Activities

1. What is poverty?
2. Why is it true to say that people in every country live in poverty?
3. Why do religions work to overcome social injustice?
4. Give some ways in which religious believers work to overcome social injustice.
5. Is there more to social injustice than poverty? Explain your ideas.

12 Diversity and tolerance

12.1 Humanity

Learning objectives
- To understand religious and non-religious attitudes to diversity
- To understand the concepts of dignity of life and sanctity of life
- To reflect on the idea of one world, one humanity

Talk it out
Why is life special?
Are there any situations in which humans do things that suggest life is not special?

Big question
Is life special?

▶ Beliefs about humanity

Humanity is a single race – one equal but diverse family – which should be united in one global society. – Bahá'í	Humans are very special – they are the only form of life which can attain enlightenment. – Buddhism	God created human beings in God's image, the highest part of creation. – Christianity	Brahman (God) is all. Nothing exists which does not come from Brahman and which does not have Brahman within. – Hinduism.
The welfare and happiness of humans must be at the centre of all ethical decision-making. – Humanism	God created all humans; they are different cultures and races because that was God's will, and they should co-operate with each other. – Islam	On the sixth day of creation, God created humans in His image, and gave them stewardship over the world. – Judaism	There is only one breath; all are made from the same clay; the light within all is the same. – Sikhism

These teachings and beliefs make it clear that humans – from every religion and none – believe that humans are special, and have evolved many extraordinary capacities that make us stand out from the rest of the animal kingdom. Linked to this is the idea of stewardship – that humans have to care for the world and all life. There are many reasons for this, including:

- God gave this duty to humans.
- Looking after the world is part of worshipping God.
- Humans live here as will their descendants – so it is important to protect it.
- It makes sense to look after the world since we live in it.

Our own experience and the stories that we see on the news also suggest that humans do not always behave as if they believe any of these things. *Can you think of some examples?*

12 Diversity and tolerance

▶ Sanctity of life

The sanctity of life refers to the belief that life is very special, or sacred, and that human life is the highest level of development in spiritual and intellectual terms. This belief comes from one or more of several ideas, for example:

- the idea of being a special creation by God
- the idea that to be reincarnated as a human is very rare so very special
- the idea that humans are the only rational beings and so hold a privileged position amongst all other species
- humans – because of their ego – see themselves as separate to the rest of nature, and above it.

Therefore, life should be cared for and protected.

This belief applies to all human life – regardless of age, gender, race, ability, status or sexuality. There is no hierarchy. Therefore, all people are equal in value and worth.

▶ Dignity of life

The dignity of life refers to the right of a person to be valued and respected for their own sake, so that they are treated fairly. If we believe that life is special and there is sanctity to life, then it follows that we should also believe there is dignity to life, and should treat people appropriately.

If a person treats someone else as less than themselves, then they are denying the dignity of that person. They are breaking the Golden Rule.

Many people say that humans are one big family. All humans are related in some way because of a common ancestry – they share the same ancestors. Many religions say that those ancestors were the first humans which God created. Science shows the genetic links between peoples – their common ancestry. This idea of all being part of one 'family' means that humans should show respect for each other, as if they are related. Most people treat their relatives well, showing them care and consideration. Imagine a world in which everyone was treated in this way.

Activities

1. Explain why human life is considered very special. Use beliefs and teachings from different sources to support your answer.
2. Explain what is meant by 'sanctity of life' and 'dignity of life'.
3. Design a poster that expresses the ideas on this page in words and pictures.
4. 'Dignity of life is more important than sanctity of life.' Give two reasons for agreeing and two for disagreeing with this statement, before writing a justified conclusion.

Values and ethics

12.2 Prejudice and discrimination

Learning objectives
- To explore forms of prejudice and discrimination
- To explore how and why people discriminate against others
- To reflect on this issue in modern society

Big question
How can we bring an end to unfair discrimination in society?

Prejudice is thinking badly of someone because of something about them. You do not have to get to know someone in order to be prejudiced against them. There are many different kinds of prejudice:

- racism – against those of a different race or skin colour
- sexism – against those of a specific gender
- ageism – against someone because of their age
- homophobia – against those perceived to be gay.

There is also prejudice against those with a disability or those from a different religion such as antisemitism or Islamophobia. The victims of prejudice are almost always in the minority; they are judged to be different in some way.

Key terms
Prejudice – prejudging someone, usually negatively; thinking badly of someone because of some characteristic they have

Discrimination – acting on prejudice, either in words or actions

Antisemitism – prejudice against Jewish people

Islamophobia – prejudice against Muslims

Activities
Read these headlines. What kind of prejudice is shown in each one?

> Women should stay at home and keep house, not go out to work

> Young people these days want paying for nothing

> Gravestones smashed and daubed with paint in hate-filled rampage

> Teenager murdered because of the colour of his skin

It is hard to end prejudice because it is what people think. No one can read or police people's minds! **Joel**

History shows us that when prejudice and power combine, ordinary people suffer terribly. **Jess**

We have to fight prejudice through education, otherwise we let discrimination happen. **Saira**

Anybody can be a victim of prejudice – I wear glasses so get called names. It just needs people to let it happen and not challenge it. **Amad**

12 Diversity and tolerance

▶ Why are people prejudiced?

Prejudice can be like a brick wall – a barrier that stops people living, working and learning together as a community.

There are five main reasons why prejudice occurs:

1. Having a bad experience with someone might make you think everybody is like that. For example, if you were frightened by a grumpy old man when you were young, you may now think all old men are grumpy, and therefore be prejudiced against all old men.
2. Being told bad things about a certain group of people by your parents or carers might make you prejudiced. Our upbringing has a big influence on us, and what we are told when we are young has a huge effect on us.
3. Having seen something in the media might make you prejudiced. You might believe something that you have seen on television or read it in a newspaper (or other form of media) that was very biased (focusing on only one fact or idea or taking it out of context).
4. Ignorance can be a reason for prejudice. If you judge someone when you actually know nothing about them or have a negative opinion about a group of people, whom you have never met or actually learned anything about, this is based on ignorance.
5. Scapegoating is when someone or a group is blamed for or used as an excuse for a problem. For example, you hang around with some friends, and one of them steals from a local shop. The owner decides everyone in the group is bad, so bans you all – even though you personally did nothing wrong, and even tried to stop the one who was guilty from stealing. The owner has scapegoated you all, and now has a prejudice against you.

▶ How do people discriminate?

Discrimination is the action taken as a result of prejudice. People may discriminate indirectly or directly.

Indirect discrimination may involve ignoring someone or what is happening to them, or making things difficult through other people; for example, by blocking appointments, influencing others, and so on.

Direct discrimination may involve using words or threats, excluding someone or being violent toward them. The extreme is to take someone's life. There are examples of governments passing laws that encourage and support discriminatory behaviour, an extreme example of this being the Nazi Government and the Holocaust.

Sociologists have drawn up the 'pyramid of hate' which shows levels of discrimination, from having a biased attitude towards someone or a group, to individual acts of prejudice, to government-supported discrimination, to direct and open violence, and finally to genocide, where the intention is to kill everyone in that group. You could find out more about the pyramid of hate for yourself.

Activities

1. Using examples, explain what is meant by prejudice and discrimination.
2. Using examples, explain why some people are prejudiced.
3. In what ways might people discriminate against others?
4. Which is worse: prejudice or discrimination? Give reasons for each, and give a justified conclusion.

Values and ethics

12.3 Religious attitudes to prejudice and discrimination

Learning objectives
- To learn some religious attitudes to prejudice
- To learn some religious attitudes to discrimination
- To reflect on whether religious people are more or less likely to be prejudiced than anyone else

Big question
Does what a person believes affect how they think of others?

The major religions around the world teach that all humans are equal (see Topic 12.1 Humanity, page 174). All humans are obviously different, and have different opportunities and live in different circumstances, but they are all of equal worth according to religion.

Most religions would see prejudice as a character flaw, something to be changed in ourselves. Some religions even see it as an insult to God, because of the belief that God created all people; by being prejudiced we imply something is wrong with God's creation. We can say that religions believe prejudice to be wrong.

Discriminating is acting on prejudiced ideas. As discrimination is usually negative (seeing someone as less than ourselves), then discrimination is hurtful. All religions teach that it is wrong to hurt someone else.

▶ Christian attitudes to prejudice and discrimination

> I'm Ben. I'm a pastor at an evangelical church. Christians believe that every single person was created by God and in God's image. It doesn't matter what they look like, how rich or poor, or even their character – Genesis tells us God made all, Jesus told us God loves all. This means there is no room for prejudice against people if you are a Christian.

Believing those things also means that Christians have to see discrimination as wrong – Jesus told us to 'Love thy neighbour'. He even told a story about it. The Parable of the Good Samaritan is about someone who helped someone else, and even went beyond what he needed to do. At the time of Jesus, the Israelites and the Samaritans hated each other. An Israelite is beaten up, has all his possessions stolen and is left for dead. People from his own country – one of them a priest – walk on by, even though they have seen him. Then a Samaritan arrives and straightaway, without thinking of his own safety, goes to help the man. He takes him to an inn and pays for him to be looked after until he's well, promising to pay any outstanding bills on his return. The two were enemies, but the Samaritan helped – and went beyond what he had to do. Of course, we learn from this that we should help people, but much more importantly, we learn that difference does not matter to God, so it should not matter to us.

The simplest teaching is: treat others as you wish to be treated. You don't want to be hurt by others – by word or action – so you shouldn't hurt anyone else. Hurting others because of discrimination goes against the idea of creation itself.

12 Diversity and tolerance

Activities

Look at the different people from our society in this artwork. They might all face discrimination. What kind of discrimination might each of them face?

How might a religious person explain why that discrimination is wrong?

> I'm a humanist. Virginia Woolfe said, 'My country is the world'. This means seeing all people as people first, not as their race, gender, age etc. first. Everyone is different and individual, but we should learn about and celebrate those differences. We all have shared needs and values – by seeing everyone as people first, we will treat others more fairly and equally.

▶ Do religious people discriminate against others?

Some people would say religious people do discriminate against others. A common criticism is that religious people show prejudice against people of other religions to their own, and those of none. Also that not all religious people accept other people's lifestyles. Some in the LGBTQ+ community feels that some Christians discriminate against them because these Christians think that their sexuality is a choice, and this choice is against God's wishes. LGBTQ+ people would say they had no choice – it is just who they are (some might say they were made this way by God). Having said that, Christians such as Quakers and the Metropolitan Community Church welcome the LGBTQ+ community. Even if some members of the Christian faith disagree with anything other than heterosexual marriage and sex, they still do not believe it is right to discriminate against others. Those who openly disagree and do discriminate are in the minority.

Others might point to the past, to the role that some rich, white Christians played in the Industrial Revolution – giving few or no rights to workers, employing children in terrible conditions for very low pay, and often building chapels with their profits so as to 'please God'. Indeed, there are many monuments, street names and memorial plaques in the UK to men who considered themselves good Christians, but still earned their wealth from these practices. We would consider that discrimination now, but it was a norm for its time.

Religious people are ordinary people, like you are – all of us can sadly become prejudiced for many reasons, and might act on those prejudices. Part of the point of following a religion is to improve oneself and to evolve spiritually, so as to recognise problems like prejudices within oneself, and stop it. Beliefs and teachings certainly don't tell people to discriminate.

Activities

1 What do religions teach about equality?
2 Explain Christian attitudes to prejudice and discrimination.
3 Retell the story of the Good Samaritan (Luke 10:25–37).
4 Do you think religious believers are more likely to discriminate against others? Explain your reasons carefully.

Values and ethics

12.4 Religious responses to prejudice and discrimination

Learning objectives
- To explore religious responses to prejudice and discrimination
- To explore an organisation that supports victims of discrimination in Wales
- To reflect on whether society does enough for victims of discrimination

Big question

Which is more important: ending discrimination or helping victims of discrimination?

Religious believers see all people as equal, and do not agree with discrimination (see Topic 12.3 pages 178–9) but most religions also teach that it is not enough just to believe something or to say something is wrong. A believer has to show their beliefs through their actions. Here are four religious believers' answers to the question: What are you doing about discrimination?

> I am a Buddhist. Discrimination is not in keeping with the Noble Eightfold Path. I go into schools to give talks about Buddhism and Buddhist values. Sometimes I go with my teacher who is a Tibetan monk. He dresses very differently from what young people see every day. We are trying to educate young people not just about Buddhism, but also that people are different, and that that is okay – not something to be feared or ridiculed.

> At our mosque, we have had lots of newcomers. Many are refugees from Afghanistan, fleeing from the discrimination they expect to receive from the Taliban. They face many difficulties and much discrimination as they start new lives. We have put welcome food packs and clothing bundles together, arranged places for them to stay and furnishings for them, and set up a translation service. We are also hosting meetings for them to learn about life in Wales.

> As Bahá'í, I accept everyone – we are all one universal, diverse family. In my dealings with everyone, I try to be calm, friendly, compassionate and helpful. Abdu'l-Bahá said that there is 'only one race', and told us to 'make everyone as friends'. If I see someone who is suffering because of discrimination, I see what I can do to help. It might be just listening to them, or doing something for them, even helping them report to the police. Part of friendship is caring enough to be there and help.

> I am a Sikh, and a barrister by profession. To do service for others (sewa), I give part of my time for free and support victims of discrimination in pursuing their case in court. I also give legal advice to organisations like SARI (Stand Against Racism and Inequality). There are many victims of discrimination who need help, which is a separate matter from ending discrimination fully.

Activities
1. What are these believers doing to help victims of discrimination?
2. What are they doing to end discrimination?
3. How important is each action?
4. With a partner, work out some things you can do to tackle discriminatory behaviour and to support the victims of such behaviour.

12 Diversity and tolerance

▶ Inclusion not exclusion – the Salvation Army

Founded in East London in 1865 by William Booth, a Methodist minister, the Salvation Army is now a worldwide organisation, serving in over 130 countries, with 35 churches in Wales, as well as shops, cafés and drop-in centres. The Salvation Army began when William and his wife Catherine decided to take the Gospel to people, instead of waiting for them to come to church. Their work has been called 'soup, soap and salvation'. They worked among the most vulnerable and marginalised people of society – those who were discriminated against by society in general, suffering from homelessness, addiction, loneliness and unemployment. They set up soup kitchens and shelters for the homeless, and found homes for those fleeing from domestic abuse. They campaigned for improvements in working conditions.

The Salvation Army's principles are based on inclusion. Discrimination is an act of exclusion – because it denies the right to the same treatment or conditions that everyone else enjoys. By being inclusive, they show that discrimination is wrong: a role model for society.

The Salvation Army's wider community work

Apart from ministry (religious work) and worship, the Salvation Army also provides many services to their local communities. Every Salvation Army church has links for:

- young people – youth clubs, fitness sessions, sports teams, leadership training, activism and mentoring
- families – crèches, foodbanks, family support
- the homeless – shelters, soup kitchens, Christmas meals, drop-ins, work in the community with the vulnerable, addiction services, life houses (homes that help the homeless to rebuild their lives)
- older people – community activities, meals, advice, care homes.

They also work with prisoners, both in prison and after release, and run lunch clubs, employment advice sessions, and much more.

Through all these things, they share their message of love for all, and the equality of all. Part of the mission is to seek ways to confront and fight racism and other forms of discrimination wherever they are found. These services give people support, making them less vulnerable to discrimination, and a place to turn if they do experience it.

> The Salvation Army's first church in Wales began in November 1874 in Butetown at the People's Hall.
>
> The Salvation Army is active in over 80 Welsh communities, covering the whole of Wales.

Activities

1. In what ways might a religious believer help those who are being discriminated against?
2. Do you think that some people are in a better position to fight discrimination than others? Explain your reasons.
3. Using the Salvation Army as an example, explain how communities that are inclusive can help fight discrimination.
4. Is discrimination the biggest issue in Welsh society today? Explain the reasons for your answer.

Find out for yourself

Find out if there is a Salvation Army corps in your town or nearby. Research what they do, especially how they help those in need.

Values and ethics

12.5 Discrimination as a religious issue

> **Learning objectives**
> - To explore examples of how religious people face prejudice because of their beliefs
> - To consider how religious believers support other religious believers in the face of discrimination
> - To reflect on whether being religious attracts discrimination

> **Big question**
> Should people hide their religious beliefs?

> **Talk it out**
> Is Wales a society that is tolerant to religion generally?
>
> What about your part of Wales? How are people treated if they are open about their beliefs?
>
> Do you know any examples, locally or nationally, of discrimination against religious people?

You have probably heard people say that the world is getting smaller. This means it is easier to travel to places almost anywhere in the world. It also means we get to see different cultures more easily, through travel, the media and migration. Turn the clock back 200 years in Wales, and practically everyone you met would have been some kind of Christian; today, go to the cities and you will meet Muslims, Hindus, Sikhs, Baháʼís, Buddhists, druids, spiritualists and many other people of faith or spirituality. This book uses examples from Welsh temples, churches, mosques, synagogues, gurdwaras and so on: Wales is a mosaic of religion!

Take a look at these real examples of things that have taken place. Do they show a society that is tolerant of religion?

- Jewish graves in a council cemetery were vandalised, stones were broken and Nazi symbols were graffitied on them.
- A secondary school renamed its Christmas holiday 'winter break' so as to not offend non-Christians. It did not, however, introduce holidays for all for Eid.
- A nurse was suspended from her hospital job because, as a Christian, she offered to pray for a patient in her care.
- A check-in desk worker at an airport was banned from wearing a cross on a necklace at work in case it offended non-Christians.
- A Muslim woman in a supermarket received loud verbal abuse from a man. When eventually he was escorted out, he waited for her outside to do the same again.

In the news, there are many examples of people being harassed, ridiculed, even assaulted because of their religion. The UK is like many Western countries: it seems more guided by science and less by religion, which can make religion and religious believers an easy target. Also, people link situations they see in other countries with a particular religion. Some scapegoat people of that religion who are living in the UK for what is happening elsewhere, and so discriminate against them. While those who carry out the violence might have some kind of religious beliefs, it does not mean that the vast majority of their fellow believers agree with them or what they do. A good example of this was seen after terrorist attacks in France – hundreds of Muslims went to the Senedd building in Cardiff and stood in silence. Many held 'Not in my name' placards, showing their condemnation of what a tiny number of Muslim extremists had done.

12 Diversity and tolerance

▶ Freedom of religious expression

In Wales today, the right to religious freedom is protected. Equality laws make persecution because of religion illegal. These laws are based on Article 9 of the Universal Declaration of Human Rights (UDHR), which states: 'Everyone has the right to freedom of thought, conscience and religion'. The right includes the freedom to:

- change religion if you want to – no one can force you to follow or leave a religion
- worship in private or in public
- carry out the rituals of a religion
- live daily life in keeping with the religion's beliefs and practices.

It also says that you have the right to express your religion as long as what you do does not break the law, or affect others negatively. The article also covers religious and non-religious beliefs, so humanists and atheists are both protected in their beliefs as well.

Activities

Read these statements. Is each person's right to freedom of religious expression being respected?

> My headteacher wouldn't let me wear a ring I was given for my Confirmation ceremony at church. Bailie

> A gang stood outside our place of worship blocking the entrance. No one could get in to join the service. Struan

> I'm a Sikh, but a man crossed the road and punched me. He shouted that I was a Muslim terrorist and deserved it. Paramjit

> I have renounced the religion I was brought up in, and decided I will follow a humanist way of thinking and life. My parents don't agree with my choice, so are not supportive. Omar

Activities

1. Why can Wales be called a 'mosaic of religion'?
2. Give some examples of how society can be less tolerant of religion.
3. What does the UDHR say about the right to religious belief?
4. Do you agree with religious belief being a human right? Explain your reasons.

Bailie – Christians do not have a duty regarding the wearing of any religious items, so wearing the ring is a choice. The headteacher was not breaching (breaking) the article.

Struan – They are being prevented from worshipping, which clearly breaches the right.

Paramjit – This was not only breaching the right; it broke the law. It doesn't matter that the perpetrator targeted a Sikh rather than a Muslim, it is still an attack on someone because of their religion, so the right has been breached.

Omar – He has the right to change his beliefs. His parents might be being difficult, but they are not trying to stop him, so they are not breaching the right.

13 The natural world

13.1 The creation

Learning objectives
- To explore the Genesis creation story
- To understand how creation stories are viewed by believers
- To reflect on the importance of religious creation stories

Big question
How did the universe begin?

Humans like to know about things – it is part of what makes us human and separates us from animals. Where everything came from is a mystery to us, because we do not have a video of the event, or any full evidence in scientific terms. However, it is something humans want to know: how did all this begin?

Some people think that we do have an explanation for how it all began; in fact, most religions have a written description in their holy scriptures. These descriptions almost always start with God, and a creation story. We will look at one of these.

▶ The Genesis creation story

This is the story for Christians and Jewish people. Genesis is the name for the first book of these scriptures; it means 'beginning'.

At first, there was nothing. Only God.

God decided to create the world, making new parts of it with each new day.

On day one, God created light. God separated the light from the dark, so there was day and night.

On day two, God created the heavens.

On day three, God collected the water together to create the seas and reveal land. God also made plants of every kind to grow everywhere.

On day four, God created the sun, moon and stars, giving lights for the day and the night, as well as to mark the seasons.

On day five, God created the fish and the birds.

On day six, God created animals, then humans. God created the humans in God's image.

On day seven, God looked at all of the creation, felt pleased, and decided the job was done. God rested.

13 The natural world

▶ Discussing Genesis

Three friends are talking about the Genesis creation story. Each has a different idea about it. The proper names for their ideas are in the box below their conversation – see if you can identify who fits each.

Bron: To me, I think this is right. I believe the prophets were told by God. God can do anything.

Ceri: Well, I can understand the story. It does more or less make sense. But I think people wrote it so long ago, they could only use the language they had then – they didn't have the science we have. I think it is a human version of what God told them – and we make mistakes.

Gwyn: I agree it makes sense. It matches the science order of things really. You know, world was a hot soupy kind of place which cooled to reveal land and seas. Insects that swam and flew were the first living things. Humans were last in the development of species. It does all fit.

Bron: So, you believe God did it?

Gwyn: I think science is humans working out how God's world works. But I think the creation story is saying God is responsible for everything there is, life and everything.

Ceri: I still think that Genesis is a version of the truth; just one that got twisted a bit in the retelling and time. We have to reinterpret some things. So, a day is a God day, not a human day. When it says 'fish', it means any water creatures, 'birds' are anything that can fly and so on.

Bron: My cousin, Win, says that Genesis can't be trusted – it's story. She says science is right as it is more reasonable, and there is actually evidence to it, not just some story someone made up. I think the Bible is the evidence. Also I like the idea that God made the world deliberately and made me deliberately.

Many Christians understand Genesis as giving key messages about God and the world: it is a good world, God loves us, we have to look after this creation which was shaped for us. This view is allegorical.

Many Christians have progressive views. They believe in Genesis, but realise that humans have affected the wording, so might have got some things wrong, but it is enough to retain their belief in God.

A small number of Christians have fundamentalist views. They believe Genesis describes exactly how the world came to be, because they believe in an all-powerful and all-knowing God.

There are many people who don't believe Genesis is the truth. Some of them don't believe there is a God at all, so the world must have happened by chance. They are atheists.

Activities

1. Draw a calendar for seven days. On each day, draw and/or describe in writing what Genesis says God did.
2. Explain different ways of understanding Genesis.
3. Do you think it matters what a person believes about Genesis? Explain your reasons.

Values and ethics

13.2 Science and the origins of the universe

Learning objectives
- To learn the main scientific theories about the origins of the universe
- To compare and contrast science with religion in relation to the origins of the universe
- To reflect on whether a person can believe science and religion in relation to the origins of the universe

Big question
Can you believe in science and religion?

Did you know? The first person to suggest the idea of a Big Bang was Georges Lemaître – a Belgian Catholic priest.

Science is a knowledge system based on observation – seeing the same thing happen most or every time gives a solid idea that that is what will always happen (in that set of circumstances, of course). It is also based on hypothesis and testing. In other words, someone makes a theory about what will happen if they do x, y, z; then they do x, y, z a number of times to prove or disprove their theory. Science is incredibly important in the modern world; you could say we live in the scientific age.

Did you know? Ancient Hindu scriptures teach that there is a multiverse with different beings inhabiting different universes.

Did you know? One Hindu creation story describes Vishnu waking and commanding the world to be created. It is created and then, after one of his days, he returns to sleep and the universe contracts to nothing again. He wakes... this process goes on forever.

▲ The Eagle Nebula, aka Hand of God

13 The natural world

Humans, being human, still want that answer to how the universe began. Almost everything we see around us and in the world and universe has a beginning and an end: we are born, we live, we will die. A seed grows into a plant, which flowers and dies. Beginning and end is what we expect based on what we experience. So, the world must have begun at some point as well.

The most popular scientific theory for the beginning of the world is the Big Bang Theory.

This theory says we have to go back about 15 billion years to the Big Bang which kick-started our universe. Before that, there was nothing but an extremely hot and dense single point. For some reason (which we don't yet know), there was a huge explosion that caused the point to inflate, first at super speed, then slower – all within a second of time. This 'explosion' generated a massive cloud of dust and gas – the building blocks that then settled into the elements of the universe. It took billions of years for the universe to look as it does today: the universe and within it, our Sun, the stars and the planets. It took until just a few million years ago for the earliest signs of life to appear.

▶ Do any scientists have any different ideas?

Some scientists believe in a multiverse, which means our universe is just one of many that are like bubbles lying side by side, each with different laws of physics. Some other scientists describe a universe that pulses – so it keeps expanding and then contracting. They believe that we are in the expansion phase. The Big Bang fits into both of these theories.

▶ Can you believe in science and religion?

The Big Bang Theory does not mention God, and there is no indication that God was involved. Scientists cannot explain why the Big Bang happened – it was just a random accident. Religions believe God was the creator. This seems to rule out believing both. If you believe Genesis is the absolute truth, it is not possible to believe the Big Bang as well.

However, many religious believers do accept the scientific theory, and believe that God was behind it all. After all, science can only give a theory, not definitive proof, and science cannot go back further than the Big Bang. If believers are right, and God is eternal and absolute, then it works.

Followers of the Bahá'í Faith believe in the importance of science together with religion as two complementary knowledge systems. All religions see the importance of science as it helps us to understand our world and can generate solutions for problems to improve life for humans. Many believers see science as revealing natural laws that God put in place.

> I think science tells us how things happen, but religion is telling us why. They complement each other and answer different questions.

> Science tells us the tested and proven truth. But we don't yet know enough about the start of the universe to say the Big Bang is that.

> Science gives me understanding of the world; religion gives me purpose and hope. For me, they don't clash.

> Read 'The Great Partnership' by Rabbi Sacks. He says that not only are science and religion compatible, but that they complement each other – and that the world needs both. It make so much sense.

Activities

1. Why do you think humans want to understand how the universe began?
2. Give a simple outline of the Big Bang Theory.
3. In your opinion, is it possible to believe in science and religion in relation to the origins of the universe? Explain your reasons.

Values and ethics

13.3 Our wondrous world

Learning objectives
- To explore the concepts of awe and wonder
- To recognise how the world inspires awe and wonder through its beauty and design
- To reflect on whether this is proof of the existence of God

Big question
What amazes you about the world we live in?

Key term
Numinous – a word invented by Rudolf Otto to describe a spiritual response caused by coming into contact with God or the divine. It gives a sense of awe and inspiration

> The thing that really surprised me was that it [the Earth] projected an air of fragility. And why, I don't know. I don't know to this day. I had a feeling it's tiny, it's shiny, it's beautiful, it's home, and it's fragile.
>
> Michael Collins, astronaut on Apollo 11

Astronauts who go into space and look down on the Earth all say the same thing – it takes their breath away – they are amazed by the Earth's beauty, and feel very privileged to have this sight of it. They feel a sense of awe and wonder. Scientists call it the 'overview effect', as astronauts suddenly begin to think of the world as a small, fragile place, protected by a very thin atmosphere. They stop thinking of country boundaries, clashes of cultures and different national groups. It becomes something that needs to be nourished and protected – by everyone.

Awe and wonder are words with similar meanings. They both describe a feeling of amazement, respect, admiration and even fear all mixed together that you feel when you are looking at something really special. You have probably felt this emotion yourself. Perhaps when you have seen a sports person show unbelievable skill or when you have seen something in nature that is so beautiful it leaves you a bit dumbstruck, and wanting to capture it by taking a picture. Those feelings of having witnessed something we couldn't do, or might never see again make us feel privileged, and – often – very small in the grand scheme of things.

▶ Rudolf Otto – the numinous

Rudolf Otto was a German theologian, philosopher and scholar who lived from 1869 to 1937. Of his many works, one focused on the feeling of awe and wonder people get from seeing nature and the world. He called this feeling the **numinous**, which means getting a sense of God or the divine. He knew that he could never prove God exists, but he was convinced that there is a God. He claimed that by looking at the world, people can get a sense of God. They sense that there is some great power behind everything they see, or that there is a design to this highly complex world. They feel humbled by what they see. For them, giving them this sense of God or the divine, the numinous, is at least an indication that God exists.

Talk it out
Can you think of any times when you felt awe or wonder?
What caused those feelings?
Might they have been caused by the numinous effect?

13 The natural world

▶ William Paley – the world was designed

William Paley was a scholar, teacher and writer, as well as the Archdeacon of Carlisle. He lived in the eighteenth century. One of the things he is most famous for is his argument to prove the existence of God, which was based on design. He said he could prove God exists simply by looking at the world. He argued that if you found a watch, but didn't know what watches were, you would still be able to say that it was something that had been deliberately made. He said that you would be puzzled by it, and perhaps amazed by it, but that you would believe that the different parts which worked together as a mechanism had been put together for a purpose.

William said that the world was like that watch – only far more puzzling and amazing. Think of the patterns in nature – the seasons, reproduction. Think of the wonderful beauty – flowers, sunsets. Think of the uniqueness – fingerprints, DNA. Think of how so many things seem perfectly suited to their environment – polar bears with their claws and fur, camels that live in the desert. The world is an amazing place.

William said that this beauty and complexity is evidence of the world being designed, and that if something is designed, it has to have a designer. To him, it was absolutely clear that the designer of the world was God. He believed he had proved that God exists.

William Paley's argument began with awe and wonder at the world around him, and used logical arguments based on the evidence of what people can see for themselves to prove that God exists.

▶ The anthropic principle

Most people believe that the Earth came about because of the Big Bang – a huge explosion billions of years ago (see Topic 13.2 Science and the origins of the universe, page 186–7). If that explosion had been hotter, cooler, stronger, weaker or different in any tiny way, there would not be life on Earth. The Earth has the perfect conditions for life, and it is the only place in the solar system that scientists know of where there is life.

There are two ways of looking at this, and both are called the anthropic principle. The strong anthropic principle says that the explanation for everything being perfect to create and support life is that it was designed that way. In other words, there is God behind everything. The weak anthropic principle says that the only reason humans can have this debate is because they are here. It is all just luck and chance. Humans have had the right amount of time for their intelligence to come up with these ideas of design.

Oh, wow!   It just is!

> Who cares if there is a God? I don't! But looking at nature, I am just blown away sometimes – so amazing, so beautiful. I do question why humans treat the world so badly – no one should need the threat of a God to look after it. Saffi

Activities

1. Explain what is meant by 'awe and wonder'.
2. Explain why you think astronauts feel the 'overview effect' when they first see the Earth. How do you think it might continue to affect them when they return to everyday life?
3. Many people believe the world looks designed, which gives them a sense of awe and wonder. Describe some of the things that might make them feel this.
4. Using William Paley's argument, explain why the world makes some people believe that God exists. Explain whether or not you find this argument convincing.
5. Strong or weak anthropic principle – which one do you favour? Explain your answer.

Values and ethics

13.4 How humans are damaging the world

Learning objectives
- To explore some of the main environmental issues faced today: pollution, climate change, extinction of species
- To research a local environmental issue
- To reflect on why humans damage their world

Big question
What environmental issues are there in your local area?

Talk it out
What environmental problems are there?

Which are the most problematic?

Why do you think individuals and businesses do things that harm the world?

Our world faces huge problems because of how we treat it. Historically, we have treated the world as our possession to do with as we wish. Henry VIII had over 100,000 trees cut down to build his Navy ships. Mines have made some families very wealthy but think of Parys Mountain in Anglesey, home to the world's largest copper mine in the 1800s, and now left as a dusty lunar landscape, with almost no vegetation. Two hundred years ago there were just over 1 billion people, now there are over 7.7 billion; more people means more demand for natural resources and living space, and more rubbish. Some people say it is too late to solve environmental problems, others that all we can do is manage the mess.

Pollution, climate change and the extinction of many species are three huge environmental issues. The three are linked, but here you will consider each in turn. As you read the information, think about your local area and whether each is an issue in your local area and whether there is a solution to the issue.

Activities
Choose one of these topics and do some research about it locally and nationally.

littering/fly-tipping

pollution

deforestation

destruction of habitats

increased carbon footprint

coastal destruction

Find the answers to the following questions and then present your findings in the form of a report.
a Is it an issue?
b Why is it an issue?
c What is being done to solve it?
d What do you think needs to be done?
e Why should we try to solve the issue entirely?

Activities
1. How are humans damaging their world? What evidence of this do you see locally?
2. Choose one of the three environmental issues from this page. Do some research to add to the information here. Write a letter to your local MP about the issue and suggest what needs to be done.
3. 'Humans are selfish – they damage the environment because they only think of themselves'. Do you agree? Give reasons for agreeing with and disagreeing with this statement.
4. Do you think more should be done in Wales to solve environmental problems? Explain your ideas.

13 The natural world

Pollution

Pollution is the introduction of something harmful to the environment, which causes imbalance and damage. Most pollution is caused by humans. There are various different kinds of pollution.

Air pollution comes from traffic and factories. In towns and cities, pollution has increased the number of cases of asthma and other breathing conditions. In December 2020, for the first time in the UK, a coroner ruled that a child had died because of the effect of air pollution on her severe asthma.

Factories and farms often release waste onto land and into rivers. Factories release chemicals; farmers use fertilisers which wash or drain into the rivers. These can pollute the water, and/or changes the balance of the ecosystem, which destroys the life in it.

It is common to see litter on our streets, in our countryside and on our beaches. It is even at sea. The Great Pacific Garbage Patch is an area of rubbish floating in the Pacific which weighs 80 million kg, and is 80 times the size of Wales. All litter is a danger to wildlife – trapping or poisoning and causing death.

Climate change

The Earth's cycle means it has hotter and cooler periods. Ice Ages were cooler periods; we are in one of the hotter periods. Scientists have been able to prove that the activities of humans over the last 250 years, especially the last 100 years, have speeded up any natural temperature change. They estimate that by 2100, the surface temperature of the Earth will increase by between 1.4 °C and 5.8 °C. The main reason for this is greenhouse gases, particularly CO_2 which is released by burning fossil fuels for energy, transport and industry.

The heating up of the world is changing our climate and we are therefore seeing more extreme weather conditions (storms, floods, etc.). Deserts are expanding and ice caps are melting. Life in these areas is affected as species have to adapt, move or die out – humans included. Some places will become too hot to sustain any life. Melting ice caps also means rising seas – a risk map for Wales makes worrying reading if you live in the south or south-east.

Extinction of species

In 2021 there were nearly 16,500 species on the endangered species 'threatened with extinction' list. This includes orangutans, tigers, Asian elephants and leatherback turtles. Puffins and basking whales, both of which are found on the Welsh coastline, are also on the list. A species is labelled as 'extinct' when no live example of it has been seen or recorded for 60 years; a species is 'critically endangered' when it is likely to become extinct. Human activity – deforestation, building, pollution, climate change, the food industry and so on – is directly and indirectly making species extinct. The World Wide Fund for Nature (WWF) estimates that for every year of your life, 10,000 species have been lost, a trend which may speed up because of what humans are doing.

Values and ethics

13.5 Environmental ethics

Learning objectives
- To explore the idea of **environmental ethics**
- To explore how religious groups have tried to act on their environmental ethics
- To reflect on the importance of environmental action

Big question
Do you have to believe God created the world to look after it?

Key term
Environmental ethics – the study of the relationship humans have with their world, and the value and status we give to the natural world and all the species within it; including ideas about what is right and wrong in how humans treat the world

▲ Fly-tipping in Cardiff

▲ Dumped chemicals killed all the fish

▶ Why should we look after the world?

- We live here. If I make a mess in my house, I have to live in the mess, and the same is true of the world.
- Others live here. The damage I do affects others. For example, if I drop litter, it makes it untidy for everyone, and my litter can also hurt animals – a discarded can is a trap for an animal, they eat the plastic, and so on.
- People will live here after we are gone. The more rubbish we leave now, the more the world that they inherit will be damaged. Much of the environmental damage that has been done was caused by people before we were born.
- For those who believe in God, this world is God's creation. Belief in God demands worship of God, and stewardship of God's world is a kind of worship. Many religious believers consider the world to be on loan, and if you borrow something, you can't give it back in a mess. They believe God will reward them (or not) for the stewardship they show.
- For those who believe in reincarnation, they will return to this world, and will see the state it is in in the future.

These ideas prove everyone has a vested interest, whatever they believe, and whether they are religious or not. This is important, because those interests are the reasons why people do things. Scientists now say that environmental issues have reached a crisis point. The only way to fix this is to take on the problem and solve it; just managing our own behaviour is no longer enough.

13 The natural world

▶ What can humans do?

With a partner, come up with as many ideas as you can.

As individuals, we can try to make our lives more environmentally friendly by recycling, reusing, not wasting, not littering, buying locally and walking rather than driving. We can join local efforts: litter picks, stream-cleaning, beach-cleaning. We can join in with campaigns and protests and donate to charities, supporting larger groups to push for change at government level.

▶ Environmental action by groups

It is not unusual to see religious groups involved in environmental actions. See page 72–73 to see an example of what some Christians did in 2021 as part of their Shore-to-Shore challenge. Combining litter-picking with beach cleaning and ministry to those who were interested, they showed that their beliefs could make a practical difference.

The Welsh Government sees religious tourism as an important source of income. There are several Pilgrim Walks in Wales, and their leaflets remind pilgrims to observe the Countryside Code for example by taking litter home with them and leaving everything as they found it.

Cyswllt Amgylchedd Cymru (Wales Environment Link) was set up in 1990 to help the different environmental organisations in Wales co-ordinate their work. The organisation helps its members to engage with Government about policies and laws, acts as a hub to link organisations, supports grant applications and publicises the work that is done. The 30 current members include organisations that are UK-wide, but many are Welsh-based and working in Wales. One example is Coed Cadw, the Woodland Trust in Wales, which focuses on tree-planting and conservation projects. Cadwch Gymru'n daclus (Keep Wales Tidy) is another, which provides the equipment for community litter picks, protects local parks, and runs the Eco-Schools programme. Afonydd Cymru manages the six River Trusts in Wales, trying to maintain good water environments. The Marine Conservation Society organises and leads beach clean-ups. Other members focus their work on marine animals, insects, footpaths, National Parks, historic buildings and so on. Each member group is active in making a difference.

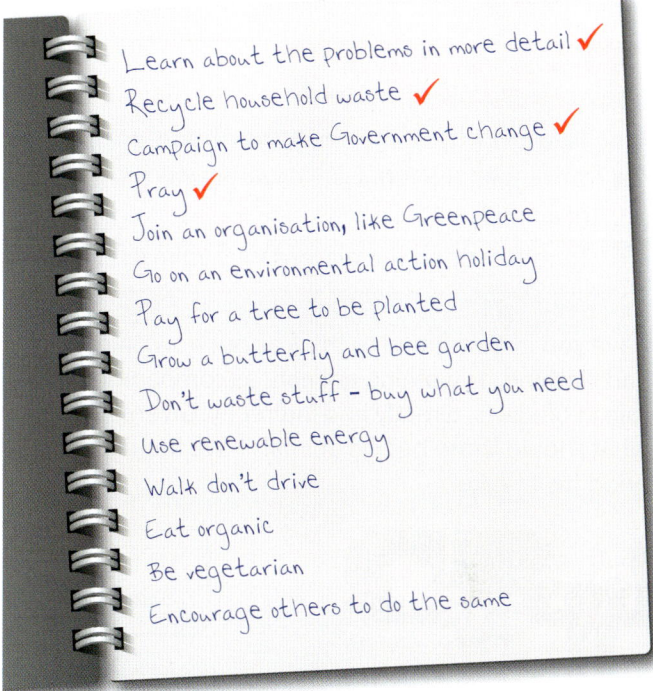

▲ All Wales is invited to act now

> I joined in Wales Climate Week last year. You can get loads of ideas by going online. I did a beach clean up and re-educated my parents about recycling and reducing waste. If everyone did something, Wales and the planet would be better off.

Activities

1. What do we mean by 'environmental ethics'?
2. Why should people be motivated to take action on environmental issues?
3. What could people in your local area do to help the environment as individuals or in groups?
4. Is it enough for an individual to be environmentally conscious and active? What about a country? Explain the reasons for your answers to both questions.

Values and ethics

13.6 Animal rights

Learning objectives
- To know what is meant by the phrase 'animal rights'
- To explore the different views people have about the treatment and uses of animals
- To reflect upon the reasons why animals should have rights

Big question

Should animals have rights?

Have you ever stopped to think about how animals play a part in our lives? We use animals in many ways: as food and clothing, as working animals, as companions, as a source of entertainment or learning. Animals play a vital role in our lives, directly and indirectly. Given the importance of animals to us, should they have rights, and if so, what should those be? Do animals have the right to be well treated, fed properly, exercised and rested, and given good healthcare?

All species are equal. Humans should not have any more rights than any other species, whether animal, bird, fish or whatever.

Animals keep us safe, even save our lives sometimes (for example, rescue dogs) and they often give their lives for humans. They deserve to have rights.

Religious people are taught to respect God's creatures. Having senses and being able to feel pain makes animals just as important a creation as humans.

Any animal we own or use has the right to be treated well. If we don't do that, they won't keep doing what we need them to do.

Animals provide love, comfort, hope, companionship and joy. In return, they should have rights.

Some animals deserve 'more' rights than 'some' humans. They are far more helpful, loyal and loving to society.

To harm animals intentionally by hunting, cruelty or abuse, putting them in cages, destroying their environments, starving them, experimenting on them is simply unacceptable. This is a human wrong that we should all be ashamed of. Humans are meant to be compassionate, not inflict pain.

13 The natural world

> Humans are superior so we should be able to use animals however we want. They are there for our needs. Human rights every time!

> Scientific experiments might seem cruel but if they result in cures for diseases that affect us, they should be done. We need to find cures and the animal suffering is worthwhile because it is for the greater good of humans.

> Humans have always hunted for food, clothing and resources, like ivory or fur. Humans use whatever is in the world, including animals and their parts, to make life easier. It's our right to have these things.

> God made humans the most intelligent and gave us power and control over the rest of his creation, so we should use that power – simple as that! Human rights take priority.

> If we want to help another human or save human life or make human life more comfortable, better for an animal to be used instead of a human. There is already too much human suffering in the world. Let's not get emotional about animals and their rights.

 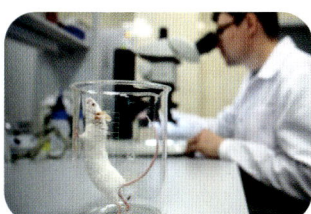  

Activities

1 What does the phrase 'animal rights' mean?
2 List some ways in which humans use animals.
3 Explain why it is important to treat animals well, whatever they are used for.
4 Read the speech bubbles on the page opposite. Write three sentences to show why animals should have rights.
5 Read the speech bubbles on this page. Write three sentences to show why human rights are more important than animal rights.
6 'Humans should be able to use animals in whatever way they want.' Do you think this is true? Give reasons for your answer. Give an alternative view.

14 Respect for life

14.1 Religious beliefs about the origins of human life

Learning objectives
- To learn some religious stories about the origins of human life
- To understand the value placed on human life by these stories
- To reflect on whether such beliefs help or hinder humans in society and the world

Big question

Is life always special?

Religions teach that human life is special. Each religion has its own version of why this is so. We will learn about some here, but there are many more, which you could do some research to find out about. There are similarities between the stories, so as you read them, try to spot these.

Christianity – the Genesis stories

Genesis is the first book of the Bible and tells of the seven days of Creation (see Topic 13.1 The creation, page 184). Genesis 1:27 says that on day six: 'God created mankind in his own image…; male and female he created them.'

Genesis 2 has a different version: God had made the heavens and earth, and made land and sea. There was no vegetation, but streams were flowing. God took the dust of the earth and shaped it to make a man. God breathed into the nostrils of this 'man' and gave him life. God then set about creating a garden for the man to live in. God created all kinds of plants and trees from which the man could eat. The Garden was Eden, the man was Adam, and his role was to tend the garden. God told Adam he was not to eat from the tree in the middle of the garden – the tree of good and evil – but that everything else was his.

Then God decided that it was not good for Adam to be alone, he needed a companion. God created birds and animals, bringing them to Adam to name them – none were suitable as a companion and helper. So, God made Adam fall asleep, and removed one of his ribs. From this rib, he made a woman, Eve, who he brought to Adam as his helper.

14 Respect for life

Islam – Surah 32

This chapter of the Qur'an is called 'Worship', but it includes a description of man's creation, which is repeated several times in the rest of the Qur'an. It says that Allah (God) began by creating man from clay, into which Allah breathed some of Allah's own spirit to give life. When Allah gave that breath, it gave man hearing, sight and intellect. 'He created man from ringing clay as baked pottery is' (Surah 55:14).

Sikhism – the Guru Granth Sahib

There is no big creation story in the Sikh holy book. Instead, there are a number of verses that mention the origins of humans, for example: 'Using the same mud, The Creator has created many shapes in many ways.'

The Bahá'í Faith – science and religion

The Bahá'í Faith teaches that science and religion are complementary knowledge systems. Abdu'l-Bahá, the son of Bahá'u'lláh, founder of the Bahá'í Faith taught that the Genesis story was an allegory – a symbolic story to explain that the world evolved gradually. He taught that God created the world and everything in it progressively through God's divine breath. He taught that there was never a time without humans, but that the form of humans has changed from very simple to the very complex state we see now. 'Gradually it passed through various conditions and different shapes, until it attained this form and beauty, this perfection, grace and loveliness.' The Bahá'í Faith seems to see the scientific idea of evolution as an appropriate way to describe the origins of human life (see Topic 14.2 Scientific beliefs about the origins of human life, page 198).

Hinduism – Purusha

One of many Hindu creation stories tells us that before the beginning of all things, there was Purusha, who is in everything conscious and unconscious in the universe now. Life started with Purusha becoming a cosmic being. He then sacrificed himself so that everything else would exist, though the world we see is only a quarter of Purusha. From his mind came the moon, his eyes the stars, his head the heavens, and his feet the Earth. From him came all the life in the world: fish, birds, animals. Humans came from his mouth, arms, legs and feet.

Activities

1. Is human life special? Explain the reasons for your answer.
2. Choose either Genesis or Purusha, and draw a cartoon strip to retell the story.
3. Why do you think religions have stories about the origins of human life? Explain your ideas.
4. Do you think that religious beliefs about the origins of human life help or hinder humans in society? Explain your ideas and opinion.

Values and ethics

14.2 Scientific beliefs about the origins of human life

Learning objectives
- To learn about scientific theories for the origins of human life
- To compare and contrast religious and scientific ideas about the origins of human life
- To reflect on whether religious and scientific ideas on this subject are compatible

Big question
Science or religion – which comes first?

Talk it out
Do you think it matters how human life began?

Why do you think some people were upset to be told that humans descended from apes?

▶ Big Bang part 2

Topic 13.2 Science and the origins of the universe (page 186) outlines a simple version of the Big Bang Theory. This is the most popular scientific theory for how the universe came to exist. It also covers how humans came to exist.

The earliest form of the world after the Big Bang was an incredibly hot place. There was no land or sea, just a sort of very hot mud, which scientists call the primeval soup. In this 'soup' were all the ingredients for life: proteins and amino acids. At some point, these got fused together to create life. For this to happen, they had to be trapped together very tightly, and in a vacuum. Study has shown that clay can make this happen: clay soaks up liquids, creating a hydrogel because it is made up of billions of tiny spaces. At some point, a reaction fused the right materials together to create life. So the first life – very simple, single-cellular organisms – were formed within clay.

Over millions of years, there was a development of these first single-cellular organisms into more complex ones. Then came insects, before fish-like and bird-like creatures. From these, developed reptiles and then mammals, and finally, humans. We call this evolution.

▶ Evolution

Charles Darwin is credited with the first complete theory about evolution. He published it in 1859 in a book called *On the Origin of Species*. He had spent years researching on a scientific ship, *HMS Beagle*, and was inspired by earlier geologists and their ideas. His book said that the world is a place of change with many thousands of species, some of which are related. The differences within and between species, he said, are the result of thousands of years of changing environment. Species had to adapt to be able to survive. He also said that because natural resources are limited, the species had to compete with each other, which meant that they had to adapt and struggle for survival. The species we see now are not the ones that existed when life first began; they are the result of evolution. This includes humans, who Darwin said had evolved from ape-like species. So, human life is the last part in a long chain of evolutionary development.

▲ Charles Darwin

14 Respect for life

At the time, people were not impressed to be told they had descended from apes – not least because there was a travelling exhibition that showed apes as snarling, aggressive creatures. Darwin's theory was not well received, and was even subject to ridicule. Today it is seen as the basis of modern evolutionary theory – which is accepted by most people.

▶ Can you believe science and religion about the origins of human life?

> Yes, you can. Darwin said 'I see no good reason why the views given in my book should shock the religious feelings of anyone.' Plus, in his book he says that God is behind everything he has proposed. If you think about it, a God that creates something that can develop and evolve is even smarter than one who makes something and then just leaves it.

> No, you can't. Science has explained it all without God, so why bother adding God in? Religion talks about God moulding man from clay, like little models and that is definitely not how science describes it.

> Yes, but that's the thing. Many religious stories say 'man from clay'. Science has shown the first life forms were from proteins and amino acids fused within clay. As long as you believe that the Genesis stories are not word-for-word truth, you can accept both.

> But that is the problem. Religious believers want to believe it all as the word of God. So Genesis is disproved by science – and science is more reliable for modern people.

▲ The scientist finally reaches the top for the truth about how humans began, just to find that theologians had been there for thousands of years

Activities

1. How did human life begin?
2. What are the main differences between the scientific and religious ideas about how human life began?
3. Are there any similarities between religious ideas about how human life began, and scientific ideas? Explain your answer.
4. Look back to page 185 at the ways in which people interpret Genesis. Can any of those interpretations fit with believing the scientific ideas about how human life began? Explain your answer.
5. 'Science and religion are two complementary knowledge systems.' Do you agree? Explain your reasons showing you have thought about more than one point of view.

Values and ethics

14.3 How important is human life? The death penalty

Learning objectives
- To explore why some countries use the death penalty as a punishment
- To consider different attitudes to the death penalty
- To reflect on whether the taking of life as a punishment is ever acceptable

Big question
Should the UK have the death penalty as a punishment?

Capital punishment, or the death penalty, is the punishment used in 58 countries around the world for crimes such as murder, but also crimes such as blasphemy, adultery, drug offences, corruption, fraud and treason. The USA is the only Western country that uses the death penalty. Most executions happen in China, Iran, Saudi Arabia and Iraq.

Each part of the UK has had the death penalty in place for part of its history. Up to 1868, executions were held in public in at least a dozen places in Wales. By the end of the First World War, there were only three places in Wales where the death penalty was still carried out: Cardiff, Swansea and Usk prisons. In the twentieth century, twenty people were executed at Cardiff prison, one of whom was female, and the last being in 1952; nine men were executed at Swansea, the last being in 1958; and four men were executed at Usk, the last being in 1922 (eight days before the prison closed). Every execution was for the offence of murder. In the rest of the UK, the death penalty was still used until its complete abolition in 1969 (1973 for Northern Ireland).

The twentieth century saw huge changes in the way society viewed criminals. The idea of reform became important – recognising that people could change for the better, and that society should encourage that. Prisons became more humane places – hard labour as part of a prison sentence was ended in 1902. Prisons began to employ teachers to help criminals improve their literacy and other skills. Young offenders became a separate category, and were treated differently from adult criminals. All this made the death penalty seem increasingly inhumane – a punishment that a civilised society should not use.

In our society today, surveys have shown that more people do not want the return of the death penalty than want it. The last time the issue was debated in Parliament was in 1998 when the Human Rights Act was being discussed. Parliament did allow for its use for murder 'in times of war or imminent threat of war'. There are crimes which lead some newspapers to call for the return of the death penalty, such as those of the Moors murderers and Harold Shipman, and acts of terrorism.

▲ Cardiff prison, one of three sites used for the death penalty in Wales in the twentieth century before its abolition

'It did not deter them then, and it had not deterred them when they committed what they were convicted for. All the men and women whom I have faced at that final moment convince me that in what I have done I have not prevented a single murder.' (*Albert Pierrepoint was the man who carried out the death penalty in the UK from 1931–56. He wrote the above in his autobiography. After leaving his job in 1956, he became an abolitionist – someone who argues for the end of capital punishment – his job had brought him to radically change his worldview.*)

14 Respect for life

▶ About the death penalty

Read these statements. Work out which ones support the death penalty, and which ones are against it.

It is the ultimate punishment to be used for the worst of crimes. Anyone who commits terrible crimes like child murder, serial killing, mass murder or terrorism deserves the most severe punishment.

The death penalty is the deliberate taking of life; it is a form of murder – which makes the State just as bad as the criminal being executed.

This is the only punishment we can use to make sure that a criminal will never hurt anyone again.

What if the person who is executed was innocent? There are cases of people being released from prison many years after they were convicted as new evidence proves them innocent. You can pardon someone who has been executed but you cannot release them.

The circumstances that lead to some criminals being as they are, and therefore committing a crime, are so unfair that we should give them help while they are being punished, not end their lives.

The USA probably has the fairest death penalty system; however, death row and execution costs more than imprisoning someone for life.

The death penalty prevents crime. Fear of being caught and being sentenced to the death penalty discourages people from committing terrible crimes.

Many religious scriptures and teachings say 'an eye for an eye', or state clearly that the death penalty should be used for certain crimes. It is justice to use the death penalty.

No matter what a person does, they can still change and improve, and their life is still special or sacred. The death penalty destroys that.

You can forgive someone, be completely sure they are guilty, and they can be reformed, but they still have to be punished in a way that fits their crime. The system in some countries, such as the USA, takes so long (many years) that it is possible to do all of these, including execution.

The best punishment reforms someone: it makes them realise what they did was wrong, and makes them want to make up for that act. All belief systems support reformation. The death penalty doesn't allow reformation because it kills the person who has committed the crime.

Activities

Look back at the ideas about the sanctity and dignity of life in Topic 12.1 Humanity (page 174). These are also important ideas for this topic. Use these ideas to help write an essay answer to this question:

Should the UK bring back the death penalty for certain crimes? Give reasons for more than one point of view, and write a justified conclusion.

Activities

1. What is the death penalty?
2. What is the history of the death penalty in Wales?
3. 'The death penalty is wrong because life is too special.' Do you agree? Explain the reasons for your answer.

Values and ethics

14.4 How important is human life? Euthanasia

Learning objectives
- To explore why some people think euthanasia should be legal
- To explore why some people think euthanasia should remain illegal
- To reflect on how strongly religious beliefs affect attitudes to euthanasia

Big question
Should people have the right to decide when they want to die?

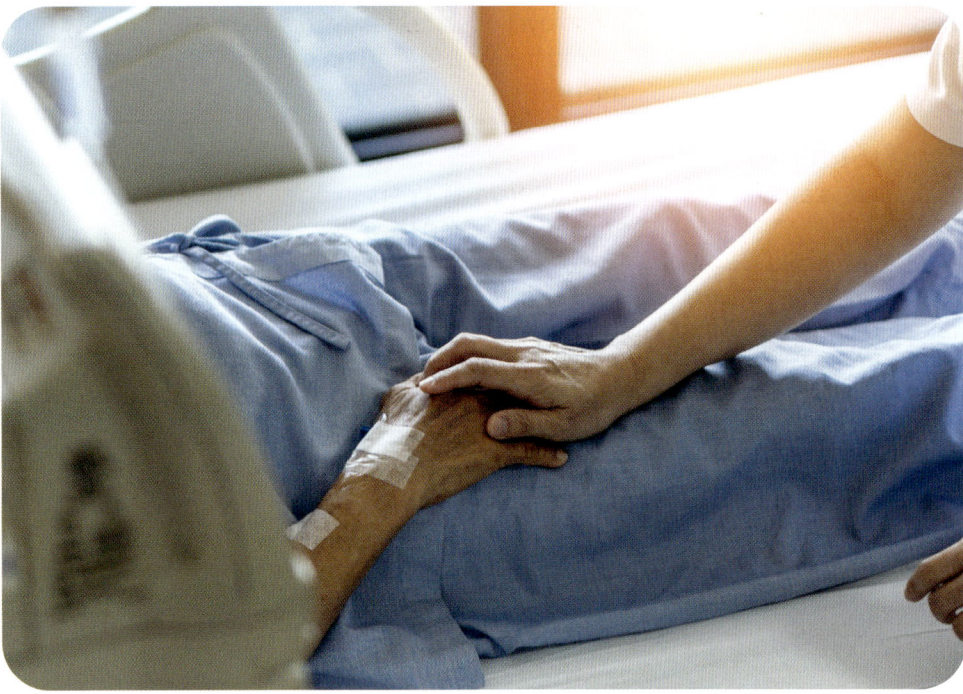

Activities
1. What is euthanasia?
2. What is the law in the UK regarding euthanasia?
3. Explain some reasons to either agree or disagree with euthanasia.
4. 'Civilised societies look after the dying, they don't kill them.' Do you agree with this statement? Give reasons for your answer.

▶ What is euthanasia?

Euthanasia means 'gentle death', and has come to mean a mercy killing, putting an end to someone's life to end their suffering. Sometimes it refers to helping someone die who is already dying – they are terminally ill – and suffering. Sometimes it refers to helping someone die who has a degenerative disease, and whose quality of life is less than they can bear. Euthanasia is done for compassionate reasons: it is an act of loving kindness.

In the UK, it is illegal to do something that will end a life, even if the person is terminally ill or suffering too much. However, a patient can be allowed to die, or they can refuse to take medication so that they die. Similarly, a patient can be prescribed drugs that will ease the symptoms of their disease, but bring their death nearer; for example, by increasing the dosage of pain killers.

Life-support machines are machines that keep a person's lungs and heart going so that they do not die, or to give them time to recover from the most serious of injuries. Some people on life-support have the chance to recover, but others will never wake up. Doctors test to see if the person's brain has stopped working. If it has, this is called 'brain death' and at this point – with the family's consent – it is legal for doctors to switch off the equipment and allow the person to die.

There is a debate in society about euthanasia, and you will sometimes hear of campaigns to change the UK law to make euthanasia legal. Dignity in Dying campaigns for the right to choose your own death; Care Not Killing is a group of organisations that fight to prevent the law being changed. Both have websites, so you could do more research on this topic.

14 Respect for life

I watched my grandfather suffer terribly before he died. Doctors knew they could not help – his pain was too great for them to manage. All they could do was make him sleep, and in his sleep he flinched and moaned. Eventually, days later, he died. This made me believe that we need to have a law supporting euthanasia. Weeks before he died, he knew he was at the end stage of his cancer, that nothing could be done and he was waiting for death. That was also the point when he could no longer do the things he enjoyed without great difficulty and pain. His bucket list of 'to do before death' was filed away. We were all very sad, and it was difficult to see his suffering increase. If he could have chosen his day of death, he would have been spared those last few days or weeks of agony. It isn't as if that time was of use, and he lost his dignity as he became so ill in the last days. A new law would be a compassionate way to deal with those we can no longer help – if that is what they want, and so long as they can make that decision without pressure from anyone.

I strongly believe that no one has the right to take life. Life is special. I am a doctor and I swore the Hippocratic Oath, in which I promised to not do anything to end life. I believe I have no right to end life, only to preserve life, or to ease pain. I understand that some pain is beyond the medicines I can give, and research continues into that. However, it is only a very few people who reach that point and for only a short time. We are still able to work with them until their death. I believe a civilised society does all it can to support life, not to prolong pain or keep someone alive unduly. It is not the mark of such a society to decide a person's life should just be thrown away. I have friends who believe that a person's suffering is part of God's plan, or allows others to learn to be more compassionate, or allows society to develop – I don't agree with any of those. Life is life: cherish it, protect it, but never end it.

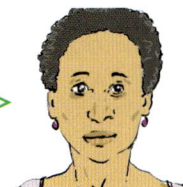

Activities

1 These are two opposing views about euthanasia. Read some other views below that are commonly used in the debate and try to identify which agree and which disagree.

- Only God has the right to take life.
- It is my body and life; it should be my right to decide.
- Helping someone die is the ultimate act of kindness and love.
- Dignity is important, and euthanasia can help preserve that.
- Euthanasia is a form of murder.
- If euthanasia was legal, anyone who feels like a burden on their family would ask for it, but not really want it.
- Miracle cures happen. People come out of comas. Euthanasia would stop both of these.
- We don't let animals suffer when they are very ill. Why are we not as compassionate to humans?
- There comes a point where the only medical care option left is euthanasia; otherwise there is no care, just medicine.
- People who are given full and proper palliative care (care that relieves pain) do not seek euthanasia.
- Euthanasia is like saying we give up on someone.

2 Look back at the ideas about the sanctity and dignity of life in Topic 12.1 Humanity (page 174). These are also important ideas for this topic. Use these ideas to help write a speech *either* supporting a new law for euthanasia *or* arguing to keep the current law in place.

Values and ethics

14.5 How important is human life? Victims of natural disasters

Learning objectives
- To understand the term 'natural disaster'
- To understand the impact of natural disasters on developing countries
- To reflect on why religious believers are involved in helping victims of natural disasters

Big question
How important are the lives of people in the developing world?

Our headline news tonight: a tsunami hit Indonesia last night, the third in two weeks as the volcano Anak Krakatau continues to erupt. Devastation and death were its gifts as the death toll has risen to over 200, with that figure expected to rise much higher. Over 1,500 people are known to be missing. The towns and villages in the path of the tsunami were wiped out, few buildings are left standing, roads were washed away, and communication and energy lines were severed. People are in a state of shock, with those lucky few survivors now camped out at schools and centres inland. Many of them are refusing to go home for fear of another tsunami.

A tsunami is an example of a natural disaster – a disaster that is not caused by humans but happens as a result of the Earth's natural processes. Other examples include earthquakes, volcanic eruptions, hurricanes, floods and wildfires. The impact of these events is often worse in poorer countries than in richer ones. This is because richer countries can afford better monitoring systems (for example, to monitor volcanoes for signs of eruption), better defences (for example, earthquake-proof buildings) and better emergency responses (for example, evacuation systems and search and rescue teams).

Activities

Think about the Indonesian tsunami described above.
1. What are the immediate problems for the survivors?
2. What problems will they have in a few weeks or months?
3. What can be done to help them?
4. Who should be helping them?

204

14 Respect for life

▶ Religious attitudes to the victims of natural disasters

All religions have a version of the Golden Rule, which is 'Treat others as you wish to be treated' or 'Do not do to others what you would not have done to yourself'. All religions see human life as special or sacred, and consider everyone to be of equal worth. Therefore everyone deserves compassion and help when it is needed.

These teachings tell us that religious believers will help those in need – if they were in that position, they would want help. As a natural disaster is no one's fault, all those affected are innocent victims. This encourages more people to help.

Read the following statements from people of faith to find out why they helped and what they did after the Indonesian tsunami.

> My religion teaches me to show compassion to others – help not harm. When I saw the news, I set up online giving to raise money quickly. We then used the money to buy emergency items – blankets, tents, medicines – and sent them to the affected area.

> My religion believes that faith without action is useless. So, as a trained medic, I offered my services to the Red Cross and Red Crescent organisation. They were sending teams to the affected area to work with the injured. Of course, I sent my prayers for them also.

> My religion believes that all life is sacred; it should be protected. So, I spoke to my temple community and we collected dried foods – rice, flour, beans, spices, etc. We then organised these into emergency packages with a pan, bowls and water bottles, so that the packages could be handed out and the victims would have the basic items to feed themselves.

> My religion believes that our wealth is a test from Allah to see if we will use it properly. So, I took time from work and travelled out there. I worked as a resettlement and support officer with the displaced people making sure they had what they needed, and could begin to rebuild their lives.

> My religion believes that we must show kindness to others – in other words, love your neighbour. So, I donated a large sum of money to a well-known charity, to help with the relief actions. I found out it had been used to provide temporary shelters for some of those who had lost their homes.

> My religion believes that we have a duty (sewa) of service to others. I think the needier the person we help, the greater the service I can do. I volunteered with Sewa International as a volunteer, paying my own expenses, and went over. I was put to work setting up tents, distributing food and clearing the debris in my three months there.

Activities

1. What is a natural disaster? Give some examples.
2. Whose responsibility do you think it is to help people in these situations? Explain your ideas.
3. Why might religious people help the victims of natural disasters? Refer back to Topic 12.1 Humanity on pages 174–5 to help with this answer.
4. How might religious people help the victims of natural disasters?
5. 'At the time of a natural disaster, which is more important: the Golden Rule, or sanctity of life?' Explain the reasons for your answer.

Values and ethics

14.6 How important is human life? The refugee crisis

Learning objectives
- To explore the reasons behind the refugee crisis in Europe
- To explore the concept of Wales as a 'Nation of Sanctuary'
- To reflect on how difficult life is for refugees and asylum seekers

Big question
What would make you leave your country of birth?

There has been lots of coverage in the news about people coming to the UK either in boats across the English Channel, or hidden in trucks. In recent years, civil wars and other conflicts in the world have meant an increase in the numbers of people trying to find better lives in other countries, and taking all kinds of risks on the dangerous routes to those countries.

If someone comes to the UK to claim asylum, there is a legal process to decide if their claim is valid. This takes around six months. During that time, they receive Section 95 funding (in November 2021, this was £39.63 a week, plus accommodation provided by the Local Authority into which they have been placed). If the individual is granted asylum, they gain refugee status. Refugees may stay in the UK for five years under a refugee visa. After five years, they may apply for further time here.

As part of the UK, Wales accepts refugees every year, mainly in Cardiff, Swansea, Newport and Wrexham.

Many people confuse **economic migrants** with **refugees** and **asylum seekers**. Economic migrants come for work, bringing the skills they need to do that work – they are drawn to the UK by the opportunity to work. Asylum seekers and refugees come out of necessity – they are pushed by circumstances in their own country. The UK sees economic migrants from all over the world, and they bring benefits to the country. Just in financial terms, a 2018 report stated that on average EU migrants contribute £78,000 more to the UK than they take in benefits and services, and non-EU migrants contribute £28,000 more than they take; UK citizens in their lifetime on average make a zero contribution (as taxation, etc. equals benefits, pensions, etc.) (data from Oxford Economics 'The Fiscal Impact of Immigration to the UK'). Our society needs economic migrants. Many parts of the workforce, such as tourism, farming and the NHS, rely on them and would not function without them.

Refugees and asylum seekers – some facts
- There are about 26 million refugees worldwide; about half of whom are under the age of eighteen.
- In 2019, 68 per cent of the world's refugees came from Syria, Venezuela, Afghanistan, South Sudan and Myanmar.
- 85 per cent of the world's refugees are accommodated in the countries directly around the one they have left; these are developing countries.
- The UK is home to only 1 per cent of the global refugee population.
- In 2020, UK asylum seekers were 57 per cent adult male; 21 per cent adult female; 15 per cent children under eighteen (5 per cent of whom were unaccompanied).
- In January to March 2021, 2,734 asylum seekers were receiving Section 95 support in Wales.

Key terms
Refugee – a person who has been forced to leave their own country to escape war, persecution or natural disaster

Asylum seeker – a person who has left their home country as a political refugee, and is seeking to be allowed to stay in another country; they are in personal danger if they remain in their own country

Economic migrant – a person who moves to live in a country other than their own for work often to improve their standard of living

14 Respect for life

▶ Wales – a Nation of Sanctuary

The City of Sanctuary movement began in Sheffield in 2005. It aimed to offer sanctuary to those fleeing persecution in their own countries. The city set up services and support for these people. The movement has since extended to many UK cities and towns, such as Cardiff and Abergavenny.

In 2019, the Welsh Government extended this movement and declared Wales a 'Nation of Sanctuary' – the world's first – in recognition of Welsh hospitality and the Welsh history of migration.

The idea behind the movement is actively to look for ways to help refugees, rather than just tolerate them within our society. For example, Swansea has a mentoring programme – refugees can ask to be assigned a mentor, who will help them get used to life in Swansea (buses, passes, places to shop, who can help and how they can help, etc.). Nation of Sanctuary co-ordinates and links refugee support groups and agencies.

When refugees are given help to settle, they begin to repay that help very quickly and are able to make the society richer both financially and culturally.

Activities

Keanan is twelve. When he gets home from school one night, he is told his family (mum, dad and sister) has to flee the country, leaving that evening, because his father's life is at risk. The family will go to a country to which he has ancestral links, but which he has never visited. He can only take what fits into a rucksack. Once there, he will live where the Government places the family. They will have very little money. The language is different and few people speak Keanan's language. The culture and laws, climate, architecture, history and civic institutions are different from those of the country in which he has been brought up.

How might he feel? What help would he and his family need? How long do you think it might take for any of them to feel settled? Will it be the same for all of them?

▶ Telling their stories

I came from Syria – civil war since 2011. The Government has bombed many of its own cities. Over 55 per cent of Syrians have fled their homes; 500,000+ are dead or missing. I escaped but lost my family. I had supported the opposition, so my life was in danger.

I am a Muslim Rohingya. The Burmese army has discriminated against us for many years. My father brought his family from Burma to Bangladesh in 1996 to refugee camps. I was 11 in 2010 when my family came to the UK. We couldn't speak English and knew nothing about the country. I felt totally excluded.

I am an Iranian man. I came to the UK on business, but learned my boyfriend had been detained by the police in Iran. We are gay, which is illegal in Iranian law and punishable by death. I applied for asylum because if I go back, I will be arrested and killed. I cannot help who I love, but I will be killed for it.

I am Ivorian. As a musician, I sang in support of the Government. When the Government was overthrown, I was put on a hit list, and had to flee.

Activities

1. Explain the difference between asylum seekers, refugees and economic migrants.
2. Explain Wales' 'Nation of Sanctuary' status.
3. Think about your town. Would asylum seekers and refugees find it easy to settle there? What could be done to make it easier for them?
4. 'Asylum seekers and refugees need our help – so we should give it.' Do you agree?

15 Peace and protest

15.1 Attitudes to peace

Learning objectives
- To learn what the terms 'peace' and 'pacifism' mean
- To explore religious and non-religious attitudes to peace and pacifism
- To reflect on whether peace is ever possible

Key terms
Harmony – when there are positive relations between all sides; when everything goes together well

Pacifism – the belief that wars and violence are wrong; that all disputes can and should be settled by peaceful means

Peace – the state of not being at war, or when war has ended; when there is calmness, friendship and **harmony** in society

Big question
What would a world absolutely at peace be like?

All religious and non-religious belief systems teach the importance of **peace**. The opposite of peace is war. During war, both soldiers and civilians get killed, either deliberately or by accident. Farming and food production is affected, as crops are left unpicked and factories get damaged, which leads to shortages. Homes are damaged through fighting and bombing. People are affected by new laws that restrict all aspects of life. Nothing is normal.

▶ What peace might mean

- An absence of war and violence.
- A commitment to understanding each other, understanding our differences, so that we can celebrate and learn from each other.
- A commitment not to harm others, and a commitment to help others.
- The belief that by working together in a friendly way, people can make life better for everyone.

▶ Why be a pacifist?

- I was brought up to see this was the best way forward in any situation for most people. Being calm, assertive and friendly gets good results; showing anger does not.

- War is good for nothing. Death, damage, so costly. Not to mention the fact that the destruction doesn't end when a war ends. Its effects ripple on for years in obvious as well as hidden ways.

- It is more pleasant to live in a place that is peaceful and harmonious. Everyone's well-being benefits and life is simply better for all.

- My religious beliefs are that peace is God's way. I should work for peace.

- Peace requires respect for the worth and dignity of humans. War is the opposite because so many lives are destroyed.

- 'If there's anything I understand from the New Testament, it is that Jesus Christ is not a militaristic person. He is the Saviour of the world, he is the Prince of Peace. Therefore those who say they are Christians, followers of Christ must reject war totally.' (T Gwyn Jones, Welsh poet, opponent of the First World War)

Religious and non-religious attitudes to peace

▲ A Quaker meeting

The Quakers (Religious Society of Friends)

This is a Christian group with a long history of **pacifism**. As a Church, they believe that they follow the true teachings of Jesus by being pacifists. The Quaker peace testimony begins 'We utterly deny all outward wars and strife and fighting with weapons for any end, or under any pretence'. This is not just a refusal to fight, but a commitment to work for peace and to protect peace. It also means working for forgiveness and reconciliation (bringing together those who are in conflict), which brings peace between individuals and groups. The Quakers believe in one universal humanity in which every person has equal worth. Peace recognises that belief, whereas war sees the other side as being of less worth, which is the only way to be able to kill. Quakers also teach that it is not enough not to be violent, that a person has to work actively for peace. Being a pacifist is therefore not a passive way of thinking, but an active and powerful force for good.

Religion as a collective voice

Generally speaking, the teachings of all religions encourage their followers to seek peace. The typical greeting for Islam or Judaism is 'peace'. Many Christians say 'Peace be with you' after an act of worship. Religious moral codes encourage peaceful behaviour and virtues such as compassion and non-violence. Religions teach that the aim of life is to attain heaven or paradise – places of peace – or to achieve liberation from rebirth – a state of bliss and contentment. For religious people, peace is a quality brought by God, and being at peace with yourself is an important part of religious devotion. If everyone was a pacifist, then peace would be experienced by all.

Humanism

In deciding what to do, humanists use reasoning and experience applied to each particular situation. This means that a humanist might say going to war is acceptable in some situations – because of the circumstances. For example, in a situation where one country has invaded another, there might be justification for fighting back. However, humanists believe in the dignity of all humans, and many believe that all peaceful attempts to calm situations should be tried before anyone starts a war. This is because humanists recognise that peace is the best way for everyone to live. Peace is seen as essential in order to uphold justice and human rights, and to ensure people's personal freedom. Any war puts life at risk, does damage to all, and affects human rights. Humanists have to work for peace, not just believe in it.

Activities

1 What is peace?
2 Why might a person be a pacifist? Use information from Topic 12.1 Humanity (page 174) to help with this answer.
3 Explain different attitudes to peace. Which principles do those who believe in peace share?
4 'If everyone believed in peace, the world would be peaceful.' Do you agree with this statement? Explain the reasons for your answer.
5 Do you think that peace is possible in the world? Explain your reasons.

Values and ethics

15.2 When conflicts happen

Learning objectives
- To learn why wars might happen
- To learn about the Just War Theory
- To reflect on whether having a code of conduct for war is practical

Big question

If you could make a set of rules for war, what would they be?

These armies inevitably used violence to maintain order, and so the Just War Theory was born: a code of conduct that said when it was acceptable for Christians to fight, gave the conditions for fighting, and stated when war must end.

▶ The Just War Theory

The principle of the Just War Theory is that sometimes war is necessary to prevent a greater evil. St Augustine and then St Thomas Aquinas – both monks – wrote versions. It is made up of a series of 'rules':

1. The war has to be started and controlled by a proper leader, such as an elected government. St Paul said that God gave power to such leaders.
2. There has to be a just (fair) cause for the war – it can't just be about invading to get land, or because a country hates its neighbour.
3. There must be a clear aim to the war.
4. War must be the last resort – every other option to resolve a situation must have been tried first, and found unsuccessful.
5. There must be a reasonable chance of success.
6. The war must be fought in a fair way: no civilians should be hurt, only reasonable force should be used, only limited damage should be caused, and so on.
7. There must be a good outcome. The war cannot aim to destroy the other side, and once the aim (point 3) is achieved, the war ends and peace is restored.

War is violent; war takes lives; war destroys communities and society – all of which goes against religious principles. However, it is clear from history, and even today in the world, that religious believers do take part in wars; some even lead them.

From the Gospels and New Testament stories of Jesus' life, we get a picture of a man who was in favour of peace rather than war. He taught that peacemakers were blessed, and that people should love their neighbour and their enemies. Even though the Christians were persecuted to death for the first few hundred years after Jesus' death, there are few records of Christians being violent towards their aggressors. Christianity certainly started out as a religion in favour of pacifism. Something changed, however.

In the fourth century CE, the Roman Emperor Constantine became a Christian. He ordered that every person in the whole of his Empire also had to be a Christian. The strength of his Empire, however, came from his many armies which controlled all of the countries within the Roman Empire – from what is now Portugal, England and Wales, down to North Africa, across to Afghanistan, and north to central Germany.

Talk it out

Read through the seven points of the Just War Theory. Do you think they are all reasonable?

Do you think that modern warfare can be fought in this way?

What do you think of rule 6?

15 Peace and protest

▶ Why do wars begin?

There are many reasons why wars begin. Whether those reasons are acceptable or not depends on which side you are on, previous events in history, where it is happening, and whether your country is involved. The diagram gives some examples of reasons for historic wars.

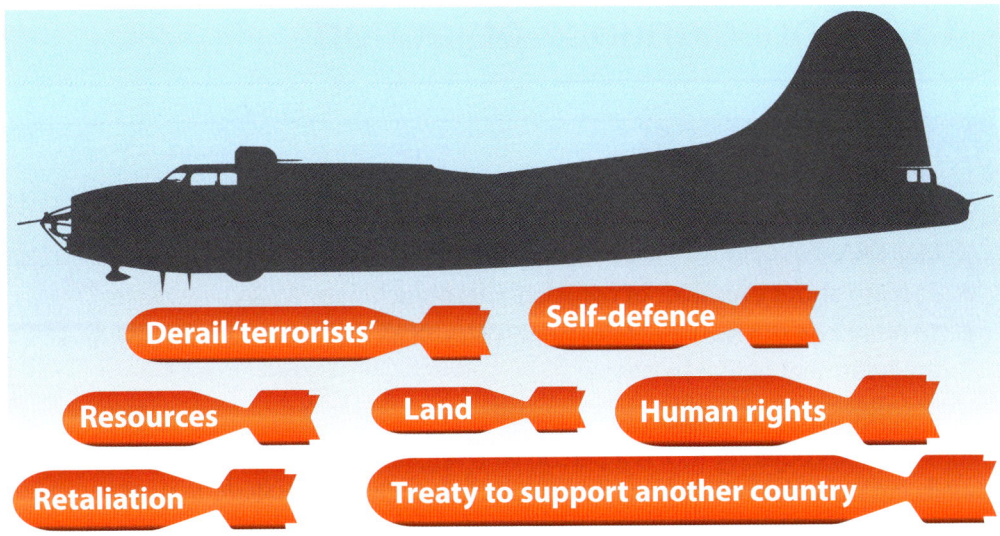

Derail 'terrorists' · Self-defence · Resources · Land · Human rights · Retaliation · Treaty to support another country

▶ The Just War Theory and modern wars

At the outbreak of the First World War, David Lloyd George, a Welshman, was a very influential politician in the UK. Lord Kitchener came to Wales to persuade men to sign up to the army. Wales at the time was dominated by Welsh Nonconformist Christian thinking, which meant non-violence and peace, so many were opposed to war. However, many did not like what they saw as German aggression, and they were influenced by Lloyd George, who was also a Nonconformist. Lloyd George used his influence over the Welsh, and especially the London Welsh at London rallies to argue the case for war. He built this case on the Just War Theory, and used two North Wales ministers to back him, preaching to the people of Wales that this war was just, and righteous, and that as Christians they had to fight. His arguments were effective, but not all Nonconformists were convinced, and this was also the start of a very strong Welsh pacifist movement. The quote by T Gwyn Jones on page 208 is an example of that disagreement. He walked out of the church that he had always attended, never to return to it, because he felt the ministers were preaching war, which was not the Christian way.

In 1990, George HW Bush announced the start of the first Gulf War. He began by saying that elected governments and organisations had made the decision after the leader of Iraq had refused to withdraw from Kuwait – a nation that Iraq had invaded several months previously. Bush continued by describing the reasons for the war. He then described at length the many attempts at a peaceful resolution, all of which had failed. Next, he gave the clear aims of the war, and outlined what the successful outcome of the war would be. He described the forces and way that the war would be carried out (largely via bombs – to protect soldiers' lives), and the military targets that would be the focus of the war (largely military installations – to protect civilians). Finally, he stated that peace would be returned to the area, and that Kuwait would be freed from the aggression of a neighbour that wanted its oil resources. He did all this in the first five minutes of his speech to the USA – to persuade the many Christians in the USA. The overall message was: support a Just War.

In 1998, Bill Clinton made a speech to announce military attacks on Iraq. His speech used the Just War principles as justification for the attacks.

Activities

1. Give some reasons why wars might begin.
2. Create a poster that uses images and text to explain the Just War Theory.
3. Why do you think that political leaders in the modern world still use the Just War Theory to announce war to their people? Explain your ideas.
4. 'A Just War is impossible in real life.' Do you agree? Explain your reasons. Try to give a different point of view.

Values and ethics

15.3 Conscientious objection

Learning objectives
- To understand the term 'conscientious objection' and know that it is an expression of deeply held principles and/or religious beliefs
- To learn about examples of conscientious objection in Wales
- To reflect on the bravery of declaring yourself a conscientious objector, and the treatment of COs by others

Big question
What beliefs and principles might lead to someone objecting to fighting as a soldier?

Key terms
Conscription – compulsory enlistment into services for the government, usually as a soldier in time of war

Facism – far-right-wing beliefs which place nation and race above the individual, for example, those seen in Nazi Germany

A conscientious objector (CO) is a person who refuses to join the armed forces (usually in times of war) because of deeply held principles or beliefs. In the First World War, up until 1916, the armies were made up of volunteers. However, this did not meet the needs of the war, so **conscription** was introduced – men had no choice about joining the army. At this point, men began to refuse – some 16,000 in total, of whom over 900 were Welsh. New laws made it easier to be recognised as a CO in the Second World War, when there were 60,000 COs in the UK.

There were four main reasons for becoming a conscientious objector:

- religious grounds – for example, Quakers are pacifists, other Christians pointed to Jesus' teachings about love, or the Ten Commandments.
- political grounds – for example, a number of left-wing activists rejected the war as they saw it as abuse of the working man to extend the power of the rich.
- personal conviction grounds – those who, without being religious, simply felt it was wrong to take life.
- the grounds of liberty – those who objected to being ordered by the Government to do anything.

COs had to apply for the status, be tested by a tribunal, and were then told an outcome: serve, serve in non-combat role, take a job in the home war effort, or be imprisoned. Some (absolutists) would not take on any role and they spent most of the time during the war in prison. One in three COs spent time in prison at least once during the war. Those in prison at the end of the war were kept there for six months so that returning soldiers could find jobs, and they were denied the vote until 1926. The attitude to COs in Britain throughout the First World War was one of suspicion and hatred. They were considered traitors and cowards, not prepared to do what all the other men in society were doing, and disloyal to their families and the country. They faced great difficulty on a daily basis, including threats, exclusion from society, assaults and even murder.

> COs military roles included working as field medics, and in bomb disposal in the UK.

> Many Quakers served in the military as medics, but not as combatants.

> International Conscientious Objectors' Day is 15 May.

Activities
1. What is a conscientious objector?
2. Why did people apply to be classed as COs?
3. Using examples, explain how difficult it was to become and then live as a CO.
4. Choose one of the three examples of Welsh COs discussed on page 213. Write a brief interview for a newspaper which shows his beliefs and how he was treated.
5. Do you think people should fight for their country, or stick to their principles? Explain your reasons.

15 Peace and protest

▶ Some Welsh conscientious objectors

About 273,000 Welshmen fought in the First World War, in spite of a divide in the Nonconformist community (see Topic 15.2, When conflicts happen, page 210). However, a strong Welsh movement in favour of pacifism existed because of conscription. COs in Wales were subject to discrimination and abuse for their decision, as they were anywhere else in the UK, and were just as likely to have their application refused and therefore be sent to fight or to prison.

▲ Engraving on Peace Monument in the Welsh National Garden of Peace, Cardiff

TE Nicholas or **Niclas Y Glais** (1879–1971) is known as the People's Poet. He was ordained a minister in the Welsh Independent churches in 1901, and held that role until 1918. He was a Christian socialist, who believed in peace and the equality of all. He disagreed with Britain joining the First World War on the grounds that it meant working-class men of different sides fighting each other for the power and glory of the upper classes, which he saw as wrong. He used his job as editor of the *Merthyr Pioneer* to voice his opinion that the war was immoral and uncivilised. In 1940, he was imprisoned – with his son – for being a **fascist** (which was extraordinary given he was a member of the Communist Party of Britain). In prison, he wrote many poems which expressed both his Christian and Communist beliefs. As an ordained minister, he did not have to apply for CO status, and in the Second World War, he was too old to be conscripted; however, he was a CO.

Ithel Davies (1894–1989) was a barrister by profession. In 1916, he received his orders to join the army, and refused. He said he would rather have died a martyr's death than 'betray the Spirit within', that Spirit being the Holy Spirit. He was a Christian who believed in love and brotherhood, both of which he said were incompatible with war. Ithel was an absolutist – he would not fight as a soldier, nor take a non-combat role, nor work as part of the war effort. As with other absolutists, he was imprisoned, but even there he refused to follow orders to do with war – he would not wear a uniform, sew mailbags for the front or take part in drills. His treatment was so harsh that it was brought up in Parliament. When released after completing one sentence, he was immediately re-arrested and sentenced to a longer period in prison and hard labour; this happened a number of times. He was eventually released in 1919.

Waldo Williams (1904–71) was born in Haverfordwest. He spoke both Welsh and English, and is a famous poet. During the Second World War, he registered his beliefs as a pacifist and so registered as a CO. At the time, he was a headmaster and, believing he would be sacked for being a CO,

he left his post. In 1953, he decided to stop paying his taxes, knowing some of these were used for National Service (compulsory time in the Armed Forces for all men). He was twice imprisoned for this, before working as a lecturer (cash-in-hand to avoid paying tax). Once National Service was ended, he returned to teaching and paying taxes.

213

Values and ethics

15.4 Keeping the peace

Learning objectives
- To learn about the concepts of peace-keeping and peace-making
- To explore examples of the work of peace-keepers and peace-makers
- To reflect on the importance of peace-keeping versus peace-making

Big question
Which is more important – making peace or keeping the peace?

Peace-making is about bringing two (or more) sides back together so that they stop fighting each other. At its best, the two sides become friends again and re-establish normal relations, putting aside any disagreements so that the earlier problem does not return. At its worst, peace-making just stops the fighting – the anger and resentment continue under the surface, just waiting to erupt again.

Peace-keeping is about a third party keeping two sides at peace with each other. Without the presence and work of the peace-keepers, the fight would start again. Usually behind the peace-keeping there are all kinds of efforts for peace-making. At its best, peace-keeping means that there is peace so that differences can be sorted out, agreements can be made, and the process of peace-making can go ahead. At its worst, peace-keeping holds the two sides apart but only in the places where the peace-keepers are, and anywhere else the fighting can start again.

▶ Working for peace – the peace-makers

Working for peace is not just something done in war time. Some people would say that our society is not a peaceful place, and that any injustice that happens is a kind of violence against people. In that case, anyone working for social reform is actually working for peace.

During war, those refusing to fight may be working for peace. Some people have used peaceful means to change society. Seeing violence in the world, some people use peaceful means to get their message heard and to convince others to change.

The Quaker ethos is one of peace, and so of active peace-making. During the First World War, many Quakers were involved in providing humanitarian relief to those affected or displaced (forced to move) by the war. This included building work, medical aid and farming. The Quakers ran a volunteer ambulance service, Friends Ambulance Unit, in Britain and in Europe.

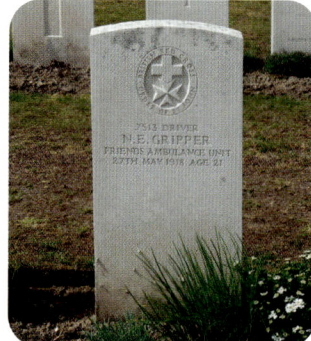

▲ A grave of a member of the Friends Ambulance Unit, killed while providing humanitarian relief in the First World War

Mahatma Gandhi was a civil rights activist in South Africa (1893–1914) and then India from 1914 until his assassination in 1948. He was involved in the protest movement which led up to Indian independence. Some of this protest was violent, not least because British rule was violent. Hinduism teaches the virtue of ahimsa (non-violence), and this was central to how Gandhi lived his life. He used peaceful protests such as marches, speeches, sit-ins, hunger strikes and discussions with authorities to bring together the power of the voices of Indians in order to achieve independence. He proved that pacifism gets results, and can be as powerful as any physical force.

▲ The statue of Gandhi in Cardiff Bay

Helen Steven (1942–2016) was a Scot with a passion for peace. In her lifetime, she shared her views at thousands of meetings as well as on TV and in print, protested at many venues and joined protest marches, and was arrested and imprisoned. During the Vietnam War, she volunteered with the Peace Corps and went to Vietnam. There she realised that justice won by violence did not last.

She believed that victory had to come without the winning side using their power in a cruel way. She also believed that only when everyone felt safe, without anger or dislike, was true, lasting peace possible. This was the motivation for her protests against war or any kind of violence. She campaigned for nuclear disarmament in the UK; was Justice and Peace Worker for the Iona Community; and set up the Scottish Centre for Nonviolence in Dunblane. Her lifetime's work for peace was recognised in 2004 by the Gandhi International Peace Award.

▶ The peace-keepers

The most famous of the peace-keepers are the United Nations' Blue Berets.

The United Nations (UN) was set up by 51 of the world's countries in 1945 after the Second World War had ended. The main aim was to promote and keep of peace across the world. One role is to maintain international peace and security. Using soldiers from all nations, loaned to the UN, their work includes:

- setting up peace-keeping operations such as protecting human rights, ensuring aid organisations can do their work, enabling free and fair elections, etc.
- the use of military force to protect civilians in war-torn countries.

At a time of crisis or war in one or more countries, UN Resolutions are agreed so that peace-keeping forces can be sent to a region.

The International Day of Peace-Keeping is on 29 May. In 2020, the theme was Women in Peace-keeping, making the point that women are essential to the process of lasting peace, as well as to making peace-keeping more effective. The UN recognises that women can bridge peace-keeping and peace-making more effectively than men. This was part of the information for the Theme for 2020.

In 2020, there were twelve UN peace-keeping operations around the world with 88,000 peace-keeping personnel involved. You can find out about the work being done at www.peacekeeping.un.org. The peace-keepers are easily recognisable – even though they wear the uniform of their own country's army, they all wear the UN blue beret.

▲ UN peace-keeper, recognised by their Blue Beret

The peace-keepers do all kinds of jobs – it really depends on where they are deployed and what the situation is. It isn't always a war situation either. During the Covid-19 pandemic, they also protected the supply of vaccines, provided medical support, and helped countries manage the difficult local situations created by shortages and fear over the disease. This work needed more experts, for example, medics and nurses, than soldiers, which shows the broadening of the UN's role in peace-keeping. The Blue Berets included soldiers, but also Armed Forces medics, and some non-Armed Forces personnel.

Activities

1. Using examples, explain the difference between peace-making and peace-keeping.
2. Create three information cards – one for each of the peace-makers in this topic. On each card include at least the following information: name, situation or context of work, activity, effectiveness, importance. Use your own opinion in providing some of this information. You could do some research to add extra detail.
3. Which is more difficult: peace-keeping or peace-making? Use examples and explain your answer.

Values and ethics

15.5 Protest

Learning objectives
- To learn about why and how people protest
- To explore examples of protest in the Welsh community
- To reflect on whether any and/or all forms of protest are acceptable

Big question
How far do you think protest should go?

Protest is the voicing of views against something. Almost every day in the news there is a story about someone somewhere in the world making a protest. There are many ways to protest: big or small, as a group or as an individual, with violence or without, actively or passively, legally or not, and more. People protest when they think there is an injustice – they hope their protest will make those with power in the situation think again and make some changes in the favour of the protest.

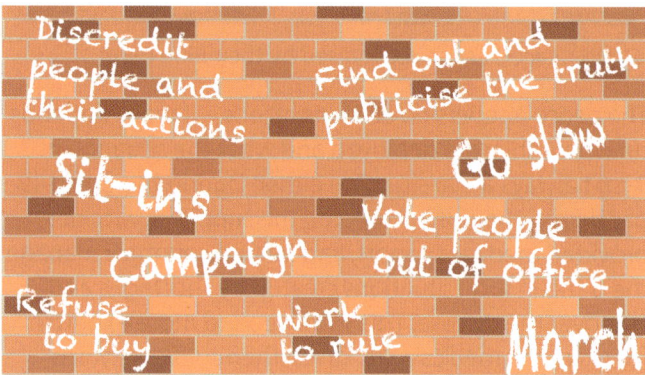

The wall suggests some of the ways in which people protest peacefully. Imagine the wall is whatever is blocking the things you want. The phrases are the ways people try to break down that barrier. Of course, protest is not always successful, and can be for something that the majority of people do not want. However, it is your human right to be allowed to protest – and we are all very different people. Something you feel strongly enough about to voice your opinion publicly might be of no matter to someone else.

In the nineteenth century, the Industrial Revolution took Wales rapidly from a mainly agricultural society to one built on factories, mills and mines. Owners got very rich; workers who left the countryside for better opportunities stayed poor and endured terrible conditions of work as well as terrible living conditions.

Activities

> I believe we are all equal, so I marched in a Black Lives Matter protest for equality.

> I think it is morally wrong to experiment on animals, so I put posters up around school and started a campaign.

> The only way to get change is to show that the voice of all the people is one. I signed a petition to save the local hospital.

> I joined others on a night vigil at the police station to protest about violence against women.

> I joined a protest group and chained myself to others across a road to disrupt the traffic and get our view heard nationally.

1. Read the statements. For each one, answer the following questions:
    - What are they protesting about?
    - How are they protesting?
    - How effective do you think this form of protest can be?
2. Is there anything that you feel sufficiently strongly about to make you join a protest? Explain your answer.

15 Peace and protest

New villages sprang up everywhere in the Valleys, to provide workers for the mines. They had no civic institutions – parks, libraries, schools, town halls, cultural facilities, etc. Life was based around three things: work, home and the chapel. For most people in Wales, early education was at Sunday School, a place where they debated and found a common voice for protest. Many social reformers of the day, who fought for better working conditions, better wages, unions and so on, started to find their voice and support at Sunday School. Topic 11.4 Social justice (page 170–1) outlines the work of Robert Owen as a social reformer.

The changes needed in social and working lives and conditions, including the vote for women, came through protest in its many forms.

▲ This is Thomas Stephens. Do some research to find out the social reforms he fought for in Merthyr Tydfil.

Activities

Modern-day Wales sees protests of all kinds. Look at these headlines about real Welsh protests. Which do you agree with and why/why not?

- Anti-vax protestors line Cardiff street
- Hundreds march with placards through city centre over benefits cuts
- Hundreds gather for night vigil outside Swansea Police station over violence against women
- Anti-war protestors gather in park to hear speeches from local, religious and political leaders
- Young Christians Climate Network Welsh members begins their protest relay march in Swansea (03/07/21) to end at COP26 (01/11/21)

Find out for yourself

Choose one of the following Welsh protests:
- The Rebecca Riots
- Alice Abadam
- Capel Celyn residents
- National miners' strike of 1984
- 2019 school strikes for the climate

Research the protest, and write a presentation that includes:
- what the issue was
- what form the protest took
- how effective the protest was in making change happen.

Activities

1. List some reasons why people protest.
2. Explain some of the ways in which people protest.
3. How might a person's principles or beliefs affect their protest – either by motivating them to protest, or in how they protest. Explain your ideas.
4. 'Protest is an important human right.' Do you agree? Explain your reasons.

217

Glossary

Absolute poverty line – a figure set by the World Bank; currently $1.90 (about £1.40) a day as minimum needed to live on (set in 2011, but still used); about 9.5 per cent of the world population or over 700 million people have less money than this to live on every day

Advocate – someone who publicly supports or recommends a person or cause

Alms round – monks going into their local community to be given food by Buddhists as a gift

Arti tray – tray used during worship; contains a lamp and representation of five elements; worshippers can take blessing from this

Asceticism – a religious way of life in which a person deprives themselves of all luxuries, and lives on the bare minimum

Asylum seeker – a person who has left their home country as a political refugee, and is seeking to be allowed to stay in another country; they are in personal danger if they remain in their own country

Awe – a sense of wonderment and amazement; linked to a sense of the divine

Baptistry – a pool in a church, used for adult baptism

Behaviour – how people conduct themselves

Beliefs – ideas we hold as true without proof, which shape our identity and actions

Belonging – the sense of being part of something (a place or group)

Blasphemy – insulting God; showing disrespect to God

Blessed – granted grace or good will from God

Bodhisattva – a person whose actions are motivated with deep, impartial, loving kindness to all beings; who has put off their own full enlightenment to be able to help other sentient beings (any being that has feelings or can feel pain) become enlightened

Cadw – The Welsh Government historic environment service, which looks after Welsh historical monuments and sites, including more than 20 religious monuments. 'Cadw' means to keep or protect

Camino – a pilgrimage walk, known in English as the Way of St James; a network of routes across Europe which go into Northern Spain and then to the cathedral at Santiago de Compostella, where St James the apostle is said to be entombed.

Census – a ten-yearly check on the population of the UK, which records various characteristics

Charismatic – appealing, captivating and mesmerising

Conscription – compulsory enlistment into services for the government, usually as a soldier in time of war

Consecrated ground – land that is declared sacred; usually for a religious building or graveyard

Covenant – a binding agreement, between God and man

Cynefin – habitat; a very personal sense of place, belonging and familiarity; the place of your birth and upbringing, the environment in which you live and to which you are naturally acclimatised; all the layers that make up the place in which you live and that make it unique

Denomination – a group within Christianity that has its own interpretation of belief and its own way to practise the religion

Dhammapada – Buddhist holy scriptures which are collections of the sayings of the Buddha; verses of truth which are the best known in the West of all Buddhist scriptures

Dilemma – a difficult choice which has to be made, often with only bad options

Discrimination – acting on prejudice, either in words or actions

Economic migrant – a person who moves to live in a country other than their own for work often to improve their standard of living

Environmental ethics – the study of the relationship humans have with their world, and the value and status we give to the natural world and all the species within it; including ideas about what is right and wrong in how humans treat the world

Evangelical – those Christian groups who see scripture as the only basis for faith, and have active evangelism (taking the Christian Gospel to others) as the most important part of what they do

Fascism – far-right-wing beliefs which place nation and race above the individual, for example, those seen in Nazi Germany

Gurmukh – being God-centred, focused on God at all times

Hadith – a collection of the sayings of Prophet Muhammad which help Muslims to do as the Qur'an says

Harmony – when there are positive relations between all sides; when everything goes together well

Glossary

Humanist – a non-religious person without a belief in a god, who advises humans to look to reason, empathy and human nature for solutions.

Identity – the qualities, beliefs, personality, looks and/or expressions that make a person who they are

ISKCON – International Society for Krishna Consciousness; a group within Hinduism who worship Krishna as Supreme Lord, and believe their duty is to show devotion to Krishna

Israelites – the twelve tribes of Israel, the ancestors of the Jewish people

Kitab-i-Aqdas – 'most holy book'; holy book of the Bahá'í Faith, written by Bahá'u'lláh while imprisoned

Laity – those people who follow a religion but are not ordained (have not taken religious vows)

Leavened – food that has used a raising agent, such as yeast, in its preparation

Manmukh – being self-centred, selfish; thinking only of oneself

Matzah – unleavened bread used specifically at Pesach

Medium – clairvoyant; a person who claims to be able to communicate on behalf of the dead to the living

Miracle – event contrary to the laws of nature, which brings a good outcome; often believed to be an act of God by religious people.

Mitzvot – commandments from God (a single commandment is mitzvah)

Monastery – a series of buildings that are home to a community who dedicate their lives to living under religious vows or promises to God

Monasticism – the practice of devoting one's life to a spiritual path, including living as part of a community of people doing the same

Monk – a man who has devoted his life to the spiritual path by taking religious vows, and lives in a community of others with the same ideal

Morality – a sense of right and wrong; principles that distinguish between good and bad behaviour

Nonconformist – Christian groups that did not keep to the rules of the established Church of England, but rather created their own forms of leadership and rituals, based on their interpretation of the message of Jesus in the Bible

Numinous – a word invented by Rudolf Otto to describe a spiritual response caused by coming into contact with God or the divine. It gives a sense of awe and inspiration

Nun – a woman who has devoted her life to the spiritual path by taking religious vows, and lives in a community of others with the same ideal

Orthodox – a Christian denomination which is the oldest form of Christianity; based mainly in the region from Greece to Russia today

Pacifism – the belief that wars and violence are wrong; that all disputes can and should be settled by peaceful means

Peace – the state of not being at war, or when war has ended; when there is calmness, friendship and harmony in society

Pentecostal – Christian groups that stress accepting the Holy Spirit into one's life

Pilgrimage – a journey to a place that is important to the religion. Many religions have places of pilgrimage. The journeys to them are often not easy, which means that greater devotion is needed in order to make the journey.

Pluralistic – where several different groups co-exist within a community, society or country.

Poverty – lack of the basic essentials for living, relative to the society we live in

Pragmatism – thinking or acting in a reasonable and logical way to get a satisfactory outcome without relying on rules or beliefs

Prayer – communicating with God; speaking to God

Prejudice – prejudging someone, usually negatively; thinking badly of someone because of some characteristic they have

Puja – act of worship in Hinduism

Quiots – a game in which rope or metal rings are thrown to catch on a stake in the ground

Refugee – a person who has been forced to leave their own country to escape war, persecution or natural disaster

Religion – a belief system that relies on the existence of a supernatural or divine being

Retreat – Buddhist practice of taking oneself away from everyday life, often to a secluded place, to spend time focused on spiritual development

Revelation – God revealed to humans; religious truths revealed by God

Revival blessing – the belief that God blessed people when they committed themselves to him during one of the revivals, forgiving their sins and giving a new start to life

Sacred scripture – holy books such as the Christian Bible, and other texts believed to hold religious truths, such as the Hadith in Islam

Secular – not connected to religion or religious matters

Sewa – selfless service to others; a duty for Sikhs

Social injustice – a situation where society is uneven, with some members affected by lack of wealth, opportunities and privileges

Spirituality – the quality of being concerned with the human spirit or soul. It is about internal calm, health and well-being, not external and material things. It is often expressed through being connected to other people, the world, life and so on

Unleavened – food that has not used a raising agent in its preparation

Values – ideas of what is important

Index

absolute poverty line 172

Adam and Eve 196

Advent (Epiphany) 48, 49

afterlife *see* life after death

aid agencies 173

akhirah 91

Al-Ikhlas Cultural and Education Centre 105

Allah 90, 91, 93, 94, 95, 96, 98

Amidah prayer 75

Amnesty International 166

Amrit Sanskar 130–1

Amritsar 132–3, 137

Amsterdam Declaration (2002) 37

animal rights 194–5

animals, endangered 191

anthropic principle 189

Arjan Dev, Guru 124, 125, 133

ark (aron ha-kodesh) 79, 81

arti ceremony 113

arti trays 111, 112, 113

asceticism 140

asylum seekers 73, 206

Awen 34

the Báb 30

Bahá'í Faith
    belief in science and religion 32, 187, 197
    comes to Wales 26–7
    daily prayer 33
    founding 30–1
    key beliefs 32, 174
    a religion for peace 27
    worship 33

Bahá'u'lláh 31

baptism 59
    adult 68–9
    infant 66–7

baptistry 68, 69

Bardsey Island 71

bedikat chametz 87

beliefs, values and behaviour 160–1

belonging 154–5

Bible 60, 61, 62
    Christian understanding 63
    Latin 11
    Old Testament prophecies 47
    translating 11
    Welsh language 10, 11, 12, 15

Big Bang Theory 186, 187, 189, 198

bimah 81

Bloom 73

bodhisattvas 152

Book of Common Prayer 61

Booth, William 181

Brahma 106, 107, 141, 152

Brahman 106, 107, 108, 109, 120

bread, unleavened 80, 81, 86, 87

Buddha, life of the 138–41

Buddhism 138–53
    beliefs about humanity 174
    comes to Wales 24–5
    key beliefs 144–5
    key teachings 142–3
    life of the Buddha 138–41
    monasticism 146–7
    places of worship 25, 148–9
    Welsh centres 146
    in Welsh community 152–3
    Wesak 150–1

Bush, George H.W. 211

Cadw 8, 15

Campbell, Betty 171

celebrants 68, 69

Celtic Christianity 4–7

Celtic crosses 5

Celtic saints 5, 6–7

census
    2001 2, 14, 20, 90
    2011 2, 14, 16, 18, 20, 22, 24, 36, 90

chapels, non-conformist 58

charismatic speakers 12, 13, 14, 50, 93

charity, giving to 100, 104

chesed 88

Christian history of Wales 4–16
    Celtic Christianity 4–7
    Christianity comes to Wales 4–5

Christianity in Wales today 14–15
    monasticism 8–9
    Welsh language and 10–11, 12
    Welsh revivals 12–13

Christianity 42–73
    attitudes to prejudice and discrimination 178, 179
    baptism 66–9
    beliefs about humanity 174
    beliefs into action 72–3
    Christmas 48–9
    creation stories 184–5, 196
    Easter 56–7
    Eucharist 64–5
    God and Trinity 42–3
    the incarnation 46–7
    key beliefs 44–5, 46, 54, 61
    life of Jesus 46–7, 48, 50–5
    pilgrimages 70–1
    places of worship 5, 58–9
    worship 60–3

Christingle 49

Christmas 48–9

Church in Wales (Anglican) 61, 65, 68

church schools 15

churches 58–9
    Spiritualist 40–1
    in Wales 5, 58, 73

citizens, religious 169

City of Sanctuary, UK 3, 207

climate change 191

conscientious objectors (COs) 212–13

Constantine, Emperor 210

Covid-19 pandemic 3, 105, 119, 137, 215

creation stories 184–5, 196–7

crucifixion 54, 56

cynefin 6, 15

Cyswllt Amgylchedd Cymru (Wales Environment Link) 193

darshan 113

Darwin, Charles 198–9

David, St (Dewi sant) 7

Davies, Ithel 213

death penalty 166, 200–1

design argument for existence of God 189

Dhammapada 152

dietary law, Jewish 83

dignity of life 175

discrimination 176–7
   religious attitudes to 178–9
   as a religious issue 182–3
   religious responses to 180–1

Divine Liturgy 64, 65

Diwali 118–19

druidry, modern 34–5

Dyfrig, St (Dyfrig sant) 6

Easter 56–7

Easter Sunday 57

Easter vigil 57

economic migrants 206

Eid ul-Adha 103

Eid ul-Fitr 100, 101

environment *see* natural world

environmental ethics 192–3

Epiphany (Advent) 48, 49

Eucharist (Holy Communion) 64–5

euthanasia 202–3

Evangelicals 14, 61

evolution 198–9

extinction of species 191

fasting 101

First World War 211, 212, 213, 214

5Ks 22, 131, 135

Five Pillars of Islam 98–102
   Hajj 102–3
   Salah 99
   Sawm 101
   Shahadah 98
   Zakah 100, 104

Five Precepts 151, 153

font 59, 66, 67

foodbanks 72, 73, 105, 121, 137

Four Noble Truths 143

four sights 139

freedom of religious expression 183

Friends of Vrindavan (FoV) 116

Gandhi, Mahatma 214

Ganges River 117

Genesis stories 184–5, 196

Gobind Singh (Rai), Guru 124, 125, 130

God, arguments for existence of
   design argument 189
   from morality 159

Golden Rule 44, 162, 173, 206

Golden Temple 132, 133

Good Friday 56

Great Commandments 44

Great Pacific Garbage Patch 191

Green Pilgrimage Network 117

Gulf War 211

gurdwara 126–7, 137
   financial contributions 135

gurmukh 123, 136

Guru Granth Sahib 125, 126, 127, 128–9, 133, 136, 197

gurus, ten 124–5
   Guru Arjan Dev 124, 125, 133
   Guru Gobind Singh (Rai) 124, 125, 130
   Guru Nanak 125, 126, 132, 136
   Guru Ram Das 124, 125, 133

Gwyn Jones, T. 208, 211

Hadith 95, 104

Hajj, Fifth Pillar 102–3

havan 113

healing, power of 52

'healing circle' 41

Henry VIII, King 9, 11, 190

Hinduism 106–21
   beliefs about God 106–7
   beliefs about humanity 174
   comes to Wales 20–1
   creation stories 186, 197
   Diwali 118–19
   holy places 116–17
   home as a place of worship 114–15
   key beliefs 106–9, 118, 120
   non-violence 214
   places of worship 21, 110–11
   in Welsh community 21, 120–1
   worship in temples 112–13

Holy Communion (Eucharist) 64–5

human life, origins of
   believing in both science and religion 199
   religious beliefs 196–7
   scientific beliefs 198–9

human rights 164–5, 166
   religion and 168–9, 183

humanism 36–9
   Amsterdam Declaration (2002) 37
   attitude to peace 209
   beliefs about humanity 174
   beliefs about morality 158
   celebrations 39
   importance 39

humanity 174–5

identity 154–5

the incarnation 46–7

India 19, 20, 23, 214

India Centre, Cardiff 110, 121

influences, good and bad 157

initiation rituals 66–9

International Day of Peace-Keeping 215

Islam 90–105
   beliefs about humanity 174
   comes to Wales 18–19
   creation story 197
   Five Pillars 98–102
   key beliefs 90–1
   places of worship 18, 96–7
   Prophet Muhammad 92–3, 94, 95
   Qur'an 93, 94–5, 197
   in Welsh community 104–5

Israelites 86, 87

Jesus
   birth 46–7
   death and resurrection 54–5
   Great Commandments 44
   miracle worker 52–3
   son of God 46, 48, 52, 54
   in support of peace 208, 210
   teacher 50–1, 178

Jones, Humphrey 13

Judaism 74–89
   beliefs about humanity 174
   celebrations 86–7
   comes to Wales 16–17
   creation story 184–5
   holy books 78–9

Index

home and daily life 82–3
key beliefs 74–5
the mitzvot 76, 77
observing Shabbat 84–5
Orthodox 77, 81
places of worship 80–1, 85, 89
Reform 77, 81
in Welsh community 88–9

Judgement Day 45, 72, 91, 94, 95

Just War Theory 210, 211

karma 108, 109, 145, 153

karma yoga 120

Ketuvim 79

Khalsa Aid 137

Khalsa Sikhs 130–1

Kirat Karni 134, 136

Kitab-i-Aqdas 30, 31

kosher 83

langars (community kitchens) 125, 126, 127, 129, 135, 137

Last Supper 54, 64

laws, religious believers and keeping 162–3, 169

Lazarus 53

Lewis, C.S. 159

LGBTQ+ people 87, 179

life after death
Christianity 45
Islam 91
Judaism 75

life and death, power over 53

Linden Church 73

liturgical worship 61, 65

'living guru' *see* **Guru Granth Sahib**

Llantwit Major 6, 8, 15

Lloyd George, David 211

Lord's Prayer 43, 60

mandirs 21, 110–11, 116
acts of worship 112–13

manmukh 123, 136

Mass, Roman Catholic 64, 65

matzahs 86, 87

Maundy Thursday 56

meditation 113, 129, 146, 149
on name of God 129, 134

Messiah 47, 75

Midnight Mass 48

miracles 52–3

Mitzvah Day 89

the mitzvot 76, 77

moksha 108, 109, 117, 119, 120

monasteries 71
Buddhist 25, 146, 147
dissolution 9
Welsh Christian 4, 6, 7, 8, 9, 11, 15, 71

monasticism
Buddhism 146–7
Welsh Christian 8–9

Mool Mantar 122, 127, 136

morality 158–9
absolute and relative 161
argument for existence of God 159
religious influences on 162–3

Morgan, David 13

Moses 74, 76, 78, 86, 94

mosques 18, 96–7

Muhammad, Prophet 92–3, 94, 95

mukti 122, 123, 124, 136

murti 106, 107, 112, 114

Nam Japna 129, 134, 136

Nam Simran 129

Nanak, Guru 125, 126, 132, 136

Nation of Sanctuary 3, 207

the Nativity 46–7

natural disasters, victims of 204–5

natural world
animal rights 194–5
awe and wonder 188–9
creation story 184–5
druids and 34
environmental ethics 192–3
helping and protecting 3, 72–3, 116, 117, 193
human damage to 190–1
science and origins of universe 186–7
stewardship 88, 156, 174, 192

nature, power over 52

Nazi Germany 16–17

Ner Tamid 81

Nevi'im 79

Nicholas, T.E. (Niclas Y Glais) 213

Night of Power 92

nirvana 145

Noble Eightfold Path 144–5

non-Conformists 12, 68, 211
acts of worship 61, 65
places of worship 58

North Wales Pilgrim's Way (Taith Pererin Gogledd Cymru) 70–1

the numinous 188

offerings 111, 113, 127, 129, 137, 149

Orthodox Church 60, 61, 65, 67

Otto, Rudolf 188

Owen, Robert 170

pacifism 208, 209, 214
Welsh movement 211, 213

Paley, William 189

Palm Sunday 56

Palpung Changchub Dargyeling (Brynmawr) 149

Panj Pyare (Five Beloved Ones) 130, 131

parables 50

peace
attitudes to 27, 208–9
-keepers 214
-makers 214–15

Pentecostalists 14, 61

Pesach (Passover) 86–7

Pharaoh 86

pikuach nefesh 88, 161

pilgrimages
Christian 70–1
Hajj 102–3
Hindu 116
Sikh 132–3
in Wales 70–1

Pilgrim's Ways 70–1

plagues, ten 86, 87

pollution 191

poverty 172–3

prayer
  Bahá'í Faith 33
  Christian 43, 60, 61
  Hindu 113
  Jewish 75, 82
  Muslim 96, 97, 99
  Sikh 128

prejudice 176–7
  religious attitudes to 178–9
  religious responses to 180–1

prison 200, 212, 213

prophets 79, 91, 92–3, 94

protest 216–17

puja 112, 114

Purusha 197

'pyramid of hate' 177

Quakers (Religious Society of Friends) 64, 209, 214

Qur'an 93, 94–5, 197

Rabbaniah Islamic Cultural Centre 105

Rahit Maryada 134

Ram Das, Guru 124, 125, 133

Rama and Sita 118, 119

Ramadan 101, 105

rebirth
  achieving liberation from (mukti) 122, 123, 124, 136
  in Buddhism 145, 153
  freedom from (moksha) 108, 109, 117, 119, 120
  in Hinduism 108, 109, 117, 119, 120
  in Sikhism 122, 123, 124, 136

Red Community Project 73

refugee crisis 73, 206–7

reincarnation *see* rebirth

religious landscape, Welsh 2–3

religious tourism 15, 70, 193

responsibilities and rights 166–7

resurrection 45, 55

revivals, Welsh 12–13

rights and responsibilities 166–7

risalah 91

Roberts, Evan 13

Roman Catholic Church 5, 9, 45, 61, 67
  Mass 64, 65

Romans 4, 34, 80, 210

rosary beads 61

rubbish and litter 191, 192

saints, Celtic 5, 6–7

Salah, Second Pillar 99

Salvation Army 64, 181

samsara, cycle of 108, 145

sanctity of life 175

Sattva, Prince 152

Sawm, Fourth Pillar 101

science
  origins of human life 198–9
  origins of universe 186–7

Second Coming 48

Second World War 17, 19, 23, 212, 213

secular 2, 39

seder meal 87

'selfless service' (sewa)
  Hindu 120, 121
  Sikh 123, 135, 136, 137

Shabbat, observing 84–5

Shahadah, First Pillar 98

Shiva 106, 107, 117

Shore to Shore 72–3, 193

shrine rooms, Buddhist 149

shrines, Hindu 110, 111, 138–41

Siddhartha Gautama, life of 138–41

sign of the cross 43, 67

Sikhism 122–37
  beliefs about humanity 174
  comes to Wales 22–3
  key beliefs 122–3
  Khalsa Sikhs 130–1
  living as a Sikh 134–5
  origins of human life 197
  places of worship 126–7
  spiritual centre 132–3
  ten gurus 124–5
  in Welsh community 23, 136–7
  worship 128–9

Sinai Covenant 76

Skanda Vale 121

Skanda Vale Hospice 121

social justice 170–1

soul
  in Bahá'í Faith 32
  in Buddhism 142
  in Hinduism 108, 109
  in Roman Catholicism 45
  in Sikhism 122, 123, 136
  in Spiritualism 40, 41

spiritual healing 41

spiritualism 40–1

spirituality 28–9

Stephens, Thomas 171

Steven, Helen 214–15, 217

synagogues 16, 80–1, 85, 89

Tawhid 90

temples, Buddhist 25, 148–9

temples, Hindu (mandirs) 21, 110–11, 116
  acts of worship 112–13

Ten Commandments 74, 75, 76

Ten Precepts 151, 153

Tenakh 78–9

Thomas, R.S. 71

Three Poisons 140, 145

Three Universal Truths 140, 142

tikkun olam 88

Tintern Abbey 8, 9

Torah 78, 79, 81, 83, 85
  scrolls 78, 79, 85

trimurti 106

Trinity 42–3

tzedakah 88

Umm al-Kitab 94

United Nations Convention on the Rights of the Child 165

United Nations Peace-Keepers 215

Universal Declaration of Human Rights (UDHR) 164, 165, 166, 168, 183

universe, origins of 186–7

Index

utilitarianism 158
values, beliefs and behaviour 160–1
Vand Chakna 135
Varanasi 117
Vishnu 106, 107, 116, 118, 186
Vrindavan 116, 117

war 210–11
  conscientious objection 212–13
Welsh language 10–11, 12
  Bible 10, 11, 12, 15
  Book of Common Prayer 61
  laws affecting 11
Welsh revivals 12–13

Wesak 150–1
Williams, Waldo 213
worldviews 156–7
Young Christian Climate Network 3
Zakah, Third Pillar 100, 104

Photo credits

p.3 *t* Young Christian Climate Network; *c* Church in Wales; **p.8** *l* © Crown copyright: Cadw; *r* © Dianamower/stock.adobe.com; **p.13** © Pastpix/TopFoto; **p.26** *l* © Casejustin/stock.adobe.com; **p.29** *l* © Reni Rudisin/Shutterstock.com; *c* © Altrendo Images/Shutterstock.com; *r* © Freebird7977/stock.adobe.com; **p.30** © EnginKorkmaz/stock.adobe.com; **p.33** © Maria Luisa Lopez Estivill/123RF.com; **p.34** © Chokniti/stock.adobe.com; **p.39** © Jon Worth/British Humanist Association/Shutterstock; **p.48** *t* © Magdalena Kucova/stock.adobe.com; *b* © Saikat Paul/Pacific Press/Alamy Live News/Alamy Stock Photo; **p.49** *t* © Richard_pinder/stock.adobe.com; *br* © Jane Williams/Alamy Stock Photo; **p.56** *l* © Peterfactors/stock.adobe.com; **p.57** *t* © Studiotouch/stock.adobe.com; *b* © Godong/Alamy Stock Photo; **p.58b** *t* © Julian Pottage/Alamy Stock Photo; *b* © Way out west photography/Alamy Stock Photo; **p.59** *cl* © Sabena Jane Blackbird/Alamy Stock Photo; **p.60** *t* © Daniel Chetroni/stock.adobe.com; *b* © Maria Marganingsih/stock.adobe.com; **p.65** *t* © Robertharding/Alamy Stock Photo; *b* © NoonVirachada/stock.adobe.com; **p.69** *l* © Homer Sykes/Alamy Stock Photo; *r* © Aliaksandr Mazurkevich/Alamy Stock Photo; **p.72** © The diocese of St Asaph; **p.73** © Linden Church **p.79** © Ira Berger/Alamy Stock Photo; **p.80** *br* © Paul Quayle/Alamy Stock Photo; *cl* Board of Deputies; **p.82** © Howard/stock.adobe.com; **p.85** *tr* © Tomertu/stock.adobe.com; *tl* © Ungvar/stock.adobe.com; *cr* © PhotoStock-Israel/Alamy Stock Photo; *br* © Katy Lozano/Shutterstock.com; **p.87** Board of Deputies; **p.89** Mitzvah Day logo designed by Graphical www.graphicalagency.com; **p.93** © ArkReligion.com/Art Directors & TRIP/Alamy Stock Photo; **p.97** *tl* Jaggery, geograph.co.uk, https://commons.wikimedia.org/wiki/File:Berea_Masjid_in_Blaina_-_geograph.org.uk_-_3659906.jpg; *tr* © Jeff Morgan 15/Alamy Stock Photo; *tcl* © Adrian Weston/Alamy Stock Photo; *tcr* © Dboystudio/Shutterstock.com; *cl* © Aleksandar/stock.adobe.com; *cr* © Alizada Studios/Alamy Stock Photo; *bl* © Fotoinfot/stock.adobe.com; *br* © Seriff/stock.adobe.com; **p.99** © PeekCC/stock.adobe.com; **p.101** © WONG SZE FEI/stock.adobe.com; **p.102** *r* © Nelen.ru/stock.adobe.com; *l* © Aidar Ayazbayev/123RF; *br* © Mohamed Lounes/Gamma-Rapho/Getty Images; **p.103** *tl* © Cem Oksuz/Anadolu Agency/Getty Images; *tr* © Mawardi Bahar/Alamy Stock Photo; *bl* © Mawardi Bahar/Alamy Stock Photo; *br* © Muhannad Fala'ah/Stringer/Getty Images News/Getty Images; **p.105** Al-Ikhlas Centre Foodband Service, Cardiff; **p.107** © ArkReligion.com/Art Directors & TRIP/Alamy Stock Photo; **p.111** *tl* © ArkReligion.com/Art Directors & TRIP/Alamy Stock Photo; **p.112** *r* © ArkReligion.com/Art Directors & TRIP/Alamy Stock Photo; **p.114** © Helene Rogers/ArkReligion.com/Art Directors & TRIP/Alamy Stock Photo; **p.115** © Rike_/ E+/Getty Images; **p.116** © Matyas Rehak/Shutterstock.com; **p.117** *t* © Wolszczak/stock.adobe.com; *b* © Copyright ISKCON Juhu & Nilachal Vedic Village, Hare Krishna Land, Mumbai, India-400049; **p.118** *b* © SD/Alamy Stock Photo; **p.119** *t* © StockImageFactory.com/Shutterstock.com; *c* © Prag bashichandra/Shutterstock.com; *b* © Michele Burgess/Alamy Stock Photo; **p.128** *bl* © Peter Marshall/Alamy Stock Photo; **p.130** © ArkReligion.com/Art Directors & TRIP/Alamy Stock Photo; **p.131** © Paul Gapper/Alamy Stock Photo; **p.132** *l* © Paul prescott/stock.adobe.com; *r* © Rafal Gaweda/stock.adobe.com; **p.135** © Michael Preston/Alamy Live News/Alamy Stock Photo; **p.137** © Peter Bolter/Alamy Stock Photo; **p.147** *t* © Kadmy/stock.adobe.com; *br* © Blanscape/stock.adobe.com; *bl* © Isabel Benchetrit/Alamy Stock Photo; **p.151** © Hanoi Photography/stock.adobe.com; **p.171** *t* © Matthew Horwood/Alamy Stock Photo; **p.181** © The Salvation Army; **p.186** © Nasaimages/123F; **p.188**; © 24K-Production/stock.adobe.com; **p.191** *c* © FloridaStock/Shutterstock.com; **p.192** *r* © Jason Mintzer/Shutterstock.com; **p.194** *tl* © Africa Studio/stock.adobe.com; *bl* © Aleksandr Lesik/stock.adobe.com; *br* © Lev Fedoseyev/TASS/ITAR-TASS News Agency/Alamy Stock Photo; **p.195** *cl* © Valery Sharifulin/TASS/ITAR-TASS News Agency/Alamy Stock Photo; *cr* © BERAUD/BSIP SA/Alamy Stock Photo; *r* © Martin Harvey/The Image Bank/Getty Images; **p.196** © Pavel Rodimov/Alamy Stock Photo; **p.197** © Teo Tarras/Shutterstock.com; **p.198** © Justine Hobson / Royal Geographical Society / Alamy Stock Photo; **p.200** © D Legakis/Athena Picture Agency Ltd/Alamy Stock Photo; **p.202** © Chinnapong/stock.adobe.com; **p.204** *l* © Alexander/stock.adobe.com; *r* © Kurniawan Rizqi/Shutterstock.com; **p.207** © City of Sanctuary UK; **p.209** © John Morrison/Alamy Stock Photo; **p.210** © Pictorial Press Ltd/Alamy Stock Photo; **p.213** *tr* © Welsh Centre for International Affairs; *l* © History collection 2016/Alamy Stock Photo; *br* Dafydd Williams, Rhuthun; **p.214** *t* © Niall Ferguson/Alamy Stock Photo; **p.215** © Bastian/Agencja Fotograficzna Caro/Alamy Stock Photo; **p.217** The Red Dragon: The National Magazine of Wales, https://commons.wikimedia.org/wiki/File:Thomas_Stephens_(1821%E2%80%931875)_(cropped).jpg.

All other photos courtesy of Lesley Parry.